Cautious Beginnings

Kurt F. Jensen

Cautious Beginnings
Canadian Foreign Intelligence,
1939-51

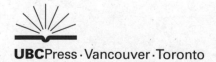
UBCPress · Vancouver · Toronto

16 15 14 13 12 11 10 09 08   5 4 3 2 1

Printed in Canada on ancient-forest-free paper (100% post-consumer recycled) that is processed chlorine- and acid-free, with vegetable-based inks.

Library and Archives Canada Cataloguing in Publication

Jensen, Kurt F. (Kurt Frank), 1946-
    Cautious beginnings : Canadian foreign intelligence, 1939-51 / Kurt F. Jensen.

Includes bibliographical references.
ISBN 978-0-7748-1482-9 (bound); 978-0-7748-1483-6 (pbk.)

    1. World War, 1939-1945 – Military intelligence – Canada. 2. World War, 1939-1945 – Secret service – Canada. 3. Military intelligence – Canada – History – 20th century. 4. Intelligence service – Canada – History – 20th century. I. Title.

UB251.C3.J45 2008   940.54'8671   C2007-907479-0

Canadä

UBC Press gratefully acknowledges the financial support for our publishing program of the Government of Canada through the Book Publishing Industry Development Program (BPIDP), and of the Canada Council for the Arts, and the British Columbia Arts Council.

This book has been published with the help of a grant from the Canadian Federation for the Humanities and Social Sciences, through the Aid to Scholarly Publications Programme, using funds provided by the Social Sciences and Humanities Research Council of Canada.

Printed and bound in Canada by Friesens
Set in Stone by Artegraphica Design Co. Ltd.
Copy editor: Stephanie VanderMeulen
Proofreader: Sarah Wight
Indexer: Patricia Buchanan

UBC Press
The University of British Columbia
2029 West Mall
Vancouver, BC V6T 1Z2
604-822-5959 / Fax: 604-822-6083
www.ubcpress.ca

Contents

Acknowledgments

This book grew from my work experience in intelligence matters and the historical interest this sparked. It is with sincerity that I express my great appreciation to Dr. Norman Hillmer of Carleton University, for his patience, guidance, and tremendous help on this project. I must also acknowledge the financial support of my then employer, the Department of Foreign Affairs and International Trade, whose Centre for International Affairs Learning and Management Development supports the educational aspirations of members of the department, and helped to make this study possible. My research would not have been successfully concluded had it not been for the many people at Library and Archives Canada and the Directorate of History and Heritage of the Department of National Defence in Ottawa whose services and advice helped me at various stages. The same is true for the Access to Information staff at the Communications Security Establishment who made available to me copies of documents as they were being declassified and released to the archives. The assistance of a colleague in arranging access to a great number of boxes at the US National Archives and Records Administration was also very helpful. I must also cite the support of my colleagues in the Foreign Intelligence Division at Foreign Affairs who granted the release of many of the documents I required, but could not find in the archives, in order to complete my research. Lastly, I want to thank my wife, Jill, and my daughters, Anna and Christina, whose support and encouragement and release from some household chores made this book possible, and have made it all worthwhile.

Abbreviations

Note: A more detailed glossary of terms can be found on p. 180.

ATIP	Access to Information Program
BRUSA	British-USA
BSC	British Security Coordination
CANUSA	Canada-USA
CBNRC	Communications Branch of the National Research Council
CIA	Central Intelligence Agency
CJIC	Canadian Joint Intelligence Committee
COMINT	communications intelligence
DEA	Department of External Affairs
DND	Department of National Defence
FBI	Federal Bureau of Investigation
HUMINT	human intelligence
MEW	Ministry of Economic Warfare
NRC	National Research Council
OIC	Operational Intelligence Centre
OSS	Office of Strategic Services
RCAF	Royal Canadian Air Force
RCMP	Royal Canadian Mounted Police
RCN	Royal Canadian Navy
SIGINT	signals intelligence
SOE	Special Operations Executive
UKUSA	United Kingdom-USA

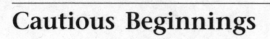

Cautious Beginnings

Introduction

Among the world's G8 nations, only Canada is without a clandestine foreign intelligence service tasked with recruiting and running agents outside the country. This is not tantamount to a conclusion that Canada does not collect or have access to foreign intelligence. Such an assumption would be wrong. Canada has considerable access to foreign intelligence and, indeed, collects much of this information through Canada's own resources. Much additional foreign intelligence is obtained through agreements and liaison relationships with the intelligence services of other nations.

The debate over whether Canada should establish its own clandestine agent-running intelligence organization, a human intelligence (HUMINT) capability, reflects an argument that has recurred roughly every five to ten years since first being raised in 1951. At that time, shortly after the end of the Second World War but with the Cold War already underway, Canada first made a decision not to establish a covert intelligence service. To fully comprehend why that decision was made in 1951, and periodically afterward, one must understand the antecedents of today's Canadian intelligence community.

During the early Cold War era, the debate over creation of a Canadian clandestine intelligence service was limited to those who were associated with intelligence work in Ottawa. More recently, as awareness and interest in intelligence matters have grown, the discourse has entered the public realm and can be found within the pages of academic journals and sometimes in the popular press. Unfortunately, the discussion has often perpetuated the misconceptions and has sometimes turned the question into one posing a choice of having or not having access to foreign intelligence, rather than focusing on the more pertinent issue of whether covert HUMINT collection is required to augment the foreign intelligence already available to Canada. While the argument over whether to establish a clandestine HUMINT organization has been both real and important, the central focus of the debate should be whether Canada has access to foreign intelligence with which to permit national policy makers to make decisions in full possession of the necessary information. Some participants in the current debate over the need for a clandestine service have known that Canada enjoys access to considerable foreign intelligence, but were often circumspect in expressing this awareness, something that may have contributed to popular misconceptions. One must recall that general information about Canada's foreign intelligence interests and capabilities was only slowly revealed to the public, beginning in the mid-1970s. However, considerable information was accessible earlier on Canada's security intelligence activities, initially on the security service within the RCMP and, after its creation in 1984, on the Canadian Security Intelligence Service, the civilian security service. Media coverage of Canadian security services goes as far back as the interwar period. Some limited information is also available about the role of military intelligence in the protection of the nation, a role that overlaps with that of foreign intelligence.

Misconceptions over Canadian access to foreign intelligence persist and are characteristic of the very limited scholarship on this facet of Canadian intelligence history. As information on this feature of Canadian foreign policy interests and tools becomes available, any misreading of Canadian involvement in foreign intelligence will diminish.

To place Canadian access to foreign intelligence in context, it is important to understand the different forms of intelligence activities in which Canada and most other nations are engaged.

A study of intelligence requires a clear definition of what constitutes foreign intelligence. Popular perceptions, the media, and the entertainment industry have contributed to definitions of "intelligence" that are at variance with the understanding of the subject within the intelligence community. Similarly, a number of terms within the genre also need to be defined to permit a full understanding of the subject.

Foreign intelligence is information relating to the capabilities, intentions, or activities of foreign states, persons, corporations, or organizations. Among the areas of interest is information of a political, economic, military, security, scientific, or social nature, obtained from overt and covert sources, which may be collected from human sources or through technical means, or through open sources. The security caveats associated with such information relate less to the data collected than the need to protect the methods and sources employed to gain access to the intelligence. Only one of many factors having an impact on political and military decision making, foreign intelligence is neither omniscient nor infallible but, rather, a tool that when used properly enhances the policy-making process.

Military intelligence greatly overlaps with foreign intelligence; the two differ primarily in the fact that the former has a greater tactical focus, while the latter is subject to a more strategic and political orientation. However, information collected as military intelligence will often meet both foreign and military intelligence objectives. In addition, military intelligence has a greater focus on collating information on hostile or potentially hostile armed forces. Nevertheless, James Eayrs is entirely correct when he "rejects as outmoded and misleading the traditional division of national security policy into two compartments, one called foreign policy, the other defence policy."[1] The two, Eayrs continues, are "indissolubly combined." While he makes his comment in the context of writing about policy making, he may as well have been discussing the policy-supporting world of foreign intelligence.

Security intelligence, which is often what the public associates with the concept of "intelligence," differs from foreign intelligence in the sense of being defensive, and has what one may call a "defence of the realm" mandate. The primary purpose of security intelligence is to protect the nation from internal and external threats. The associated tasks include counter-intelligence (countering the activities of hostile foreign intelligence services), counter-terrorism, countering political violence, and preventing threats to democratic society. A broad grey area exists where security and foreign intelligence overlap. Security intelligence, a substantial study in its own right, is covered only tangentially in this book.

Canada possesses a broad and vibrant intelligence community in which foreign intelligence collection and evaluation are significant and largely effective. Certainly, an important dimension would be added if Canada did possess a clandestine HUMINT organization, if only to place Canada on an equal footing with its key intelligence partners. However, Canada is a risk-averse, cautious, and frugal nation that throughout the passage of the past half century repeatedly made decisions not to embark on this type of collection activity.

In today's more open societies, an argument can also be made that the role of secret agents has been partly bypassed by history. That statement may come as a surprise, but it is generally agreed in intelligence circles that as much as 80 percent of the contents of today's intelligence assessments is gathered from open-source material – that is, information that was not obtained through secret or clandestine means. The remaining approximately 20 percent is derived from secret sources, most often through signals intelligence (SIGINT) or other methods euphemistically listed as national technical means, as well as from human sources.

Secret intelligence is not solely limited to clandestine or "black" sources. Human sources may also provide "grey" intelligence or information not normally accessible to the public (i.e., open sources) but not obtained through clandestine means. The classic example is the debriefing of prisoners of war and defectors. However, intelligence organizations also devote considerable resources to interviewing other individuals who may have gained valuable insights through travel, business dealings, academic activity, and so forth. Similarly, one of the most valuable intelligence tools is the activity of diplomats stationed abroad conducting bilateral relations or involved in more directed information-gathering mandates. A primary role of diplomats is to know and understand the environment in which they operate. Diplomatic activities provide highly valuable intelligence on foreign states, both friends and adversaries.

The intelligence collected by secret agents can be extremely valuable when reflecting access to the thinking and policy making at the apex of a foreign country's leadership. Nothing would surpass the admittance to the thought processes of a foreign leader. However, that sort of insight is rarer in real life than in spy fiction. Much information collected by clandestine agents does not represent direct access to foreign leadership and is more likely to be similar to open source and grey information. In fact, many agents simply pass on information learned from following the media or from working and circulating within a given society. This does not mean that it is without value. Such information can be difficult to obtain from outside the society and can gain value by being filtered through the insights and knowledge of the person making it attainable.

In a new age of increasing threats of terrorism, one might argue that the need for HUMINT is increasing rather than diminishing. This is a valid argument and would be true if it were feasible to develop human sources within terrorist organizations. However, HUMINT from within terrorist organizations is extremely difficult to access, although this situation may improve with time as terrorist organizations grow in membership and the ideological fervour of members of such organizations diminishes and becomes more susceptible to the traditional factors influencing a person to become a HUMINT source.

Today, Canada has a wide range of intelligence materials available that largely meet its national needs. A dependence on allied and liaison relationships exists; therefore, one might argue that Canadian intelligence sovereignty no longer remains. However, given costs and other political realities, it is unlikely that intelligence sovereignty is attainable by any country or, indeed, necessary in an increasingly interdependent world in which no nation can have independent access to all of the foreign intelligence required to act in full confidence and awareness of political factors that can have an impact on foreign policy. The scope for collecting intelligence probably exceeds the resources available to any one nation.

Canada's intelligence community today is complex, relatively large, and very effective, given its limited resources and the lack of a clandestine HUMINT collection service of its own. This is not to say that more could not and should not be done, particularly in terms of diplomatic and grey intelligence collection. Canada's resources in these areas are few and have eroded over the years.

The Canadian intelligence community has its shares of problems and interdepartmental/agency strains. It is a complex community encompassing a wide variety of mandates and interests. Security intelligence falls within the Canadian Security Intelligence Service but also includes national security law enforcement by the RCMP. The RCMP also has separate criminal intelligence responsibilities. Additional organizations have substantial resources directed to customs intelligence issues, border control intelligence, and immigration intelligence. The foregoing all fall under the umbrella of Public Security Canada. Several other departments also maintain small specialized intelligence units directed at securing information on pandemic health issues, food inspection, and so forth. In addition, there are departments and agencies with specific and significant foreign intelligence mandates. These include the Department of Foreign Affairs and International Trade,[2] parts of the intelligence function of the Department of National Defence (in addition to the overlapping traditional military intelligence function), and SIGINT activities of the Communications Security Establishment, an organization reporting to both the DND and the Privy Council Office. As well, the Privy Council Office exercises a coordinating role for the entire Canadian intelligence community as well as maintaining a centralized assessment service.

Strains within such a complex range of mandates are natural. The strengths and weaknesses that exist today reflect the strains, compromises, and working relationships that constitute the evolutionary development of the Canadian intelligence community.

This book sets out to describe how one portion of Canada's intelligence community was established and to outline its developmental path during the early formative years. Canada's foreign intelligence activities are not of long duration, having only truly begun with the onset of war in 1939. This book will also demonstrate that Canada developed a foreign intelligence architecture that was not perfect but seems to have largely met the requirements of the foreign policy decision-making establishment. As a minor but not insignificant international player, Canada has a demand for foreign intelligence. The foreign intelligence community that was developed during the war, and adapted afterward to the postwar environment, has generally met the needs of the nation while accommodating Canada's cautious approach to matters of intelligence and a general reluctance to spend significant sums on such matters.

Canada entered the Second World War on 10 September 1939, ill-prepared for what would follow. With a weak industrial base, an inadequate military establishment, a very small and insufficient diplomatic service, and a lack of necessary economic resources, Canada did not have the tools with which to wage war.[3] Canada was a nation of over 11 million people in 1939, which grew to 12 million by 1945. The economic improvement that had begun in 1935 as the country slowly emerged from the ravages of the Depression was reflected by a growth in the gross domestic product to just over $5 billion in 1939 (a figure that had been previously reached in 1927). The GDP more than doubled to nearly $12 billion by 1945.[4] Although industrial plants existed, particularly in Ontario and in Quebec, Canada's economy was still driven by primary commodities. This changed with the war, during which $1.3 billion was invested by the government in industry, the effects of which were felt almost immediately. Between 1939 and 1941, the GDP increased 47 percent as primary commodities production doubled and secondary manufacturing tripled.[5]

When war broke out, Canada's Department of External Affairs (DEA) had a staff of 174 people, 68 in Ottawa and 106 assigned at diplomatic missions abroad. At the time, the diplomatic staff numbered only twenty-nine officers, ten of whom were in Ottawa. Canada also had a High Commission in London and five delegations: Washington, Paris, Tokyo, Brussels, and The Hague. In addition, there was the delegation to the League of Nations.[6] By 1945, the number of staff had grown to 107 of diplomatic rank and 391 clerical, with 26 missions abroad, figures that by 1950 had increased to over a thousand staff stationed at home and abroad in thirty-three countries.[7]

The need for a foreign intelligence capacity was not obvious to Canadian policy makers as the world approached war in 1939. In fact, as noted above, the country was still building its diplomatic service. Canadian political leaders did not discuss or establish an intelligence capability in the period leading up to war. What information Canada possessed at the time about international events was derived from the reports of a handful of Canadian diplomatic missions abroad and from selected British diplomatic and intelligence reports that were forwarded to Ottawa, sometimes on subjects far removed from Canadian interests. No independent access to foreign intelligence was available to Canada as the country approached war, and the realization of the need for such a resource to meet Canada's national requirements came slowly.

The creation of a Canadian foreign intelligence capacity was the result of a steady, incremental effort by a handful of individuals in positions of importance throughout the Canadian government, who laboured to assemble the rudiments of a foreign intelligence community. A blueprint for the wartime intelligence effort was quickly agreed upon once war began, but it was not until after the Dunkirk evacuation and the fall of France in 1940 that urgency was evident and a more active approach was directed at the problem of intelligence gathering. The clear menace to the supply lines between North America and Europe posed by the North Atlantic German U-boat campaign was among the early catalysts creating the momentum toward the establishment of a foreign intelligence organization.

The innate minimalist approach of the Mackenzie King government and the perennial Canadian caution and penuriousness ensured that Canada's foreign intelligence collection community, even in wartime, remained small. The creation of a foreign intelligence organization was further complicated by the fact that many persons who would have been of great assistance to intelligence work quickly became involved in other wartime ventures; thus, the intelligence organizations often faced challenges in meeting staffing requirements. Wartime intelligence activities also brought to light the lack of coordination between the armed forces intelligence services, the DEA (the earlier name of the Department of Foreign Affairs and International Trade)[8], and the RCMP, the latter being a member of the wider intelligence community with responsibility for security matters but with little involvement in foreign intelligence issues.

Over the course of about a decade, Canada's foreign intelligence capability grew from a small and limited existence within the prewar bureaucratic confines of the DND to a community comprised of not only the DND but also the Privy Council Office, the DEA, and a host of lesser players, including the RCMP and the National Research Council of Canada. It was some time before progress in the establishment of an intelligence community was apparent.[9] Once formed, however, the resources of the intelligence community provided Canadian decision makers with a uniquely Canadian information perspective. It was at this same time that the DEA formalized its foreign intelligence activities through the directed activities of individuals who worked at identifying requirements and exploring opportunities for obtaining required intelligence. The collection and processing of SIGINT was also begun in earnest. Soon after, Canada established the Royal Canadian Navy's (RCN) operational intelligence centre to support the battle against U-boats in the North Atlantic, and the DEA created the special intelligence centre within Canada's cryptanalysis organization, the Examination Unit, to exploit the intelligence that became available through signals interception.

When the war ended, the Discrimination Unit (signals collection) and the Examination Unit (signals decryption and evaluation) merged into a single integrated SIGINT service, the Communications Branch of the National Research Council, while several intelligence units, the Canadian Joint Intelligence Committee (CJIC), the Canadian Joint Intelligence Bureau, and the Canadian Joint Intelligence Staff, were established or expanded as the functional units of foreign intelligence activities. Lastly, the Defence Liaison 2 Division, a more formal acknowledgment of intelligence duties, was created within the DEA in the early days of the Cold War. The foreign intelligence activities of the DND's military intelligence divisions were partly reduced after the war and subsumed within traditional military intelligence activities.

As the end of the war approached, Canada had already begun a review of its foreign intelligence elements in preparation for the transition to a postwar society. This process was launched before the Cold War became entrenched, and it is remarkable how little direct impact the East-West confrontation had on the postwar foundation of Canada's intelligence resources; nowhere in the archival material is a link drawn between the growing East-West confrontation and intelligence reorganization. Rather, intelligence was required primarily as a support tool for Canada's growing international interests. The intelligence review lasted into the late 1940s. At the time, caution and fiscal concerns dominated policy decisions. Disagreement abounded over the extent to which Canada should become involved in the field of foreign intelligence. The organizational structures that emerged at the end of the postwar reorganization defined Canadian engagement in foreign intelligence for many years.

Canada chose a "safe" road for postwar foreign intelligence collection. No covert foreign HUMINT service was established between the end of the war and 1951, the date at which this study concludes. Canadian decision makers were never willing to accept the financial burden or the potential political risks arising from the kind of embarrassing disclosures that can be associated with a clandestine foreign intelligence service. SIGINT, the passive collection of radio signals from the air waves, was continued and expanded in the postwar period. A more structured intelligence analytical capability was also established after the war.

Canada created its foreign intelligence capability in the midst of war and, after the conclusion of hostilities, it restructured much of what had been created under the pressures and constraints of conducting a war effort. In presenting the first comprehensive account, based on primary sources, of the birth and postwar reorganization of Canada's foreign intelligence community, this book focuses on the intelligence services' contribution to the war effort and on the way in which wartime experience was adapted for a postwar mandate.

The bureaucratic relationships between the various intelligence entities, most of which existed within the DND and the DEA, will be explored, and the study records how the DND slowly ceded a greater role over foreign intelligence to the DEA in the postwar period. This book is the administrative history of the makings of a Canadian foreign intelligence capability and how this addressed the perceived needs. The study documents that Canada's foreign intelligence activity in the early postwar period accomplished little more than ensuring membership in the postwar co-operative community of the US, British, Canadian, Australian, and New Zealand intelligence services, an achievement that was to pay untold future dividends for Canada. The findings demonstrate that the restructuring of Canada's postwar intelligence community was afflicted with conflicting bureaucratic responsibilities because no clear department was in overall charge of intelligence.

They also show that the independent intelligence fiefdoms in various departments, which had been a problem during the war, remained largely unchanged. Because the political leadership of Canada clearly yielded to senior civil servants the responsibility for intelligence matters, this may have been the pattern destined to emerge. Nevertheless, in the postwar period External Affairs slowly came to dominate all intelligence committees and organizations in Canada. This did not discourage the other intelligence community partners from expressing firm views during administrative deliberations, but External Affairs assumed a central coordination role for foreign intelligence.

This book is also a case study of how a government responded in the midst of a crisis to the need for an independent means to fill an information vacuum. In the process, the government laid the foundations for the foreign intelligence capability that exists to the present day. The institutions created by Canada during the war to address the lack of information consciously reflected a British approach to intelligence management. The British model represented an unstructured and informal committee format with vaguely defined relationships and reporting lines among the constituent elements. Administratively, this structure functioned quite well as long as Canada's intelligence community was in its infancy, but proved to have many deficiencies when applied to the postwar environment in which the several poorly resourced units seemed excessive for the mandate.

This study also serves a greater purpose. It documents the changes in some aspects of Canada's foreign relations during 1940-50 as the historical ties to Britain slowly loosened while those with the United States, already strong, became more entrenched. This was not a shift in "dependency," with Canada jettisoning the vestiges of colonial ties to Britain in favour of military-industrial links with the United States. Such labelling oversimplifies the complexity of the events that occurred. Canada's drift away from Britain was a progressive twentieth-century occurrence facilitated by the exceptional circumstances of the Second World War.

The transition began in the years immediately after the end of the Second World War. While the intelligence links with Britain remained exceedingly strong, they were no longer exclusive. The strengthening of ties between Canada and the United States may have been affected by the threatening environment of war but was a logical outcome of geographic proximity, cultural affinity, and a commonality of interests. While Canada certainly took the initial steps toward a "partnership" with the United States in the postwar world, it was a partnership that would be mutually advantageous and was embraced by Canada because the international circumstances dictated this as being in the country's best national interest. For the United States, the initiatives toward a partnership were equally welcomed; it was important to have a northern neighbour whose politics were predictable, whose friendship was assured, and whose landmass was not an undefended invasion route. The partnership, which began in the early postwar period, was not rooted in ideology or a negation of Canadian sovereignty but, rather, premised on mutual respect and self-interest. What emerged was a pragmatic partnership between sovereign states entered into for reasons of national self-interest. The establishment of an autonomous Canadian foreign intelligence capability, modest as it was, provided Canada with one set of tools for exercising sovereignty.

Canada's involvement in foreign intelligence, while neither significant nor adequately resourced, reflected a maturing of the nation in its international engagements. More precisely, this study addresses particular questions. Did a concerted Canadian interdepartmental vision exist for creating a foreign intelligence capability? Was there a clear political commitment to the creation of foreign intelligence bodies, and, following the experience of the Second World War, did Canadian policy makers possess a clear vision of the foreign intelligence capacity they wanted to retain for the postwar world? Was the elected government actively engaged in the drafting of Canada's wartime intelligence structures and the revision of the foreign intelligence assets during the early postwar period?

Only limited analysis of why various directions were pursued at different moments in the evolution of Canadian foreign intelligence is included in this book. In published material on intelligence matters, the introduction of analysis of why things happened is often a mask for lack of clarity in the limited available resources. In the case of Canada, the accessible archives are far from complete. Past studies have reflected the paucity of material. Analyses in earlier studies have been proven wrong when additional archival material was released.[10] Intelligence literature has often had a short shelf life because inferences are drawn and conclusions reached based on limited information. Subsequent scholarship points out the weaknesses of drawing too many inferences when the primary sources are not entirely accessible. In the interest of providing insight into Canadian foreign intelligence that is sufficiently robust to accommodate future archival revelations, this study is cautious about advancing analysis based on speculation or drawing conclusions from limited archival material.

The story begins with a description in Chapter 1 of Canada's foreign intelligence capability on the eve of war and during the dramatic early days of the conflict. The most significant intelligence development in Canada was the creation of SIGINT expertise, the early evolution of which, as the following chapter illustrates, was accompanied by confusion as both the DND and the DEA launched separate SIGINT initiatives that were not complementary. The third chapter records the early efforts in building intelligence alliances between three principal partners: the United Kingdom, the United States, and Canada. The partnership began before the United States became belligerent, and was cemented after the Americans joined the common battle.

The initial and modest Canadian engagement in HUMINT is presented in the fourth chapter. While Canada did not send covert operatives abroad during the war, considerable valuable HUMINT was obtained through censorship activities and debriefing POWs and others. A blending of HUMINT and SIGINT efforts is illustrated in the following chapter by an early and largely unique operation within the United States during which Canadian representatives collected raw communications products for SIGINT exploitation. Chapter 6 describes how the intelligence entities coordinated their activities to have an impact on the conduct of the war in its middle and later stages.

A discussion of the intelligence planning for postwar SIGINT, which was well underway long before hostilities were concluded, is outlined in Chapter 7. In Chapter 8 we find the story of the creation of postwar intelligence structures, dealing primarily with collating and evaluating foreign intelligence. This subject proved critical in defining the future shape of Canadian foreign intelligence as policy makers vacillated over whether or not to continue foreign intelligence collecting activities. The chapter provides an overview of decisions made during the postwar period to establish the foreign intelligence machinery, and outlines the manner in which many pieces of the wartime intelligence establishment were restructured. A critical decision made in 1951 to not establish a Canadian clandestine intelligence service forms the conclusion to the chapter. The final chapter looks at postwar SIGINT collection and discusses Canada's participation in a five-power alliance with the United States, the United Kingdom, Australia, and New Zealand that provided communications intelligence coverage of most of the world.

Few academic studies of Canadian foreign intelligence have been published. Much of the existing literature on intelligence in Canada has been anecdotal in nature and has often focused on security intelligence.[11] A country with little public knowledge or culture of foreign intelligence, Canada has not highlighted this side of its history.

Some Canadian literature on intelligence suffers the same weaknesses as sometimes occurs in the intelligence literature of other nations. Particularly in non-academic writings (but not limited to such) there is occasionally an analysis of events that reflects assumptions and fills gaps in the available archival material. Although many egregious examples of this phenomenon exist, the evolving interpretation of the unique achievements of British SIGINT at Bletchley Park in breaking the Enigma code illustrates the problem. Until recently, books on the breaking of Enigma ignored the role of the Polish and French. The Polish built an Enigma machine in the 1930s (when the British failed), and the French obtained vital information from an agent on how the ciphering worked. An early British writer on the subject, F.W. Winterbotham, first introduced the world to Ultra (decrypted intelligence) in his book *The Ultra Secret*. However, basing his information on what he had heard from intelligence colleagues who also were not fully informed, he had only limited knowledge of how the achievement had been reached. Some of his conclusions were conjecture. Parts of the true story eventually emerged but not all of it. A subsequent writer, Anthony Cave Brown, took some of the story revealed by Winterbotham and added details for his book, *Bodyguard of Lies*, that have not stood the test of time. A third book was William Stevenson's *A Man Called Intrepid*, which further changed the details in Cave Brown's book and improved upon them, again with little basis in fact.[12]

Although the three writers were not writing for academic audiences, some of their mistakes have crept into academic studies. All of this is simply to say that analysis of limited resource material can be dangerous and can misdirect historians. Therefore, the present study has been cautious about interpreting material unless it was known to be correct. This makes for a book drier than some but hopefully with fewer errors, which will allow it to stand as a resource for much needed work on Canadian foreign intelligence.

The first book to treat the question of Canadian foreign intelligence in depth, and the only previously published study that attempts to present a detailed picture of one important element of Canada's wartime foreign intelligence community, is John Bryden's *Best Kept Secret: Canadian Secret Intelligence in the Second World War*, published in 1993.[13] This study has a clear focus on wartime SIGINT collection.

Prior to Bryden's book, there had been little published in Canada on the nation's foreign intelligence activities. Some specialty studies, such as *Scarlet to Green: A History of Intelligence in the Canadian Army, 1903-1963* by Major S.R. Elliot, which contributed insight into the military intelligence of that period, presented extensive details about certain elements of Canada's intelligence community. Similarly, David Stafford's *Camp X: Canada's School for Secret Agents 1941-45* provides very useful details on the relationship between Canadian foreign intelligence activities and British Security Coordination (BSC) in the United States.[14] Stafford makes a significant contribution to an understanding of Canada's wartime foreign intelligence activities through his study of a British Special Operations training facility located in Canada. Although that facility, Camp X, was a British site during its early period, its establishment and operation was conducted with the clear cooperation of Canada. Camp X was used by both countries until, toward the end of the war, it was turned over for the exclusive use of Canada. The Camp X story focuses on a narrow segment of Canada's foreign intelligence experience but does it well.

J.L. Granatstein and David Stafford's *Spy Wars: Espionage and Canada from Gouzenko to Glasnost* is an excellent primer on intelligence issues relating to Canada.[15] Reflecting first-rate scholarship, given the sources that were available at the time, it captures the essence of the story. The book makes little distinction between security intelligence and foreign intelligence, and much of the book is focused on the former.

Quite revealing is BSC's own "lost" history, *British Security Coordination: The Secret History of British Intelligence in the Americas, 1940-1945*.[16] Written in 1945 by an associate of William Stephenson, who is incorrectly identified as "Intrepid" by some authors,[17] the book was not published at the time. It was prepared at Stephenson's behest and for the purpose of lauding his operation in North America. When the book was completed, the files and archives of BSC were destroyed.[18] The book was not written for an academic or popular audience but as a record of how an intelligence organization could be used to influence a foreign government, in this case that of the United States. As such, the book provides examples of how BSC achieved its objectives rather than recording historical events in detail. In addition, the original draft, prepared in the closing months of the Second World War, is concerned with maintaining security of information and is often vague or cryptic when describing people and places.[19] Nevertheless, the book appears factually correct; in instances where references in the book can be tested against information held at Library and Archives Canada, it has proven accurate.[20] The book was accessible for many years only to select British authors on intelligence matters, but was made available to the public in 1998. The copy of the original unpublished study given to the Canadian government in 1945 appears to have been lost.

Canadian studies on intelligence face a particular challenge. The wealth of archival material that exists for British and American intelligence studies will never be available for Canada. Material is lost or otherwise irretrievable (seemingly including many early intelligence assessments), and Canada operated on a much smaller scale with much less material committed to paper and far fewer persons in the know. In the meantime, what information is available on Canadian foreign intelligence warrants being made accessible to the general public.

Much of the serious scholarship on Canada's foreign intelligence activities, however, has been in the form of academic articles. These began to appear by the mid-1980s and became progressively more revealing as new material was unearthed in Canada's National Archives.[21]

A number of books and articles written from British, American, and Australian perspectives have discussed the intelligence relationship between the United States, the United Kingdom, Canada, Australia, and New Zealand, which developed during their wartime alliance and became entrenched in a series of early postwar treaties.

The most important of the studies that look at the overall Anglo-Saxon intelligence relationship is Richelson and Ball's *The Ties That Bind: Intelligence Cooperation Between the UKUSA Countries.*[22] Probably the premier study of the postwar US-Commonwealth intelligence relationship, this book achieves a high degree of accuracy and depth of detail. Numerous other studies make reference to Canadian participation in the five-power intelligence-sharing club, but few reflect as clear an understanding of the subject or provide as many details as Richelson and Ball. While the Anglo-Saxon intelligence partners increasingly reveal details of their intelligence relationships, none of the countries in the UKUSA alliance has acknowledged full particulars of the treaties governing their intelligence-sharing co-operation.

There is relatively little credible information in the public domain that throws light on the technicalities and manner of collecting and decrypting SIGINT in the postwar period. Because of the incremental way in which new information becomes available, books on postwar SIGINT activities have not always aged well. Most of the literature on this facet of intelligence is focused on the United States, which has intelligence organizations so vast that diligent journalists and academics regularly uncover important new details. One of the prime authors on the subject, and likely the premier student of the architecture of the American intelligence community, is Jeffrey T. Richelson, whose *The U.S. Intelligence Community* is an exceptional resource, particularly on electronic intelligence gathering.[23]

Among the better material paralleling the coverage of Richelson's book are Richard Aldrich's *The Hidden Hand: Britain, America and Cold War Secret Intelligence* and "British Intelligence and the Anglo-American 'Special Relationship' during the Cold War."[24] The article summarizes the thesis of Aldrich's book; both are excellent studies of British intelligence and the relationship with America. Christopher Andrew's article "The Making of the Anglo-American SIGINT Alliance" covers the birth of the SIGINT relationship and is laudatory of the value of this tool in deciding the outcome of various facets of the Second World War.[25]

Much of the documentary evidence recording the development of foreign intelligence activities by Canada was inaccessible to scholars and the public until very recently. This book is the first to bridge the wartime and postwar periods, drawing clear links between the two, correcting and expanding on the existing literature. In addition to providing new details on previously known aspects of the Canadian intelligence story, this study also makes available for the first time information on previously unknown Canadian intelligence activities, including the Mousetrap collection activities in the United States, HUMINT collection from POWs and returning Canadians from enemy-held areas, details of a SIGINT project conducted by Canadians in Australia toward the end of the war, and others. Many of the earlier historical studies have suffered from a limited access to archival material or have a very narrow focus. Corrections to egregious errors in earlier studies are contained in the text where making such corrections is important. Nevertheless, this study does not devote extensive space to correcting earlier errors in interpretations where such are likely to be apparent to scholars.

Spurred on in part by the terrorist attacks of September 11, a growing number of students and academics are beginning to study subjects relating to intelligence. The focus remains on security and terrorism issues, particularly among those scholars from a political science discipline. However, responding to the ever-growing body of archival material, a small number of historians are looking at facets of Canada's foreign intelligence history, though much remains to be researched and published.

A great deal of the archival material in Canada pertaining to intelligence subjects is interspersed with other documentation and is not always easily retrieved. This is changing daily as Canadian documents relating to foreign intelligence become available to the public. A great deal of intelligence-related archival material has also reached the US National Archives and Records Administration, where a significant number of files concern Canadian wartime intelligence efforts. Some material can also be gleaned from the British public records. The situation will be eased when Canadian government departments that have been engaged in intelligence matters decide to release their records to Library and Archives Canada. That has not yet happened and is probably hampered by the sheer cost of vetting the files, a necessary prelude to their release for public examination.

A number of in-house histories of Canada's SIGINT organization have been released under the Access to Information Program (ATIP) and have contributed to this study. While Library and Archives Canada holdings of material relating to intelligence are constantly expanding, much of the material has not been processed or, if processed, remains closed and only available through ATIP challenges. However, ATIP is not always an option. The glacial pace of the ATIP process is a growing concern. At the present time, it often takes twelve months or more to have material reviewed under ATIP. If consultations on the contents are then required, it can take two and a half years or longer to receive access to documents. A contributing factor is the intelligence agreements between Canada and the United States, the United Kingdom, Australia, New Zealand, and, for some material, other nations. Material that does or could contain information from an allied intelligence organization must be vetted by any possible contributing organization before being released. This can be a protracted process.

Considerable historical material is also available at DND's Directorate of History and Heritage, which is open to scholars and students. This reservoir of archival material contains a great deal of data relating to intelligence matters that is not available at Library and Archives Canada. A large volume of classified documents has also been individually released by Canadian government departments under ATIP. Much of this information is readily available to researchers. This is especially true in the case of the Communications Security Establishment, a key entity within Canada's foreign intelligence community, whose various internal histories have all become available with little more than technical information apparently having been excised.[26] The Communications Security Establishment has stated that all its file material up to the end of the Second World War has now been released to Library and Archives Canada.[27]

It is difficult to assess what significant archival gaps remain in the story of Canadian foreign intelligence. Relatively little material has been released by the Privy Council Office and the Department of Foreign Affairs and International Trade, although the unreleased material would probably serve only to round out an understanding of the issues rather than reveal much information requiring a reinterpretation of the story. Many of the documents relating to the special intelligence section of the Examination Unit, the Canadian Joint Intelligence Bureau, and to a lesser extent the CJIC remain unavailable, particularly the intelligence assessments, virtually all of which are absent from Library and Archives Canada. Some file material explains what has likely happened. A significant number of files relating to intelligence assessments contain only the file covers, some of which carry a notation indicating that the file contents were transferred to files that remain active.[28] Whether the file material is indeed active or whether this is a ploy to prevent release of the information to the public cannot be determined.

Access to individual intelligence assessments would have proven beneficial to this study. Very few are available. Most of the assessments may well have been destroyed over the years. While they would have contributed to an understanding of the areas of interest and possible sources of information, the intelligence assessments are not likely to have provided direct insight into the formulation of foreign policy. The nature of intelligence assessments is such that they inform policy but do not formulate policy. Hence, those persons who prepare policy options for the prime minister or foreign affairs minister will have had access to intelligence material and hopefully will have reflected its value in the policy proposals sent forward to decision makers. Based on the author's own experience, it is difficult to imagine a memorandum to the prime minister or foreign affairs minister including a line that stated that based on certain foreign intelligence, a specific course of action was recommended. Rather, the intelligence would be reflected in the advice provided without explicitly confirming a tie to intelligence. This is not for reasons of secrecy but simply because policy decisions are based on a host of factors, some of which are intelligence related in origin.

A foundation for further studies exploring the relationships and structures that define Canadian foreign intelligence can be established only by understanding the dynamics contributing to the creation of a Canadian foreign intelligence infrastructure during the Second World War, and the critical intelligence developments that followed during the early postwar years. This study looks at the administrative evolution of the Canadian foreign intelligence segments from the beginning of the war until 1951. That year was crucial and marked the emerging of a new era. While Canada formed its intelligence structures during the Second World War and reorganized these for peacetime activities from the end of the war until roughly 1950-51, a number of events heralded changing international realities. The Russians had made great strides in consolidating their hold on eastern Europe and had demonstrated their nuclear prowess. The Korean War had begun in 1950. The McCarthy era of treasonous allegations and flaunting civil liberties was creating an environment of fear that influenced American domestic and international policies.

The changing political climate, a Cold War in full flux, brought new realities and pressures to bear on Canada's intelligence community. The architecture that was in place by that time would govern Canadian intelligence activities until the present day. This book describes the creation of that intelligence architecture. The manner in which this story unfolded continues to influence the shape of Canada's foreign intelligence community today.

1

Foreign Intelligence
at the Beginning of the War

The coming of war in 1939 did not surprise Prime Minister King or his close advisors. O.D. Skelton, the under-secretary of state for External Affairs and a staunch nationalist, was frustrated by the loss of Canadian independent control of its destiny as it was drawn into the coming conflagration in Europe by "policies and diplomatic actions initiated months ago without our knowledge or expectation."[1] At the time of the Munich Crisis, Lester B. Pearson of the DEA wrote to Skelton from London, "It seems necessary to draw the conclusion that in the present state of Canadian opinion no Canadian Government is likely to be able to keep Canada out of a great war in which the United Kingdom is engaged." He continued, "Canadian self-government obviously is incomplete so long as the most vital decision which can arise in the life of a nation is not taken in fact as well as in form by the leaders of the Canadian people."[2]

Mackenzie King was asleep at his beloved Moorside at Kingsmere in the Gatineau Hills near Ottawa when the German armies rolled into Poland on 1 September. Arnold Heeney, principal secretary to the prime minister, was finishing breakfast at 6:30 a.m. when he heard the news on the radio.[3] He immediately telephoned Mackenzie King to inform him of the events. After quickly conferring with Norman Robertson of External Affairs and following directions from Mackenzie King, Heeney raced to the East Block on Parliament Hill to arrange for a 9:00 a.m. meeting of Cabinet to discuss the events in Europe.

Following the Cabinet meeting, Mackenzie King issued an announcement he had prepared in anticipation of the outbreak of war, stating that Parliament would meet six days hence and, in the event of the United Kingdom becoming engaged in war, the prime minister would seek the agreement of his fellow parliamentarians to stand by Britain's side. When Parliament met on 9 September in a special war session, Mackenzie King secured the widest possible approval for Canada's entry into the war. War, for Canada, began the following day, a Sunday. The date was 10 September 1939.

Throughout the final crisis in the countdown to war, Britain had kept Canada informed of developments, but it had never consulted Canada. As a result, Canada was uncomfortable with elements of British foreign policy. No Canadian interpretation of events was asked for by London, and none was offered by Canada.

Canada and its civil servants may have been concerned by the country's slow path toward embroilment in the coming European war, but Mackenzie King was a political realist. There was never a moment when he doubted that Canada would have to stand shoulder to shoulder with Britain if ever the British Isles and the imperial homeland were threatened. Although attempting to follow a policy of isolation, and despairing of Great Power politics, Canada was grudgingly drawn toward inevitable war in Europe in the shadow of the United Kingdom.

While the coming danger of war was acknowledged, little was done by Canada's political leadership to provide the country with an independent source of information to corroborate and complement the sparse diplomatic reports of the DEA and various (not always reliable) news sources. Canada had long been receiving British diplomatic and intelligence reports to supplement its own meagre resources. Sometimes voluminous and generally informative, the British reports were selected to meet a British interest as well as to address a Canadian information need, and were often late in arriving. However, they were not unwelcomed by the Mackenzie King government, which had little hard diplomatic intelligence on which to base a firm stance on issues.[4] Pearson had acknowledged the dilemma in early 1939 when he wrote Skelton that "the Foreign Office, in certain telegrams which they send to the dominions, are more interested in making a case than in providing information. I do not mean that they are attempting to expound in their telegrams, but that by careful selection and emphasis they can create an impression which may not always be strictly justified by the information on which the telegram is based."[5]

No Canadian diplomatic network existed beyond a small number of representatives at core centres of power. No independent sources of information were available to test and corroborate information made available through diplomatic sources. Canada did not have a foreign intelligence service to ferret out the shards of information that could confirm or deny reports that became available through other means. Nor did Canada have an intelligence resource to provide contextual knowledge to information already obtained through more accessible means. Although Canada's reliance on Britain's Secret Intelligence Service (more popularly known as MI6) and the Government Code and Cipher School (Britain's SIGINT service) proved valuable, these were not a substitute for an independent Canadian source of information.

Canada's lack of a secret intelligence service must be viewed in the context of the times. The DEA had only been in existence for about thirty years and was grossly understaffed, having only a handful of diplomatic missions around the world. The United Kingdom still played a large role in formulating Canada's view of the world. That Canada did not create a foreign intelligence service before the Second World War is understandable; the limited resources available to the country could more effectively be directed at expanding Canada's diplomatic eyes and ears to obtain openly available information. However, as the world was drawn toward war, little was done by Canada to expand its diplomatic resources.

With few Canadian diplomatic missions in existence, access to independent sources of information was limited. No Canadian diplomatic mission was present in Berlin, although there was an important presence in Tokyo. Nevertheless, Canada was well served by its small diplomatic service, which sought to collect and collate information of benefit to Canadian decision makers.

Rather late, as events turned out, Canada came to understand the need for a foreign intelligence capability. None existed within the sphere of foreign policy making. Some rudimentary intelligence gathering was already available within the Canadian armed forces, although much less than required and not always under direct Canadian control. Each of the armed services had a unique approach to intelligence gathering. With few exceptions, there was little effort among the services to coordinate intelligence activities, and intelligence gathering within the services was conducted with limited effectiveness until shortly before the war. The lack of effectiveness reflected limited resources, deficiencies in leadership, complacency, and an absence of co-operation between the services.

The intelligence efforts of the Canadian Army, a small service with an uncertain focus as to where future danger might lie, were inconsequential. What foreign intelligence Canada collected, or received from the United Kingdom, had little applicability to Canada's limited areas of foreign policy interests. Nearly all intelligence relating to matters beyond the shores of North America seems to have come from the British War Office or the Dominions Office. During this period, Canadian military intelligence, an area greatly overlapping with foreign intelligence in methods, sources, and focus, was little more than a library receiving and filing British reports, which were often unread.

The root cause of the poor quality of Canadian military intelligence was the paucity of resources. With very limited staff dedicated to intelligence matters, it was all they could do to keep their heads above water. No structured intelligence collection or analysis of received information was possible with the few people available to carry out the task. Since available information was often of tangential interest only, it was impossible to establish a readership of the material among decision makers whose immediate priorities often lay elsewhere.

In the decade following the First World War, the military conducted only one training course on intelligence. In January 1929, shortly after becoming Chief of the General Staff, General A.G.L. McNaughton wrote his minister, seeking guidance. He noted, "Most of the incoming [intelligence] information stops in the Department [of National Defence] and ... I do not think that we as a country are getting all the benefits out of it that we should."[6] McNaughton wanted to make the intelligence available to the DEA and the Department of Trade and Commerce.

After discussing his proposal with Skelton of External Affairs, an intelligence exchange was begun. The DND forwarded to the DEA what information was available to it, while the latter provided copies of the foreign intelligence documents the British Dominions Office sent to the governor general to inform the Canadian government. As it applied to areas outside Canada, foreign intelligence and military intelligence were interchangeable and of interest to all departments with a foreign policy mandate. The foreign intelligence documents included such series as the "Special Monthly Secret Intelligence Summary," "Confidential Intelligence Summary" (monthly), "Weekly Secret Intelligence Summary" from India, and various intermittent reports from elsewhere in the Empire, as well as copies of British diplomatic reports. A review of some of the intelligence reports that reached Canada at the time makes one wonder as to the applicability of such minutiae to Canada's circumspect foreign or defence policies. While the benefits of McNaughton's intelligence-sharing initiative may well have been limited at a time when there was neither appreciation of the need for intelligence gathering nor much of a Canadian-directed intelligence collection program with which to balance the flow of British material, his effort probably constituted the first step in forming the entity that became the Canadian foreign intelligence community.

The thrust of Canadian military intelligence efforts in the latter part of the interwar period was directed toward support for fighting forces. Intelligence training and preparation were limited to teaching officers the rudiments of field reconnaissance. Much of what limited intelligence collection was carried out by the Canadian military focused exclusively on the United States. The Directorate of Military Operations and Intelligence, the then military intelligence unit, controlled intelligence funds, which in 1927 amounted to a mere $1,500. In 1932, only $750 was expended on the purchase of 2,625 maps of New York, Pennsylvania, Illinois, Indiana, Michigan, and Wisconsin.[7] During the fiscal year of 1933-34, the five military districts in Canada received a total of $250 (the lowest allocation was $30, while the highest was $70) for "intelligence services," which seem to have consisted of subscriptions to local and US newspapers, and the purchase of maps, reports, and League of Nations Armaments Year Books.[8] As late as

1938, the funding for intelligence-related activities in the military districts (of which there was now a greater number) remained roughly the same.[9]

The preoccupation of Canadian military intelligence with the United States during much of the interwar period reflects an ill-conceived effort to return to perceived normalcy following the end of the First World War. Preparation to meet a possible invasion of Canada by the United States was, rightly or wrongly, considered a valid requirement. During the early 1920s, the prime preoccupation of military intelligence and planning was Defence Scheme No. 1, the Canadian response to an attack by the United States.[10] It is questionable how seriously this scheme was taken by Canadian decision makers at the time. Nevertheless, supporting activity continued well into the 1930s and reflects the limited resources devoted to military intelligence and its entrenched mindset that favoured support for the status quo. By way of balancing the foregoing, Defence Scheme No. 3, preparing for Canadian engagement in war beyond the North American continent, was launched in 1927.[11] Very little planning had been carried out for this scheme before Canada found itself involved in a European war.

While symptomatic of the lack of support given to intelligence matters during the period leading up to the Second World War, these allotments reflect only the resources made available to military districts, which had no substantive intelligence collecting role at the time. More funding was clearly made available at the national level.

The near lack of involvement of Canada's army in intelligence matters had a number of causes: the army was small in peacetime with insufficient resources to do everything that was necessary; the absence of a credible military threat for much of the interwar period contributed to a disinterest in the mundane tasks that governed much of daily intelligence work; and the popular articulation of Canadian nationalism that identified Canada as part of North America, increasingly divorced from European affairs, influenced the thinking of many people involved in policy making. Mackenzie King, who had returned to government in 1935, was intent on minimizing international commitments and maximizing international trade as a way of escaping the impact of the economic depression.[12]

While the Canadian Army hardly rated an acknowledgment of having had a viable foreign or military intelligence program during most of the interwar period, the situation was different for Canada's small navy. The evolution of engagement in intelligence matters in the RCN had come about differently. The Royal Navy was the premier force within the British armed services, and close links had long existed with the naval resources of the dominions in effort to control the communications lines between parts of the Empire. The RCN's more significant imperial role in the early part of the twentieth century ensured a more effective engagement in all facets of naval duties, including intelligence. Consequently, the interwar intelligence role of Canada's navy was more determining but still must be viewed in the context of limited resources and a mission that remained largely one of support for imperial objectives. Efforts by the RCN to define an intelligence role for itself had begun in October 1910, four years before the beginning of the First World War, when G.J. Desbarats, Canadian deputy minister of the Department of Naval Services, wrote to the assistant secretary to the Admiralty in London, advising that the Canadian Naval Service was "desirous of establishing a Naval Intelligence Branch and would be glad to receive the advice of the Admiralty as to its proper organization."[13] Desbarats went on to seek guidance on establishing arrangements for an interchange of intelligence material between the imperial and Canadian navies, especially concerning the United States, Central and South American powers, and China and Japan in the Far East.

The following December, an imperious reply from the Admiralty advised, "The Canadian Naval forces have not yet reached such a development that it was necessary to establish a separate Naval Intelligence Department on the lines of the Naval Intelligence Department of the Admiralty."[14] The Admiralty then proposed to send to the Department of Naval Services "such intelligence as [the Admiralty] consider[s] will be of use to the Canadian Naval forces."[15] In exchange, the RCN was asked to report to the Admiralty the intelligence it had collected. In what may have been symptomatic of friction in the United Kingdom over control of intelligence matters, the Admiralty proposed that the Department of Naval Services arrange with the Canadian Militia Department that the monthly intelligence diary, which the latter prepared and forwarded to the War Office in London, go to the RCN for collation with its own material before everything was sent directly to the Admiralty.

The proposal was taken to heart. From the vantage point of today, the arrangement appears as a constraint on Canadian sovereignty. At the time, however, the British proposal was accepted as reasonable and an appropriate means of gaining access to such intelligence material as the Admiralty deemed appropriate to Canadian needs. The Canadian offering was likely modest (no copies of Canadian reports have been located) and was viewed by Canadian officers, most of whom were British-trained, as a proper contribution to a collective imperial undertaking. There is no indication that political sanction for the inter-services arrangement was sought in Canada.

With the outbreak of the First World War, the RCN was placed at the disposal of the Royal Navy. Canada's minuscule naval intelligence organization became an element of British naval intelligence. At the end of the war, the RCN sought to establish a permanent Canadian naval intelligence organization. This was driven, in part, by a Royal Navy plan to relocate the existing regional headquarters of the West Indies and North America (Intelligence) Station from Halifax to Bermuda.[16] The proposal was rejected and

Canada got its naval intelligence organization, but the earlier ties to Admiralty intelligence remained intact.

The early post-First World War Canadian naval intelligence organization amounted to little more than a few officers (three in 1921), a couple of "lady clerks," cramped quarters, and a large number of shipping and marine journals as well as newspapers.[17] The Canadian naval intelligence service did little more than study the naval affairs of nations in its area of interest.

By 1920, a wartime arrangement for Admiralty naval intelligence coverage of the coastal and ocean areas contiguous to North America was reorganized and became the Ottawa (Naval) Intelligence Area, which absorbed responsibilities hitherto allotted independently to the naval stations in Halifax and Esquimalt.[18] The intent was to extend the Canadian naval intelligence coverage, still under the auspices and direction of the British Admiralty, as far as the coasts of Central America, with control centralized in Ottawa. During the 1920s and 1930s, the Ottawa (Naval) Intelligence Area sent Canadian naval intelligence officers, on behalf of Admiralty intelligence, to conduct annual tours of each of the American coasts, and to meet with British Consular Reporting Officers residing in British consulates in coastal cities. The collected information consisted largely of details of US naval fleet movements, visiting warships, shore facilities (dry docks and other infrastructure), coastal defences, and communications capabilities. Given the single annual visit of only one coast, the collected information must have been terribly outdated by the time it was collated. No urgency was associated with this activity and one can surmise that much of the information was pro forma and destined for a filing cabinet without being assessed. Most of the information was clipped from newspapers with news of US naval movements often ceasing whenever the United States undertook even the most rudimentary forms of concealment. The consuls were willing and anxious to assist, even though not all were British subjects, but they complained about the difficulty of obtaining naval news.[19]

The management of naval intelligence in much of the western hemisphere by Canada's navy on behalf of the British Admiralty was not always smooth. One minor incident marred the operation in 1921 when the British naval attaché in Washington, DC, was curtly told by his superiors to cease interfering with British consuls in the United States who were reporting on naval matters to the Canadian naval intelligence organization.[20] The British naval attaché was to restrict himself to the official intelligence exchange with the United States, for which he was accredited. This implies that the contacts the Ottawa (Naval) Intelligence Area had with the British consulates in the United States may have constituted a form of covert intelligence gathering unknown to the United States. If such was the case, the intelligence gathering was quite benign.

The Ottawa (Naval) Intelligence Area continued its activities in the United States after the outbreak of the Second World War. There is some evidence that the Canadian naval officers may have gathered intelligence from Americans supporting Allied aims. This activity may not have been clandestine in nature, but more likely simply represented information provided openly and freely by friendly and helpful Americans unaware that it might constitute intelligence activity.[21] By 1942, collection of naval information had been transferred to a new British unit in the United States, the amorphously named Consular Shipping Advisers, who continued reporting Canadian naval intelligence, but now in co-operation with US authorities.

In addition to maintaining the Ottawa (Naval) Intelligence Area as an adjunct to British Admiralty intelligence throughout the interwar period, in 1925 the Admiralty also asked the RCN to establish a wireless and direction-finding station at Esquimalt on Vancouver Island. The station, which was a link in a growing British effort to maintain global surveillance of radio communications, would work in tandem with a similar station in Singapore. The Royal Navy trained the SIGINT collection staff at Esquimalt, and may have supplied their own intelligence staff. Details are sketchy but it seems possible that the RCN was not aware at the time of all of the intelligence-gathering activities carried out by the British at Esquimalt. All intercepts and direction-finding data were forwarded to the Admiralty for processing.[22]

While the RCN co-operated closely with the British Admiralty on SIGINT matters, other small SIGINT activities had been quietly launched during the interwar period elsewhere in the Canadian government. A signals communications subcommittee had been established by the DND as early as June 1921 to collect information on existing systems of signals communication and on technical equipment.[23] By 1930, the committee had been made a subcommittee of the Joint Staff Committee. The subcommittee, which included representation from the RCMP but not from the DEA, was directed to collect and study existing systems of signals communication and to examine all facets of operation, maintenance, and technical resources. The goal of the subcommittee was not to establish a Canadian intelligence collection program but, rather, to prepare for a potential capability in a vague and distant future. Few resources were available and existing efforts appear to have been directed toward identifying the assistance that Canadian telegraph and telephone companies could provide for the army in time of crisis.[24]

Apparently unrelated to the cautious Canadian initiatives outlined above, a meeting took place in London on 28 July 1937 to establish co-operation in wireless interception. No details of the actual meeting are available but the Dominions Office wrote to Dominion high commissioners on 30 August 1937, asking them to name a national authority for wireless interception. Canada nominated a representative of the Department of Transport.

Some unclear link with Canadian naval authorities, whose intercept station at Esquimalt "had done work on American and later Japanese traffic," was maintained under this initiative.[25] Very little is known of this, which at face value appears separate from other ongoing wireless intelligence initiatives primarily with Canada's navy. Some contact, presumably by the British SIGINT service, was maintained until after the beginning of the war. In early 1939, a program of work was assigned to each dominion; Canada was responsible for intercepting Japanese commercial radio stations linking North and South America with Japanese merchant shipping in the North Pacific. Newfoundland, a separate dominion, was responsible for German stations directed at the United States, and German shipping in the North Atlantic. However, such activity amounted to little more than listening stations feeding collected information into the British SIGINT effort.[26]

The army's Royal Canadian Corps of Signals was not part of the foregoing arrangement. Already beginning in 1924, the Corps of Signals operated the commercial stations of the North-West Territories and Yukon Radio system as well as maintained wireless beacons and other radio stations in support of the Trans-Canada Air Route. These stations were gradually taken over by the newly formed Department of Transport during the 1930s. They had no intelligence-related purpose when first established but would later become vital cogs in the wartime SIGINT machine.[27]

The first Canadian-directed effort in modern foreign intelligence collection occurred on 5 April 1938, when Major W.H.S. Macklin, a member of the general staff at army headquarters in Ottawa, made a proposal for wireless intelligence collection. This proposal went to Colonel H.D.G. Crerar, director of military operations and intelligence, soon to become Chief of the General Staff and leader of the First Canadian Army during the Second World War.[28] Taking advantage of Mackenzie King's 1937 rearmament initiative, which included a decision to prepare coastal defences, Macklin set out, under the rubric of the coastal study, to make a case for establishing a comprehensive system for wireless intelligence gathering in Canada. At the time, wireless intelligence was restricted to the derivation of information from the nature of the signals intercepted, or to the deduction of information from the number, nature, activity, and frequency of stations heard. No cryptographic analysis – code breaking – was involved. Macklin also suggested that intelligence could be gathered through position-finding methods – that is, determining from triangulation the location from which a signal originated, a strategy that would later prove critical during the North Atlantic U-boat war.

Macklin underscored the complexity of the task. The necessary equipment had to be capable of handling weak and fading signals on all frequencies as well as those transmitted at high speed, sometimes in a foreign language or in code. There had to be sufficient stations to permit the triangulation of signals in order to determine their geographic origins. More was needed than just the ability to intercept signals. Familiarity with foreign signalling procedures and knowledge of the type of equipment being used by other countries was necessary. In addition, operators had to be able to understand foreign language signals practices and Morse code for symbols not found in the English alphabet or in Latin script. A support structure had to be in place to handle foreign language messages. Staff had to be identified and trained to collate, study, and interpret the information collected. All this had to be carried out under rules of exceptional secrecy.

Macklin bolstered his proposal by citing examples from the First World War of the effectiveness of wireless intelligence. In fact, in making reference to the success of wireless intelligence in Canada during the earlier war, he asserted that "the use of the method did not cease with the armistice," but he did not amplify by explaining that what was actually done was very limited in scope. He saw his scheme as potentially vital not only to the army but also to the RCN and the air force, but Macklin acknowledged that he did not know "what stations, if any, of this nature are operated secretly by the Naval Service." The proposed scheme would "be indispensable from the very outset of the war, and indeed probably even more so during a time of strained relations."[29] He urged that the stations be equipped with modern receivers and be supported by properly trained, skilled operators. Macklin had made a revolutionary proposal. If one acknowledged the value of such intelligence gathering, it followed that all three armed services stood to benefit. Since the militia had the trained men, Macklin proposed that it operate the wireless intelligence gathering on behalf of all three services and make the findings available to all.

The Canadian Army's director of signals, Colonel Earnshaw, was already in the United Kingdom learning about British successes with interception of wireless signals at the time that Macklin's proposal was being circulated.[30] Earnshaw's assistant, Major H.A. Young, immediately grasped the importance of the proposal and quickly volunteered a small number of trained operators. He also recommended the appointment of Major R.A.H. Galbraith, an experienced officer who had done direction-finding work during the First World War, to the position of Officer Commanding the Fortress Signals Establishment (the proposed name for the unit charged with wireless intelligence collection).[31]

Both the chief of the naval staff and the senior air officer informed the Chief of the General Staff of their strong support for the proposal. The RCN admitted that its own small efforts had suffered from insufficient resources.[32] Later, under pressure from the British Admiralty, the navy abandoned its support on the basis of "over-riding considerations."[33] This was an obvious effort by the Admiralty to maintain the covert wireless intelligence station that had existed at Esquimalt since 1925. The difference between the Admiralty effort at Esquimalt and what was contained in Macklin's proposal was that the material collected at Esquimalt did not remain in Canada but was sent by surface mail to Britain, where it was processed by the British SIGINT agency. Canada benefited from this program only indirectly through whatever information Britain chose to send as decrypted and assessed material. From the available files, it is unclear whether British Admiralty intelligence was concerned with ensuring the continued smooth functioning of its existing SIGINT efforts, which included Esquimalt, unhampered by Canadian interference, or simply did not want Canada to have access to an autonomous source of intelligence.

In an obvious attempt to build on the initiative begun with the Macklin proposal, on 19 March 1938 Crerar proposed to the three service chiefs that a joint service intelligence section be formed as a subcommittee of the Joint Staff Committee.[34] His goal was to eliminate duplication of effort and make the best use of the very limited Canadian resources dedicated to intelligence work. By April a subcommittee of the Joint Staff Committee had been formed to consider and report on the feasibility of inaugurating a joint service intelligence section.

Crerar's initiative was really only the expansion of something already largely in existence. The army and air force intelligence sections had been amalgamated six years earlier (at a time when the air force was at minimum numbers). By extending army-air force intelligence co-operation to include the navy, it was hoped that a force multiplier would be achieved through better use of existing resources. The joint service intelligence section would collate and correlate all sources at one central agency: more information would be more easily available for exchange among the services, a duplication of effort would be reduced, savings from pooled newspapers, periodicals, and other public sources would permit an increase in subscriptions, and, most importantly, inter-service co-operation would be enhanced to extend coordination of intelligence interpretation, and all the parties would share a common perception of events.[35]

The navy was initially cryptic in its response to Crerar's proposal. At the beginning of May 1938, it recommended "a closer co-operation between the intelligence sections of the three services as at present constituted. This must be largely a personal matter."[36] None of the other parties to the discussions seem to have understood the response from the navy. However, it quickly became clear that the navy was opposed to the idea of inter-service intelligence co-operation beyond very limited coordination. The navy thought its own intelligence efforts more focused than those of the other services and claimed that "the creation of a war room in which operational movements and Intelligence obtained from the separate sections may be coordinated requires further thinking." This response was seen as the stalling tactic it clearly was and the navy was pressed for an unambiguous position. The answer was negative: the "Canadian Naval Intelligence and Plans Division is part of the world-wide British Naval Intelligence Organization and is responsible, through the Chief of the Naval Staff, to [the British] Admiralty for the collection of intelligence in the North American area."[37]

At the same time the navy was rejecting the proposal for a joint service intelligence section, on 3 May 1938 the Minister of National Defence appended his approval of a memorandum that outlined the Macklin proposal for wireless intelligence collection as being of great value to Canada's defence in the event of war. The memorandum to the minister underscored that Canada had to rely on its own intelligence resources in the event of war with Japan, and that the wireless system could not be hastily improvised in the midst of an emergency.[38] In case of hostilities, Canada could expect to receive less assistance from the Royal Navy in defence of Canada's Pacific coast than would be available in the Atlantic. The necessity for great secrecy was stressed; the stations were to be provided security covers as the signals system of fortresses and port defences. The minister agreed to the initial establishment of two or three wireless intelligence stations along the Pacific coast with attendant administrative and technical support.

Within days of receiving the ministerial approval, Colonel Crerar had established a subcommittee of the DND's Joint Staff Committee. The first meeting was held with representatives of the three service intelligence units on 18 May 1938; no representation was accorded to civilian organizations, including the DEA.[39] The RCN, while supporting the effort launched by Crerar, was not prepared to assist in a practical sense: "The commitments for Naval Signal personnel make it impractical for the Naval Service to provide any personnel for this service [i.e., the project prepared by Macklin] now or in the near future."[40] The navy was totally committed to its own limited direction-finding signals efforts, conducted at the behest of the British Admiralty. The navy's attitude did change later as a result of influence from the Admiralty, which eventually saw the benefits of a more holistic approach to wide interception of radio signals.

Although preparations for establishing wireless intercept stations were begun in 1938, there were no stations in place and operational when the Second World War began. The first army wireless intercept station became operational in the fall of 1939, some time after hostilities had commenced.[41] The breakdown in co-operation between the army and navy in allotting resources to the project was just one of many setbacks experienced during the early SIGINT efforts. Nevertheless, had preparations for SIGINT gathering not begun until after September 1939, the implications for the North Atlantic U-boat war would have been greater. Major Macklin and Colonel Crerar were exceptional for their time in having the foresight to argue persuasively for the establishment of a Canadian SIGINT facility in the face of great competition for limited military funding and insufficient understanding of the importance of the future wireless war.

While the Macklin initiative for an integrated tri-service approach to Canadian SIGINT collection had been defeated by naval intransigence, the RCN continued its own SIGINT efforts in co-operation with the British Admiralty. A new Canadian director of naval intelligence, Commander E.S. (Eric) Brand of the British Royal Navy, was appointed in June 1939 with primary responsibility for overseeing what was expected to be a vital convoy link between Canada and Britain. At the time of his appointment, Canadian naval intelligence was expected to continue as an adjunct of Admiralty intelligence. Before proceeding to Canada, Brand met with the British SIGINT service, where he learned of the existence of the RCN's SIGINT station at Esquimalt. The British SIGINT service made it clear that the Admiralty would continue to provide tasks and direction to the Esquimalt facility. The Canadian contribution was solely to pass on the collected data without efforts at assessing or interpreting the information.[42] The Admiralty also asked Brand to establish a direction-finding intercept station in the vicinity of Halifax as a link in the chain of the stations the Admiralty thought necessary to protect its trans-Atlantic supply lines.[43]

When Brand assumed his duties in Ottawa on 28 July 1939 at the Naval Service Headquarters on Queen Street, between Metcalfe and Elgin, he found that only four reserve officers had been mobilized as intelligence officers at the outbreak of war. All had been commanded in March 1939 to be available at a moment's notice in the event of war. One of the four officers was Lieutenant Commander John (Jock) Barbe-Pougnet de Marbois of the Royal Navy Reserve. De Marbois was already fifty-one years old when war began and previously a language teacher at Upper Canada College. He had been born on an island in the Indian Ocean near Mauritius, had run away to sea at age twelve, sailed around the world twice, survived shipwrecks and a bloody mutiny, became a British liaison officer on a Russian cruiser during the First World War, and escaped from the Bolshevik revolution with his Russian countess fiancée. After stopping briefly in Nigeria, de Marbois settled in Canada.[44]

Brand selected de Marbois to build the RCN's knowledge of SIGINT. By this time, Brand was no longer satisfied with having all SIGINT direction come from the British Admiralty, and must have been given some Admiralty latitude for building the Canadian organization. De Marbois was placed in charge of a small unit named the foreign intelligence section, with the responsibility of passing Canadian naval SIGINT to the Admiralty as well as of instituting a system for collecting "Y" discrimination data (the triangulation of radio signals) and plotting the locations of enemy vessels.[45]

De Marbois would later recall arriving in Ottawa to find a naval SIGINT organization that was little more than a post office forwarding collected material to the Admiralty for processing. De Marbois viewed the arrival on "virgin ground" as an opportunity to build a Canadian direction-finding organization that was "more progressive and modern in every point of view than the Admiralty."[46] Although hardly modest, de Marbois was probably correct in his recollection. By the middle of the war, his collection of geophysicists and other scientists recruited from the National Research Board had sharpened the collection of direction-finding bearings to take into account earth magnetism, meteorology, and auroral activities to provide more precise pinpointing for intercepting radio signals. De Marbois' scientific approach would later be copied by the Admiralty and the other Allied SIGINT services.[47]

One of the reasons for de Marbois' success was his rapid assembly of a Canadian naval "Y" organization, using triangulation to identify the origin of signals. Among the first to whom he sent a call for help was C.H. (Herbie) Little, a teacher at Upper Canada College who had been one of de Marbois' German-language students there. Little, a naval reservist, arrived on 13 October 1939 to assume charge of all documents and books and to assist de Marbois with translations.[48] Little and others quickly formed the nucleus of an intelligence unit that came to have an impact on winning the U-boat war in the North Atlantic.

De Marbois did in fact receive a great deal of assistance from many of the individuals who ran the British Admiralty's own direction-finding operations. This assistance came in the form of personal letters from Captain H.R. Sandwith, who ran the Admiralty's direction-finding operation, and Admiral Clayton, a senior officer in Admiralty intelligence. The British had their own interests in establishing a credible Canadian SIGINT unit. The Royal Navy urgently required stations in Canada to assist in plotting direction-finding bearings to help locate the enemy in the Atlantic. At this stage of the war, no one knew whether Britain itself would be invaded, forcing any remnants of Admiralty intelligence units to flee to Canada. Also, perilously close to the centre of the war, the Admiralty's SIGINT stations could be disabled through aerial bombardment.

Because of the unavailability of navy radio receivers, de Marbois set about procuring assistance from the Department of Transport. This was not as novel as it might seem, since the department had been providing the Admiralty with wireless traffic for years.[49] Brand had already been in contact with Commander C.P. Edwards, the head of the Radio Division of Transport, and a former radio intercept officer during the First World War.[50] During a 5 September call from de Marbois to Edwards, the latter agreed to full co-operation.[51] It is important to note the date of this meeting. Britain had declared war two days before, but it would be another five days before Canada formally went to war. It is also interesting to note that de Marbois, a reservist to be called up in the event of war, had reported for duty before Canada's declaration of war.

Before long, Edwards agreed to use Transport funds to build a direction-finding signals station at Hartlen Point, near Halifax. The station was placed on a strip of land at the eastern gateway to Halifax harbour with a clear view of the sea in all directions. The station was controlled by Department of Transport staff, and did not become operational until late 1941 or early 1942. After that, however, Hartlen Point became a vital link in direction-finding SIGINT, and was critical in locating and attacking German submarines operating in the North Atlantic.[52] Before long, the station at Hartlen Point, in co-operation with other stations in Bermuda and Jamaica, could use triangulation to pinpoint the location of German submarines in the North Atlantic.

The first Department of Transport radio station to be pressed into service for the RCN on "Y" efforts was in Strathburn, Ontario, assigned on 8 December 1939 to watch for German naval ciphers sent from German commercial stations.[53] The station suffered from lack of proper equipment (not even a clock to record the time of transmissions) and it was some time before it functioned properly. Other Department of Transport radio facilities the RCN pressed into service when war began included stations in St. Hubert in Quebec, Shediac in New Brunswick, St. Louisbourg in Nova Scotia, Forrest in Manitoba, and Botwood in Newfoundland. Use of Botwood, which had been operated by the Department of Transport on behalf of the Air Ministry, required the approval of Britain, since Newfoundland was now under direct British control.

As the Canadian naval SIGINT operation grew, there came with it a natural inclination toward greater autonomy. In early 1941, the British Admiralty sought to reassert its control over Canadian operations by having the Canadian stations become subordinate to the British admiral in Bermuda, and the collected data passed through British naval headquarters in Bermuda before reaching the Admiralty Operations Centre in London. De Marbois, by this time promoted to commander, made a visit to Bermuda in an attempt to resolve the matter, but was not successful. The problem was solved only when the Canadian chief of naval staff informed the British naval headquarters in Bermuda that the unique situation in Canada, involving many stations, some of which were manned and operated by the Department of Transport, necessitated that Canada deal directly with London for the sake of efficiency.[54]

While Canada's navy approached the coming war with the rudiments of an intelligence base because of its collecting ties to the British Admiralty, the Canadian Army started with an even weaker foundation. Canada's first army SIGINT station, which was inaugurated in October 1939, was located at army headquarters at Rockcliffe Airport in Ottawa. The station had the designation VER, the international radio call letters assigned to Canadian army headquarters. Located in the basement of one of the airport buildings (formerly a garage), the station initially consisted of three operators, two of whom were brothers, under the command of Major W.J. McGill of the Directorate of Signals.[55] By November 1939, responsibility for the Rockcliffe station had passed to Captain H.D.W. Wethey as commanding officer of the Royal Canadian Signals Experimental Section. Captain E.M. Drake was second in command. The early mandate of the Rockcliffe station is unclear, but the very limited resources available to the station suggest that little of consequence could have been accomplished.

In November 1940, the Canadian Army sent Drake on a mission to Washington to seek assistance and advice from the United States on the establishment of a cryptographic bureau in Canada. Ostensibly, the reason for the visit to the United States was for Drake to obtain technical information on certain radio equipment manufactured by American firms, to assess their performance, and to determine if appropriate equipment could be purchased by Canada.[56]

It was while preparations for Drake's visit were still underway that planning assumed a new direction. Lieutenant Colonel H.E. Taber, the Canadian Army's acting director of signals, informed Drake that his mission now had an additional fourfold purpose.[57] Drake's primary objective became to assess the feasibility of organizing a Canadian cryptographic section within the Canadian Army's Signal Corps, essentially an expansion of the work Drake was already conducting. Canada knew that the United States was carrying out cryptographic work, although there does not seem to have been any understanding of the details. Drake's second objective was to assess whether there was scope for wireless monitoring co-operation with US services. He was also to learn of any US experience using radio amateurs for monitoring duties and to seek access to a US monitoring station to study its organization. Nothing sinister needs to be read into the changes to Drake's purpose in visiting the United States. Almost certainly, this was merely an effort to make use of his presence in the United States to speak with American officials about Canadian plans for a cryptographic bureau and to benefit from US knowledge on the subject.

The Canadian Army's decision to send Drake to Washington instead of London is inexplicable. Nothing in the files suggest any motivation, nor do available documents allude to any consideration being given to visiting London. While close co-operation existed between Canada and Britain in all defence matters, exchanges often involved administrative issues rather than innovative initiatives. The decision in favour of visiting Washington may have resulted from as mundane a reason as less expensive travel costs, or may have been tied to the original purpose of the visit, which was to secure equipment. More likely, it reflected an assumption that the United States would be

more receptive than Britain to a request for assistance in creating an autonomous radio intercept facility. However, it must be remembered that at the
time of the visit, Canada was at war while the United States was neutral.

The Canadian military attaché in Washington arranged for Drake to meet
with Major General Joseph O. Mauborgne, chief signal officer of the US
Army. Drake's meeting with Mauborgne on 19 November lasted two and a
half hours, an indication of their mutual interest and importance given to
the talks. Mauborgne was surprised that Canada did not have a cryptographic bureau and made it clear that he thought it vital for a nation at war
to have access to the type of information that might be derived from SIGINT.
Although forthcoming and helpful, Mauborgne explained that the United
States was not at war and that, as such, details of the activities and locations
of US Army monitoring stations could not be discussed. He was clearly surprised that the Canadians even knew the stations existed. He did admit that
much of the US SIGINT collection effort was carried out in co-operation
with the US Federal Communications Commission.[58]

Much of the meeting centred on a discussion about breaking enemy codes
and ciphers. It was Mauborgne's opinion that Canada should not become
involved in cryptographic work with less than a staff of about 200 people.
To assist the Canadians, Mauborgne would arrange for them to receive various US cryptographic training manuals. For his part, Drake informed the
Americans of signals and call letters originating in the United States from
stations the Americans had not known existed, and which the Canadians
had been intercepting. Drake also gave Mauborgne the details of several
German stations and frequencies that Canada had recorded.

In response to the question of closer and ongoing co-operation that was
raised during the discussions, Drake was informed that there were already
talks underway between the Federal Communications Commission, Canada's
Department of Transport, and the armed services of the United States,
Canada, and Britain.[59] Mauborgne cautioned the Canadians that because of
the US status as a non-belligerent, the US Army Signal Corps would want to
keep its activities hidden from the public. The Canadian military attaché
accompanying Drake responded that the question of formal and ongoing
co-operation would be a matter that could be referred to the Canada-US
Permanent Joint Board on Defence, the bilateral defence forum that permitted a measure of Canadian-American military co-operation notwithstanding US neutrality. Mauborgne was supportive of the Canadian suggestion
but the US record of the meeting also states, "Nothing was said about existing proposals along this line."[60]

Mauborgne suggested that the Canadians discuss their proposal with the
British, and recommended that Canada ask the British for copies of available German, Italian, Russian, and Japanese codes or cipher systems as the
first step in launching a cryptographic effort. It must have become apparent

to him during the meeting with the Canadians that such codes and cipher systems had not been provided to Canada. The US Army Signal Corps was encouraging and willing to assist the Canadians but also cautious of the American political position; the American notes of the meeting record a willingness to assist once the Signal Corps had been provided with the policy direction to do so.[61]

As a result of Drake's visit, a recommendation was forwarded to the Canadian Chiefs of Staff Committee, proposing the establishment of a cryptographic bureau of approximately 200 people, including cryptographic specialists, translators, and clerks. Because so many staff members were required, it was recommended that a conference be held among the three Canadian armed services to arrive at a decision on creating a joint operation. Perhaps recalling the earlier failure of the 1938 Macklin initiative, the drafters of the recommendation stated that if the navy and air force did not want to participate, the army should begin organizing its own cryptographic section with whatever resources could be made available.[62]

On 11 December 1940, the Chiefs of Staff Committee turned down the proposal for a Canadian military SIGINT bureau because the cost was too great. The decision by the Chiefs of Staff Committee must be seen in the context of the times. Canada was newly at war and resources were at a premium. There was no guarantee at the time that the cryptographic effort would be effective. The navy was opposed to the idea, stating that such a bureau duplicated existing facilities in London and Washington.[63] It is not entirely clear whether the RCN understood that cryptographic activity was not the same as "Y" work, the direction-finding activity that was so vital to the navy in the North Atlantic U-boat war and that was the only SIGINT activity with which the RCN was engaged. Furthermore, there is no evidence that US cryptographic-derived intelligence had been made accessible to Canada up to this time.

No information has been unearthed on what foreign intelligence activities may have been initiated during the period up to 1940 by the DEA. Most likely there was little explicit intelligence-related work being done. The department was in the midst of a great expansion of its diplomatic activities during the early part of the war; in 1940 there were still only forty-four officers and 328 other staff in the DEA.[64] However, there was obviously ongoing intelligence liaison work with the British, as had been the case for many years. Contacts existed between the Canadian High Commission in London and the British Secret Intelligence Service. This was a one-way relationship, providing Canada with intelligence that had been interpreted through the eyes of Britain. Prior to the outbreak of war, the flow of intelligence was of little direct benefit to Canadian decision makers, who maintained very narrow foreign policy interests. The flow of information did not alter in quantity or quality until the war, when the volume increased so significantly that it caused Winston Churchill in December 1940 to decry the scattering of "so much deadly and secret information over this large circle."[65]

By the end of 1940, Canada had been at war for more than a year. France had fallen to the German onslaught; Scandinavia and the Low Countries had earlier succumbed. Though far from disinterested, the United States remained neutral. Britain was not quite alone. Beside her stood Canada, already thought of as a refuge for the British government and the Royal Navy should the home isles be successfully invaded by Hitler. In addition, the remainder of the British Empire, primarily Australia, New Zealand, South Africa, and India, became important players.

Between the outbreak of war and the end of 1940, the DND budget rose from $112 million in fiscal year 1939-40 to $647 million in the next. The number of Canadian men under arms doubled to 124,800 by 1940, in addition to some women in auxiliary roles.[66] That Canada did not do more to harness the various and disjointed efforts to engage in foreign intelligence activities at this juncture in the war is understandable. Foreign intelligence was viewed as important but not vital, given the scarcity of resources. Some intelligence initiatives were launched and proved successful at this stage, as was the case with the navy's operational centre. In other cases, as with Drake's unsuccessful effort to establish a cryptographic unit within the DND, there was failure, perhaps because the impact on the overall struggle was less immediate and less discernible.

For the first year and a half of war, establishing a Canadian foreign intelligence program was not a Canadian policy priority; it was an issue on which the government was not actively engaged. There were many reasons for this. Not only was there no substantial experience with or understanding of the concept of foreign intelligence, but also Canada's overtaxed and limited resources, coupled with the more immediate need of creating an army of substance and building an industrial base for war, relegated foreign intelligence to secondary importance. And there was virtually no existing intelligence infrastructure on which to build.

Notwithstanding the competition for resources, some steps had been taken by 1940 in the direction of intelligence collection. Canada's rudimentary interwar intelligence efforts within the DND provided little foundation on which to establish wartime intelligence needs. Perhaps because the navy was so close to British Admiralty intelligence, it had a clearer understanding of its priorities and was more active than the other services in intelligence matters. Co-operation with the other Canadian services in intelligence matters was not among the navy's priorities, but protecting the North Atlantic convoy route was. By the end of 1940, the RCN had a respectable SIGINT operation covering high frequency, direction finding, and "Y" activities using stations at Hartlen Point, St. Hubert, Botwood, Esquimalt,

Ottawa (Rockcliffe), Strathburn, Forrest, and Vancouver. A staff of more than 110, using more than forty receivers and other equipment, collected and processed the signals.[67] By early 1941, there was even talk of establishing an intercept station at Julianehaab, Greenland, to extend the range of signals that could be collected.[68]

Not until 1941 did Canada establish foreign intelligence priorities and create the supporting infrastructure, and success was not immediate. Failures and lack of clear direction marred the journey, but before the end of the following year, Canada had elaborated most of the instruments of foreign intelligence collection that remained in place for the duration of the war.

The first challenge was for Canada to establish SIGINT capability. Captain E.M. Drake's visit to the United States in November 1940 had been a disappointment since the Chiefs of Staff Committee turned down the proposal for a cryptographic bureau. The story might have ended there but for the foresight and determination of a handful of individuals set on providing Canada with a sovereign source of intelligence. The creation of a Canadian SIGINT agency called the Examination Unit was the first step.

2
The Birth of the Examination Unit

At the beginning of 1941, Hugh Keenleyside, a sombre, precise person known for his managerial skill, and who represented the DEA on the National Research Council's (NRC) War Technical and Scientific Development Committee, enquired of the DND whether it had carried out any work toward creating a cryptographic capability. Near the end of January, he received a reply from Captain E.S. Brand, director of naval intelligence, briefly stating that the Chiefs of Staff had reviewed the issue in December and had deferred the matter until a later date.[1] Believing his department should have been informed about this, Keenleyside expressed surprise that this was the first intimation the DEA had received of the Chiefs of Staff Committee's decision.[2] Since the DEA was at that moment conducting its own study on the creation of a cryptographic unit, he asked for the rationale behind the Chiefs of Staff Committee's decision. Brand's response, quoted directly from the minutes of the Chiefs of Staff meeting, conveys the pervading institutional attitudes in Canada. He states, "The Committee decided they were unable to recommend the institution of a Cryptographic Branch in Canada, and felt that we should continue to use the United Kingdom facilities for this work. In the event of these being seriously interfered with by enemy action, a similar organisation exists in the U.S.A. which would be available to assist in the event of the United States' entry into the war. They also considered that the cost of such an organisation in Canada could not possibly be justified at the present time."[3]

In fact, at the time that he received the response, Keenleyside was very likely already aware that the DND had turned down the proposal to establish a cryptographic unit. Captain E.M. Drake, the signals intercept officer who had gone to Washington to discuss a Canadian cryptography unit, and Lieutenant C.H. Little of Naval Intelligence had already been in contact with T.A. Stone, the officer at External Affairs charged with foreign intelligence matters, to discuss the possibility of External Affairs establishing a cryptographic unit. That the relatively junior Drake and Little took this initiative without the knowledge or consent of their superior officers (who likely would have denied them the authority to proceed) was a very serious matter in the midst of a war. Having been briefed by Drake and Little, Stone had discussed the proposal with Norman Robertson, the recently appointed[4] under-secretary of state for External Affairs, and received his support to actively pursue the matter.[5] Nothing is known of Drake's motivation for speaking with the DEA about the DND's decision to reject the proposal for a cryptographic unit. In postwar articles about his experience, Little is mute about any contacts of this nature that he or Drake had with Stone. Perhaps it was simply an innocent conversation bereft of insubordinate intent. Whatever the cause, Drake was highly regarded by the DEA for the rest of his career.

At about the same time, Norman Robertson received a letter from Lester B. Pearson, who was posted at the time at the Canadian High Commission in London. Pearson wrote that the British War Office was reluctant to continue decrypting intercepts from the Vichy legation in Ottawa, which the Rockcliffe station was recording and forwarding to British intelligence for processing. The War Office asked whether Canada was giving any thought to establishing a cryptographic bureau of its own, and offered to provide assistance.[6]

Several months elapsed before a meeting occurred on 22 April 1941 between the DND and the DEA to discuss the advisability of establishing a cryptographic unit as well as constructing a Canadian government cipher, a coding key created by Canada for use in encrypting classified messages. Canada had hitherto used British-produced ciphers. The meeting was reported to Norman Robertson, revealing that the DND remained opposed to the idea of establishing a cryptographic bureau of its own in view of the earlier Chiefs of Staff decision. Robertson decided to have the DEA proceed with the study.[7]

The acting president of the NRC had already sent letters to Canadian universities in January enquiring about the availability of mathematicians with an interest in cryptography. Keenleyside, who was shepherding the project for the DEA, was surprised by the large number of responses, but knowing little about cryptography himself, admitted defeat at assessing whether the many respondents claiming knowledge of codes and ciphers actually possessed any real skills.[8]

Among the names sent to Ottawa in response to the NRC query were those of Dr. Gilbert de B. Robinson and Dr. H.S.M. Coxeter, who had been proposed by the president of the University of Toronto. Neither of the two heard anything from the NRC until April, when they were suddenly invited to a meeting in Ottawa. Dean C.J. Mackenzie, head of the NRC, introduced the two to Lieutenant Little of Naval Intelligence, who explained that the DND collected radio signals and that the NRC would make available a room in which a small number of individuals could work on decrypting the messages.[9] Inexplicably, Little did not brief the two on Captain Drake's earlier visit to Washington, of which he must have been aware. Similarly, no rationale is evident for Little's briefing of the two mathematicians, given that the DND was not involved in exploring creation of a cryptographic unit. One can only surmise that, with the small circle of individuals engaged in SIGINT matters, the DEA had asked Little to carry out the briefing because of his greater technical expertise.

Robinson and Coxeter were recruited for the summer university break, and Dean C.J. Mackenzie suggested that they begin their task with an exploratory visit to Washington. As it happened, both were well acquainted with Dr. Abraham Sinkov, a cryptanalyst with the US Army's office of the chief signal officer, with whom they were expected to meet to discuss possible training facilities, the organization of a cryptographic bureau, and the profile of the sort of person best suited for the type of work involved.[10]

Coxeter and Robinson arrived in Washington on 1 May 1941, a Thursday. After a preliminary meeting on the same day with a US Army Signal Corps officer, they were informed that Major General Joseph O. Mauborgne, chief of the Signal Corps, would receive them on Friday morning. Mauborgne opened the meeting the next day by enquiring about the connection of the visit of the two mathematicians with that of Drake the previous November. Coxeter and Robinson were stupefied, knowing nothing of the earlier visit, and could only say that they were there representing the NRC. Probably cautious about dealing with disorganized Canadians, Mauborgne was unwilling to go into details of his own organization and its links with other US intelligence agencies.[11] He wondered aloud why the United Kingdom was unwilling to assist the dominions, adding that he had had a similar approach to that of the Canadians from the South Africans.

As he had with Drake, Mauborgne suggested that any cryptographic bureau should be centralized and would need about 250 staff (he had told Drake 200). He also indicated that the training material that had been put together for Canada in response to a request from Drake could be made available. National Defence had never followed up with an official request for the promised training material, which thus remained packaged and ready on a shelf. Mauborgne added that a skilled instructor would be needed and that he could not spare any of his staff, although he proposed that Canada contact either Rosario Candela, a wealthy Italian man lecturing on cryptanalysis at Hunter College in New York City, or Major Herbert O. Yardley, founder of the US cryptography bureau.[12] Yardley had recently returned to Washington from China, where he had worked for the Kuomintang government, and was now without a job.

Returning to the Canadian Legation, Coxeter and Robinson received authority by telephone from Mackenzie to contact Yardley. They also briefed

Hume Wrong and R.M. Macdonnell of the Legation on their meeting with Mauborgne, and Macdonnell reported separately on the meeting to senior officials at the DEA.[13] Arrangements were made to meet Yardley at the Legation the same day at 4:00 p.m.

Yardley met with Coxeter, Robinson, and Macdonnell to describe for them his intelligence work in China. He was of the opinion that cryptographic training under his direction could be shortened to about six weeks and that a smaller staff of ten to fifteen members was all that was needed to begin. This was welcome news to the Canadian representatives, who intuitively knew that Ottawa was unlikely to be receptive to the staffing projections presented by Mauborgne.

A seasoned and effective diplomat who had been a teacher of history at the University of Toronto when recruited for the DEA, Wrong sent a reporting telegram to Ottawa dated 3 May (Saturday), two days after Coxeter and Robinson's arrival in Washington.[14] One of the surviving copies of the message indicates that the telegram was referred to the Secretary of State for External Affairs, Mackenzie King, who was also prime minister, and a copy was sent to the Minister of National Defence. This suggests that King was kept briefed and may have had an interest in the issue.[15] There may also have been some urgency associated with the visit to Washington, given the speed with which meetings were held and decisions made. A decision to proceed with a cryptographic bureau must already have been made.

The message of 3 May is important for other reasons. According to Wrong, while Mauborgne supported the Yardley candidature, he had been frank in providing details of Yardley's lack of favour in Washington because of his bestselling book on American SIGINT experience, *The American Black Chamber*, which was perceived by some US officials as a betrayal of trust. In Washington, Wrong also recorded that Keenleyside had telephoned him at the Legation to ask him to arrange an invitation for Yardley to visit Ottawa, and to instruct Wrong that the US Department of State was not to be consulted at this stage. This decision is important and inexplicable in light of what later happened. If Keenleyside did not want the state department to know about any Canadian ties to Yardley, it could only have been because he anticipated what the response might be. If such an assumption is correct, it is hard to understand why he proceeded. At the NRC, Mackenzie was nervous about Yardley's background and wrote a couple of days later cautioning against an invitation "until the matter had been canvassed diplomatically."[16] But it was too late. Keenleyside responded that an invitation had already been extended to Yardley and that he would arrive within a week.[17]

The decision to recruit Yardley is inexplicable. Keenleyside, who made the decision to override the concerns raised by Wrong at the Legation in Washington, provides no indication of his motivation. Although the British had earlier recommended that Canada establish a cryptographic unit, there had been no direct proposal to assist Canada. There was probably also present concern that Britain would want to have a Canadian cryptographic unit subservient to British interests, as was already evident in the control exercised over Canadian naval intelligence. A Canadian desire to create an organization obligated to no one may also have existed. Perhaps tipping the balance was the endorsement Yardley received from Mauborgne. Yardley was available and qualified. Although he had made a serious mistake with the publication of his book on US SIGINT activities, he seemingly had the support of responsible US SIGINT officials.

Yardley came to Ottawa on 12 May and met with the Interdepartmental Committee on Cryptography, the ad hoc working group Keenleyside had assembled to launch the cryptographic bureau. The group met in the East Block of the Parliament buildings, the home of the DEA. In addition to Keenleyside, who chaired, and Yardley, the meeting was attended by T.A. Stone from the DEA, Captain E.S. Brand and Lieutenant C.H. Little of Naval Intelligence, Lieutenant Colonel W.W. Murray of Military Intelligence, and Miss D. Geary, representing the absent Dean C.J. Mackenzie of the NRC.

The meeting began with a statement from Lieutenant Colonel Murray stating the military's view that it was "futile to embark now on any expensive undertaking to break down high-grade cipher, and that our efforts should be confined to comparatively simple activities such as interception and deciphering of the illegal wireless messages being sent from stations" in the western hemisphere. Lieutenant Little added that the breaking of simple agent codes was already being done in co-operation with the RCMP.[18]

When it was Yardley's turn to outline his thoughts on a Canadian cryptographic facility, he stated that he was of the opinion that it would be best to start small but with work carried out on both illegal agent traffic and diplomatic material. He suggested that activity begin on Japanese diplomatic material, with which he was already familiar because of his activities in China. The Japanese codes employed a transposition system that was relatively easy to decrypt. Yardley was averse to attacking the German codes, which were complex and would require that an intelligence service buy information about the code books from German traitors. He proposed a staff made up of himself, an assistant cryptographer, two typists, and "someone with a good brain." Yardley indicated that there was an experienced woman working for Mauborgne in Washington who possessed particular skills in deciphering Japanese codes, and whom he thought he could arrange to have released to assist him.[19] The report provides no additional information on this woman, Edna Ramsaier, with whom Yardley had an affair.[20]

When the Interdepartmental Committee on Cryptography met again the following day, Keenleyside stated that he was inclined to recommend to the War Technical and Scientific Development Committee that the sum of $10,000, which had been allotted for cryptography, be used to establish a small unit under Yardley's direction.[21] This money was possibly part of the $25,000 that had been made available to the NRC in March 1941 "in connection with experimental work upon, and manufacture of radio equipment."[22] Keenleyside set out three objectives for the unit: continue and expand the interception of illegal code traffic already being done by Lieutenant Little; attempt to break the Japanese diplomatic code; and act as a cryptographic training unit. The unit would be given funding for six months, during which it would have to prove itself. At this point, Brigadier Maurice A. Pope intervened to express the DND's support for ongoing financial assistance if the experiment proved successful. This heralded a significant departure from previous DND positions.[23]

Yardley and Ramsaier were to be offered six-month contracts, Professors Coxeter and Robinson from the University of Toronto were to be offered positions (only Robinson accepted), and additional support staff were to be recruited. It was agreed that the cryptographic unit was to be administratively housed within the NRC but was to report to the DEA. For the sake of security, Yardley was asked to assume an alias so that his notoriety, from the publication of *The American Black Chamber,* would not draw attention from the media. He would use the name Herbert Osborn during his stay in Canada.[24] This was the same name he had used in China where his activities were known to US authorities, and was a ploy unlikely to fool anyone.[25]

The RCMP was asked the following week to participate on the cryptographic bureau's supervisory committee and to provide a Japanese translator (the RCMP was unable to meet this request).[26] Space for the unit was found at the NRC's Montreal Road Laboratories in Ottawa. Canada's new cryptographic unit was to be called the Examination Unit, an ambiguous title that would be acceptable as the name of a department of the NRC.[27]

The Examination Unit came into being on 9 June. Yardley reported to the Supervisory Committee, Examination Unit, NRC, which had succeeded the Interdepartmental Committee on Cryptography.[28] The new committee had the same mandate as its predecessor, with the addition of postal censorship – that is, reviewing mail for disclosure of information useful to the enemy.[29] The first organizational meeting of the Examination Unit took place on 11 June. A week later, the training material promised by Mauborgne arrived.[30] A month after that, having by this time seen some of the Canadian decrypted product, Mauborgne sent an additional thirty sections of the American cryptanalyst manual to the Examination Unit.[31] The released files are silent on how Canada came to share its decrypted SIGINT reports with the United States, at that time still a neutral power while Canada was a nation at war. Possibly, the decision was made under the auspices of the cooperation envisaged by the Permanent Joint Board of Defence, or it was done administratively in acknowledgment of the importance of future cooperation with the United States.

The day-to-day intelligence tasks at External Affairs were run by T.A. Stone, whose intelligence activities were shrouded under the guise of responsibility for economic warfare, which allowed him to obtain information through censorship activities and other sources of intelligence.[32] A short, stocky man, Thomas Archibald Stone hailed from Chatham, Ontario, where he was a childhood friend of Lester B. Pearson, one of Canada's senior diplomats and an eventual postwar prime minister. Stone was educated at the University of Toronto and the École Libre des Sciences Politiques in Paris, and had originally joined External Affairs in 1927 but resigned in 1935 to marry an American heiress from Charleston. However, he returned to the DEA with the coming of war, and is remembered by one of his closest wartime associates as "the most alive and enthusiastic kind of person. He was always wanting to start something new."[33]

Among Stone's responsibilities was oversight of the Examination Unit and other foreign intelligence matters, whose activities were scattered among a host of fiefdoms, civilian and military, and whose heads were more preoccupied with protecting their independence than with banding together to achieve a significant impact. Stone sought to bring the various Canadian intelligence units into harmony by arranging greater coordination among them. At a 5 June meeting with the National Defence intelligence services, he had underscored that Naval Intelligence conducted a great deal of wireless interception, much of which was passed directly to London. Only some of it circulated to various departments in Ottawa. Although Canada's security operations were working well, Stone explained, there was a need for "some central organization in Ottawa, through which the activities of the various Intelligence Branches could be co-ordinated."[34] While Canada's various foreign intelligence organizations continued to co-operate and exchange information, throughout this period there was a strong reluctance from the National Defence intelligence services to extend co-operation to any endeavour that might threaten their own powers. Such an attitude was not unnatural. The DND intelligence chiefs had assumed their positions during the prewar period when the DEA had demonstrated little interest in foreign intelligence. The military, still seeking to define its own intelligence role in support of its fighting men, was cautious about succumbing to the embrace of the DEA on intelligence matters.

On 5 June 1941, the DEA had instructed the High Commission in London to inform the British authorities about Canada's recruitment of Yardley. Canada welcomed any British suggestions that might be helpful and offered co-operation with British cryptographic efforts.[35] By the end of July, after only one month of operation, the Examination Unit appeared well launched. There was early and considerable success in decrypting intercepted messages that involved a transposition cipher. Four copies of decrypted material were made: one file copy, one each to Military Intelligence and

Naval Intelligence, and one to Stone at the DEA. There had been some successes against the Vichy ciphers, and German traffic between Hamburg and Rio de Janeiro was also being deciphered. Expenditures for the month had totalled just over $2,600. The Japanese diplomatic section of the Examination Unit began operating on 8 August 1941, and quickly provided a satisfactory output of reports in terms of quantity and quality. By now, the staff of the Examination Unit had grown to a dozen. There had already been one notable success when SIGINT, decrypted by the Examination Unit, led to the arrest of a German agent by the FBI in June.[36]

Then disaster struck. A month after the Canadian High Commission had been instructed to inform British authorities about the new Examination Unit, a strange telegraphic query was received from London about a Mr. Emeley, a name cited in the 5 June message from Ottawa on the recently appointed head of the Examination Unit. The High Commission wondered whether it could be the same person as H.O. Yardley since the alleged Emeley had also worked in China and had written a book on American cryptography.[37] The encrypted message to the High Commission in London naming Yardley as the new head of the Examination Unit had been garbled – Yardley had been rendered as Emeley – when the message reached London.

The DEA knew that Yardley had a checkered past for having disclosed the secrets of American cryptography and breaking Japanese codes during the interwar period. Replying to the telegraphic query from London, Norman Robertson informed Vincent Massey, high commissioner in London, about the error in ciphering in the earlier message and acknowledged Yardley's checkered career. Robertson underscored that Yardley had made his peace with the US intelligence services and that close co-operation now existed with them. Indeed, he explained, the US Army's SIGINT service continued to furnish secret training material to the Examination Unit. Robertson added that the FBI, which was maintaining an interest in Yardley, had informed the RCMP that its intelligence sources indicated that Yardley was working in Canada under the alias "Osborn"![38]

Lester B. Pearson, who by now had returned to Ottawa from his post in London, was anxious to enhance the cryptographic relationship with Britain and to allay British concerns over Yardley. In a message to Massey on 22 August, Pearson encouraged him to impress upon the British the high desirability of closer co-operation.[39] Eventually, the British sent to Canada two senior intelligence officers who made it clear that there could be no co-operation between British services and the fledgling Examination Unit as long as Yardley remained in Canada's employ. One of the British representatives was Alastair Denniston, head of the Government Code and Cipher School (the British SIGINT service), who had been in Washington to negotiate a work-sharing arrangement with the Americans. Denniston added that Canada should also expect no co-operation from the Americans if Yardley remained.[40] Canadian protestations that Yardley had been hired on the recommendation of Mauborgne were for nothing. Mauborgne's views, the response went, were his own and were not shared by the US intelligence services. To soften the blow, the British offered to supply one of their own cryptographic intelligence officers to assist Canada. However, Canada had signed a six-month contract with Yardley; two and a half months of it remained.

Pearson quickly asked Vincent Massey to inform the British of a decision not to renew Yardley's contract, and to assure them that Yardley had had access to no information he could use to his own benefit. He told Massey that Canada welcomed the offer of a senior British officer for SIGINT work. Upon informing the Canadian Embassy in Washington of the decision on Yardley and while seeking clarification of US attitudes toward Yardley, External Affairs learned that Mauborgne had retired and that the US State Department had probably never been made aware that Yardley was in Canada.[41]

In the interim, the Examination Unit continued to function effectively under Yardley, still locally known as Osborn. Throughout this period, Yardley had no intimation of the discussions being conducted concerning his future. The Examination Unit successfully continued to decipher both Vichy diplomatic and German agent traffic. Canadian authorities finally confronted Yardley in November. After securing confirmation from London that Britain would lend Canada an experienced cryptographic expert, Pearson and Stone met with Yardley on 22 November to ask if he would extend his six-month contract by three weeks until 1 January 1942, after which his services would no longer be needed. What followed was "a most unpleasant half hour" as Yardley indignantly claimed that Canada had picked his brains dry and was now dismissing him. The tirade unsettled Pearson and Stone, who became unsure of themselves, and arrangements were quickly made for Pearson to visit Washington to clarify "vague and unsatisfactory references to the book which [Yardley] published."[42]

When Pearson arrived in Washington with Lieutenant Little, they learned that there was relatively little concrete information against Yardley beyond his penchant for self-promotion and an American feeling of betrayal arising from the publication of his book on American SIGINT collection during and after the First World War. The extent of the evidence against Yardley, following a number of meetings with senior US intelligence representatives, amounted to his being "unreliable and untrustworthy." An informal meeting with Dr. William Friedman, the chief cryptanalyst in the US War Department who would come to be viewed as the father of postwar US cryptography, elicited the information that the hostility toward Yardley was almost exclusively tied to the publication of his book, which was said to have damaged US interests.[43] Friedman speculated that as a result of the publication of Yardley's book, the United States had lost access to Japanese codes, which had hitherto been easily solvable. The American attitude toward Yardley was framed by emotion, but would almost certainly preclude co-operation be-tween the Examination Unit and US and British intelligence services.

The documentary evidence is clear that Britain would not deal with Canada's Examination Unit as long as it was under Yardley's direction. The British knew of American objections to Yardley and shared concerns about his possible future revelations. They also wanted to exert a measure of con-trol over the direction of the nascent Canadian SIGINT activities in order to secure their own more important Ultra efforts, the decryption of German machine-encrypted messages, of which Canada might become aware. This could most easily be accommodated by having someone from the British Government Code and Cipher School assigned to manage the Examination Unit. Yardley's departure from the Canadian organization would also per-mit Britain to champion a trilateral intelligence relationship.

John Bryden, in his *Best Kept Secret: Canadian Secret Intelligence in the Sec-ond World War,* argues that Britain wanted Yardley out of the way as a means to gain access to Canadian success in "breaking South American [German] traffic that neither the British nor the Americans had mastered."[44] Bryden asserts that Britain wanted to bolster the position of William Donovan, US Coordinator of Information, the forerunner to the Office of Strategic Ser-vices (OSS), who was working very closely with British intelligence and who was experiencing heavy opposition from the FBI and the armed services, both of which resented Donovan's incursion into foreign intelligence. Un-der existing procedures, the Examination Unit under Yardley was handing to the RCMP decrypted material about German spies in the western hemi-sphere. The RCMP passed it to the FBI. However, in Bryden's view, Britain wanted to pass the information through its own intelligence services to Donovan so he would reap the credit. Yet there is no documentary evidence in the archives to support Bryden's interpretation.

It is unlikely that the Examination Unit's products were of such quantity and consistent quality that they could significantly impact the intelligence relations of two major nations such as Britain and the United States. Pearson's meetings with the Americans in Washington about Yardley's employment by Canada underscore the fact that the US opposition to Yardley was vis-ceral. From his talks with the Americans, Pearson emerged with little more than an American sense of betrayal stemming from Yardley's decision to publish his book. There was no wider conspiracy by Britain to gain influ-ence over American intelligence through championing Donovan.

Meanwhile, Yardley was mustering his defences. These included inter-ventions with Eleanor Roosevelt, wife of the US president, conducted by George T. Bye, his friend and literary agent, who knew the First Lady well.[45] An attempt was made by a friend of Yardley to meet with President Roosevelt, but there is no evidence that such a meeting took place. Nothing came of these efforts.

Canada was prepared to sacrifice Yardley in the interest of gaining access to broader intelligence co-operation with Britain and the United States. Canada's situation is summed up in a letter from Pearson to Massey in London. Pearson attributed much of the American objection to Yardley to the "professional jealousy involved in this business" and acknowledged that Yardley had been "industrious, reliable, and most efficient."[46] Anxious to have Yardley and Edna Ramsaier, whose employment was also to be terminated, end their sojourn in Canada without animosity, External Affairs arranged for their assignment on "special duty in Washington" for two and a half months, to cover transitional financial needs and to overcome an unresolved issue of a Canadian income tax liability.[47] Yardley and Ramsaier left Canada just before the Japanese attack on Pearl Harbor.

The attack on the American fleet at Pearl Harbor altered the nature of the war. In the interregnum between Yardley's departure and the arrival of his successor, British High Commissioner to Canada Malcolm MacDonald had asked Norman Robertson whether Britain and Canada could coordinate their joint activities and eliminate duplication in their SIGINT intercept activity. The British proposed that they themselves should assume responsibility for all European and trans-Atlantic traffic including that between South America and Europe. Britain hoped that Canada would assume responsibility for trans-Pacific traffic. It was important to have access to Japanese communications traffic with the western hemisphere, Malaya, and the East Indies. MacDonald explained that the United Kingdom authorities "would deeply appreciate it if the Canadian service (whose efficiency in intercepting enemy secret service wireless traffic is well known and is most highly valued) could give first priority to this work from the earliest possible moment."[48] Britain was prepared to send a trained officer to assist with Japanese encryption techniques. Before Canada formally responded, Pearson telephoned the British high commissioner to accept the loan of a British officer. Canada's response a few days later agreed that it was time to distribute assignments among all intercept facilities available to Commonwealth and Allied countries.

Canada astutely set conditions for agreeing to the British proposal. Canada would cease all interception of German agent traffic between South America and Europe if they received deciphered British copies of those intercepts. Intercept collection in support of Canadian naval activity would not be curtailed at stations such as Esquimalt, Forrest, and Hartlen Point, which covered the Pacific, but some additional resources could be made available at Victoria and Point Grey to collect Japanese traffic.[49] Pearson met with army, navy, and Department of Transport representatives at the end of January 1942 to obtain agreement to the new collection regime. The following months were taken up with finding the necessary linguistic skills to meet the new tasks.[50]

The decision to set conditions on co-operation with Britain reflected a protracted effort to wean the motherland away from the notion that the Dominion was merely a cog in the British machinery. While Canada remained dependent on Britain in many areas, there also existed a determination to make autonomy an objective and dependence a diminishing condition.

The War Committee of the Cabinet was informed on 26 January 1942 of Yardley's departure from the Examination Unit. An update on the SIGINT collaboration then emerging between Britain and the United States was provided at the same time, stressing that Britain hoped Canada and the other dominions would participate in the new cryptographic structure, and that Britain was prepared to send Canada a cryptographic specialist to replace Yardley.[51] Because of Yardley's departure, the Examination Unit was accorded a more formal stature as associate committee of the National Research Council, with $100,000 appropriated for its work in the next fiscal year.

True to its word, Britain lent Canada a replacement for Yardley. Prior to being sent to Canada, the selected candidate, Oliver Strachey, had headed the British Government Code and Cipher School team working on German overseas intelligence ciphers. When he assumed responsibility for the Examination Unit on 15 January 1942, Strachey was already sixty-seven years old. His arrival in Canada has been described by historians J.L. Granatstein and David Stafford as "Canada's willing surrender of its independence as the price of joining the global signals-intelligence war."[52] The fact is simply that Canada, because of its prewar neglect of intelligence matters, had no option but to seek help from the Americans (Yardley) or the British (Strachey). No matter what impact key intelligence functions being directed by foreign nationals (and, indeed, Strachey continued to be paid by London) had on sovereignty, Canada had no other option if it wanted to play a significant role in SIGINT; at the time, Canada did not have the domestic talent to provide the training to develop the skills to operate a cryptographic organization. Strachey brought with him the benefits of British strides in SIGINT collection and cryptography. He had extensive knowledge of and experience with the current techniques and cryptographic tools. In addition, Strachey brought assurance of British commitment to assisting Canadian SIGINT efforts and, by extension, the potential for a more formal tie to the United States.

Within days of Strachey's arrival, the ad hoc committee responsible for the organization and work of the Examination Unit was reorganized under External Affairs direction. The new title was the Advisory Committee on the Examination Unit and it was to function as an associate committee of the NRC.[53] Membership included Dean C.J. Mackenzie of the NRC as chairman, Lieutenant Colonel Murray from the DND, Little from Naval Intelligence, Group Captain R.E. McBurney from National Defence for Air,

Inspector C. Batch from the RCMP, and Lester B. Pearson from the DEA, as secretary. Oliver Strachey was an ex-officio member.[54]

The spring of 1942 was one of expansion for the Examination Unit. Additional staff was found. Some came from the British censorship office in Vancouver; others were reassigned from the armed forces. The United States, finally in the war, was moving rapidly forward in mobilizing for the conflict. After tremendous effort and brilliant research, Britain was experiencing greater successes with its attacks against the German Enigma codes. Strachey had brought with him cipher keys for German non-Enigma and Japanese traffic, although Canada's own set of keys to German traffic was found nearly as complete as the set provided by London.[55] Prior to Strachey's arrival, ties between the Examination Unit and British and American SIGINT organizations had been informal and infrequent. Deciphered text was indirectly forwarded through the RCMP or British Security Coordination (BSC) in New York. However, co-operation with other SIGINT centres began that spring under Strachey's tutelage. By March, the growing Examination Unit had run out of space at the facilities provided by the NRC. New quarters were located at 345 Laurier Avenue East, Ottawa, a stately Victorian house of about 5,500 square feet, available at a rent of $300 per month for a period running to six months after the end of the war. It had all the comforts of home. Work was conducted in bright, airy rooms and there was a convenient kitchen with a stove and icebox and the necessities for tea. The lovely enclosed garden allowed the staff to relax outside.

Because the house on Laurier Avenue East was bigger than the growing Examination Unit required, it was arranged that the army's Discrimination Unit, when it was formed on 12 June 1942 under Captain Drake, would share the premises. This was the group tasked with the non-cryptographic interpretation of collected signals (identifying stations, unit call numbers, frequencies, etc.). Up until then, the army's intercepted signals traffic had been forwarded to the director of military intelligence and the Royal Canadian Navy's (RCN) operational intelligence centre and its foreign intelligence section under Commander John (Jock) de Marbois.[56] With the Examination Unit finally coming of age, the army was also restructuring its SIGINT service to operate on a more sophisticated level.

The Discrimination Unit was on the main floor and the Examination Unit was on the second floor of the Laurier Avenue house. Shortly after arriving at the house on Laurier Avenue, the Examination Unit established secure communication links with BSC in New York (which passed messages to London) and with Arlington Hall in Washington, the former private girls' school that housed the American army's SIGINT agency. In spite of cohabiting, there was no thought at the time to amalgamating the Examination Unit and the Discrimination Unit. Indeed, there is no evidence that this possibility was even raised. No consideration was given to a more centralized approach instead of the patchwork series of governing committees that were the Canadian norm.

The house on Laurier Avenue was next door to the home of Canada's prime minister. Mackenzie King was probably aware of his new neighbours; he did not like surprises and officials in External Affairs or the Privy Council Office would have kept him apprised. Certainly, he was aware of Canada's SIGINT efforts.[57] Later, members of the Examination Unit recalled that King always courteously tipped his hat to the staff he encountered while out strolling with his dog.[58]

Strachey lasted only about seven months in Canada. Although bearing his years well, he was a man from an earlier generation and was not one to develop existing talent within the Examination Unit. He could recognize the skills of individual staff but could not nurture latent abilities. Clearly, as Gilbert de B. Robinson, author of the 1945 internal history of the Examination Unit, writes, Strachey was "a man whose best work [had] been done."[59]

Strachey's successor, and the third director of the Examination Unit in less than a year, was F.A. Kendrick, who took over in July 1942. Kendrick was in his thirties, rather shy, and more dynamic than Strachey, although suffering from a handicap (possibly polio). He was better qualified to decrypt modern machine-encrypted messages; both Yardley and Strachey had been more familiar with older transpositional types of encryption. Kendrick was interested in research into individual ciphers, including those that were machine generated. Once he had mastered a problem, he was inclined to pass the results to his staff to carry out the ongoing decipherment. The Examination Unit began to flourish under Kendrick, and extensive work was carried out on both French (Vichy as well as Free French) and Japanese traffic. Training by Britain's Government Code and Cipher School was provided for some staff. With the passing months, the work began to shift toward coverage of Japanese traffic. The Examination Unit continued to grow until space again became a problem. Eventually, in the fall of 1942, the army's Discrimination Unit moved out of the house on Laurier Street.

A small organization called the Examination Unit Information Centre was established in the spring of 1942 to provide researchers, translators, and cryptographers with information facilities. For example, the Information Centre would track down press releases referred to in Vichy intercepts. Having the full and correct text of something that might be quoted in a ciphered message could help break the code for that segment by providing a string of words of known text, or "crib," thereby giving insight into the working of the entire cipher. The Information Centre acted as an autonomous advisory authority in the manner of a specialized library.

The DEA was the prime consumer of the SIGINT provided by the Examination Unit. The material collected was often of limited value unless placed in context and evaluated as to meaning and importance. Often, several reports had to be collated before valuable intelligence could be extrapolated. Concerned with making the best use of the intelligence collected, particularly the Japanese material, T.A. Stone established a special intelligence section of the DEA in September 1942 under the direction of E.H. Norman, who had recently been repatriated from Japan where, as a member of the Canadian Legation, he had been interned after the outbreak of war with Japan. William Stephenson, the Canadian head of BSC in New York, may have encouraged Stone to establish the unit as a way of having an External Affairs office with which BSC could liaise on SIGINT.[60] Although the officers of the special intelligence section were drawn exclusively from the DEA, albeit with support personnel supplied by the Directorate of Censorship, the section was housed with the Examination Unit at 345 Laurier Avenue East.[61]

Norman's principal work was to prepare intelligence reports that brought together secret information from various sources concerning Japan and the Far East. These were prepared biweekly and distributed to the prime minister, Norman Robertson, and the three service chiefs.[62] Herbert Norman had full access to all SIGINT material as well as all significant information passing through the various divisions at External Affairs.[63] He remained focused on Japanese diplomatic decrypted traffic; few Japanese economic and military intelligence reports were prepared. During the first year of operation, the reports were largely edits and interpretation of individual intercepted messages. After awhile, however, this was changed to using the contents of several messages to prepare longer reports.[64]

Norman was joined in November by A.R. Menzies, who assumed responsibility for interpreting the French traffic, primarily Vichy but later also Free French. However, Norman retained responsibility for purely Far Eastern French traffic, which was studied against Japanese traffic for more insightful analysis. As a result, the analysis of events in French Indo-China, for example, achieved a high level of detail and accuracy.[65] Menzies, who had no prior experience in intelligence and who defined his job as doing "what Norman did not want to do," also did some work on Spanish language intercepts that were decrypted by the Examination Unit.[66] He stayed with the special intelligence section until February 1944, when he was replaced by G.W. Hilborn.[67] The special intelligence section was never staffed by more than two officers at any time, who were supported by appropriate administrative assistance.

The Japanese diplomatic traffic provided an intelligence insight into anywhere Japan had diplomatic missions. While Japan still had missions in some Latin American countries, it was possible, through the Japanese intercepts, to gain insights into the personalities and activities of pro-Axis politicians in countries such as Chile and Argentina.[68] Excellent Japanese diplomatic reporting was also obtained from their missions in Moscow,

Finland, Bulgaria, Romania, Sweden, Portugal, Berne, Turkey, Afghanistan, and elsewhere. The smaller Japanese missions seem to have also been used for collecting and forwarding intelligence. As Japanese missions in these areas became increasingly isolated, diplomatic couriers could no longer bring new ciphering systems and the Japanese traffic could more consistently be decrypted and followed.[69]

Many of the Japanese missions in Europe, with the exception of Moscow, repeatedly reported on the expectation that the Soviet Union would end its alliance with the Anglo-Saxon countries. The Japanese diplomatic traffic was particularly beneficial to the Allies because of the exceptional reporting by the Japanese ambassador in Moscow, who was an objective and intelligent diplomat, but also because it provided a window to the situation in countries where the Allies had little or no diplomatic access. As well, policy telegrams from Tokyo often provided clues to Japanese estimates of Allied plans and policies, in addition to information on the Japanese home front.[70]

By the fall of 1944, the special intelligence section was no longer considered essential, given the staff shortages being experienced by External Affairs, and a decision was made to draw down the section and have Norman and Hilborn return to the department the following January. However, after his return to External Affairs and to new responsibilities, Norman continued to review Japanese diplomatic traffic on behalf of the DEA, but the practice of preparing more extensive intelligence reports on the intercepts was discontinued.[71] The files that the special intelligence section had created were considered valuable and were transferred to External Affairs.[72]

Now, the special intelligence section files no longer appear to exist, although the material was transferred to the DEA after the section was wound up. Menzies has stated that he "doubts this stuff [section reports] got into the archives."[73] However, the raw decrypts of Japanese, German, and French (Vichy and Free French) diplomatic traffic have recently been made available at Library and Archives Canada.[74] Only one report of the special intelligence section, prepared by Herbert Norman, has been recovered, and it is one he wrote on the basis of interviews and readings collected in Washington during a visit to the Office of Strategic Services. The report on the Japanese in the Dutch East Indies was prepared in 1943, and is a well-written analysis of Javanese and Sumatran society, nationalism, ethnicity, and the impact of the Japanese occupation.[75] One cannot say with certainty, but it is very likely that this report was typical of the sort of intelligence analysis prepared by the special intelligence section. As time went on, the special intelligence section was also tasked with conducting "specific research topics" relating to acquisition of strategic war supplies by the enemy.[76]

Today, Norman is not remembered for his wartime involvement in Canadian intelligence but as the brilliant scholar-diplomat who, because of a youthful flirtation with Marxism, was hounded by American McCarthyites in the postwar period until, while stationed as Canada's ambassador in Cairo in 1956, he leapt from a building to his death.[77] In 1942, however, Norman was a junior External Affairs officer, recently repatriated from Japan and noted for his Japanese language skills (he was born in Karuizawa, Japan) and his seminal doctoral dissertation and subsequent book, *Japan's Emergence as a Modern State*.

By the time the Examination Unit was on its third director, co-operation with the army's Discrimination Unit under Lieutenant Colonel E.M. Drake was well entrenched. The move of the Discrimination Unit from 345 Laurier Avenue East, when space proved insufficient, did nothing to hamper a close working relationship. The Discrimination Unit was relocated to the third floor of the La Salle Academy, between St. Andrew and Guigues Streets in Ottawa. Drake had joined the Royal Canadian Corps of Engineers' "Experimental Station" in Rockcliffe, Ottawa, in March 1940 as a lieutenant. While still a captain and stationed at Rockcliffe, he had taken a great personal risk after the military establishment had rejected the proposal for a cryptographic unit by turning to the intelligence managers at External Affairs and planting the idea with them for SIGINT work. Two years later, in June 1942, Drake had been transferred to DND headquarters and was immediately promoted to major and established as head of MI2, the organization within Military Intelligence responsible for the Discrimination Unit. By the fall he was a lieutenant colonel.

By the spring of 1942, the army operated the Rockcliffe station, by now called No. 1 Special Wireless Station, in Ottawa. The No. 2 Special Wireless Station was located in Grande Prairie, Alberta, and the No. 3 Special Wireless Station was in Victoria, British Columbia. Through wireless intercepts, the Rockcliffe station had assembled the order-of-battle for the Spanish army, navy, and air force, as well as the identity of the head of the Spanish secret service.[78] In addition, fifty-two foreign agents had been identified around the globe.[79]

The stations were also equipped with direction-finding apparatus. Still, none of the stations had their full complement of signals operators, although additional staff members were expected shortly. Negotiations to hand over to the army two or three Department of Transport stations, apart from the three existing facilities, were also underway. The resources were totally inadequate for the task at hand, given the size of the country, but the Canadians can be commended for what had been accomplished in so short a time. It was during this same period that the army assumed full responsibility for intercept coverage of diplomatic and commercial traffic, something that was previously shared with the RCN.[80]

Naval Intelligence had not been idle, and by 1942 the navy was obtaining intercepts and direction-finding signals from about nineteen sites.[81] The RCN's "Y" organization, the direction-finding function, was working well and had materially assisted the war effort in spite of a shortage of staff and equipment. One weakness was the shortage of Kana operators – operators trained in the Japanese Morse system – which left much Japanese naval communications traffic untranscribed for the cryptanalysts.

Planning was underway for doing the SIGINT job well, although shortages of personnel and equipment continued to plague the Canadian effort. This was somewhat offset by greater understanding of what was needed and what could be done by the different organizations. It had been about a year and a half since Keenleyside had prompted the National Research Council's War Technical and Scientific Development Committee, in the weeks before Christmas 1940, to look into cryptography as a tool to aid in the war effort. The decision to establish a cryptographic bureau had acted as a catalyst to provide direction to the disparate SIGINT efforts underway within the armed forces.

Finally, there was a Canadian purpose to the activities. No longer was Canada merely a supplier of raw material, collecting opportunistic radio waves that traversed the sky and were easily captured for onward passage to the British. Two years into the war, Canada was making a contribution on the intelligence front, albeit at a level significantly lower than those of its allies and involving less complex decryption tasks. And although the Examination Unit was directed by a representative of the British Government Code and Cipher School, it remained largely a homegrown enterprise. Detracting from an otherwise exemplary performance was the absence of integration of foreign intelligence efforts. Collection was carried out by the military services, while decryption was done by the Examination Unit, and interpretation of the material was conducted by the special intelligence section of the DEA.

Canada's early success in SIGINT was heavily dependent on the assistance of Britain and the United States. While Canada had the capacity to collect signals from the atmosphere, there existed no homegrown skills with which to exploit the material through decryption. The decryption process was initially entirely attributable to imported skills and talents, first from the United States and later from Britain.

Canada had no illusions about its ability to start and manage a sovereign intelligence facility without outside assistance. Close ties existed with both Britain and the United States, and it was natural for Canada to turn to these countries for support and eventual closer ties through intelligence alliances that extended beyond the SIGINT sector.

3
Building Alliances

Canada lived under a geopolitical protective umbrella during the Second World War. Both the United Kingdom and the United States shielded Canada for reasons of their own self-interest, as well as because of their historical and familial ties to Canada. Britain saw in Canada both a fighting ally in the war and a supplier of raw materials; the United States wanted the continuance of a stable, independent North American continent. For historical, geographical, and traditional reasons, Canada derived benefit from its position between the two.

Canada played on its symbiotic relationships with Britain and the United States to full advantage, leaning first toward one country and then toward the other. In the realm of foreign intelligence collection, Canada followed a pattern of balancing between the two powers. Canada sought assistance and guidance from the two more powerful nations and thought it natural that it, in turn, should do everything it could to assist the others. However, Canada never acted as a catalyst to bring the other two countries closer together in matters relating to foreign intelligence. The intelligence relationship that developed between the United Kingdom and the United States even before the two were formal allies in the Second World War occurred for reasons of state. The relationship easily and naturally drew Canada into its fold.

The early and cautious intelligence mating dance between Britain and the United States has been well documented in such studies as Bradley F. Smith's *The Ultra-Magic Deals and the Most Secret Special Relationship, 1940-1946*.[1] Smith makes late 1939 the starting point for US-British intelligence sharing, when William Stephenson arrived as head of British intelligence in the United States.[2] Inexplicably, Smith gets the date wrong, since Stephenson arrived at the British Consulate in New York in June 1940, assigned as the British passport control officer, the conventional and paper-thin mask for British Secret Intelligence Service officers operating abroad under official cover (i.e., as declared diplomats).[3] The amalgamation of the Secret Intelligence Service office with other British security agencies in the United States under a single head, namely Stephenson, came later.

Neither side was quite certain how much intelligence to provide the other, nor at what cost. Smith states that by May 1940 (again, the date must be wrong), Stephenson had taken on the task of slipping "Most Secret"-sourced intelligence to the Americans.[4] This was not as exceptional as it may seem. Intelligence services often shared intelligence with the services of other states with which they were not allied, but only when the sharing of information satisfied a policy objective. Probably a more appropriate date for the start of the British-US intelligence relationship is August 1940, when Commander Alastair Denniston of Britain's Government Code and Cipher School (the SIGINT service) agreed to exchange cryptanalytic data with Dr. William Friedman, of the US Army's SIGINT service.[5] Ultimately, the meetings between British and American intelligence officials gave rise to the Ultra-Magic deal, the exchange of the key cryptographic achievements of the two countries, namely, the British decryption of the German Enigma coding machine (Ultra) and the breaking of the Japanese Purple code (Magic) by the Americans.

Canada became a real intelligence partner of Britain and the United States with the establishment of the Examination Unit, since Canada's earlier role had been relegated to that of a supplier of raw – that is, undeciphered – SIGINT traffic for the British. During the Yardley era, the Examination Unit passed decrypted SIGINT to the RCMP, which then forwarded the material, through its existing liaison channels, to the FBI in the United States. The intelligence links between the three countries remained informal arrangements that had been quickly crafted in the midst of rapidly changing circumstances, as the three countries established and then expanded their intelligence resources before the United States finally joined the war effort. The early, informal SIGINT-sharing arrangements worked well but were initially limited to exchanges of strategies for attacking encrypted enemy messages; only later did they evolve to include extensive exchanges of decrypted traffic, sometimes hampered by a duplication of effort. Co-operation between the intelligence partners, which Britain initiated, developed slowly, with many faltering steps and with no template for establishing the intelligence relationships. It was clearly Britain's decision to initiate the relationship, since at first the United Kingdom was the only one of the partners able to make a substantial contribution. However, the relationship between Britain and the United States was entrenched by the American decision to share Magic, the US ability to decrypt Japanese enciphered communications. This cemented the relationship between Britain and the United States, which was later extended to include Canada and others in full and unfettered co-operation.

An early effort to structure the emerging intelligence-sharing activities was launched by the FBI in late 1941, and did not involve SIGINT but, rather, conventional intelligence gathering. In November 1941, the US State

Department extended an invitation to Britain and Canada to attend a Washington meeting arranged by the FBI, to be held in January 1942, "to discuss organization of Intelligence Services in the Western Hemisphere."[6] The FBI initiative was very likely tied to the struggle over control of foreign intelligence that was taking place in the United States between the FBI, the various armed services intelligence organizations, and William Donovan, who was trying to establish a civilian foreign intelligence organization, the eventual Office of Strategic Services (OSS). The FBI invitation was extended prior to the 7 December Japanese attack on Pearl Harbor. At that time, the United States was still a neutral non-combatant; many Americans did not support the United Kingdom. No one could have anticipated that the United States would be at war by the time the conference occurred.

There was much uncertainty within America's fledgling intelligence establishment. The Coordinator of Information position, the predecessor to the OSS, with William Donovan as its head, was only created by the US president on 11 July 1941, after some initial wrangling between the US armed services.[7] At this time, and for some time following, the FBI retained responsibility for US intelligence activities in the western hemisphere, although the demarcation of authority between the FBI and virtually all others became increasingly contested. Since both the armed services and Donovan's organization were also engaged in foreign intelligence work, this was a period of confusion and uncertainty as the US intelligence community attempted to create itself and develop relationships and inter-connectivity.

The FBI conference proposed to limit itself to "establishing a more closely correlated and official machinery for handling of investigative activities in the Western Hemisphere." The goal of the meeting was to improve exchanges of information, establish liaison representatives among the parties, and create "an International Body to convene from time to time for the purpose of outlining investigative and operational procedure as joint undertaking and on a hemispheric basis."[8] Canada was interested in attending the meeting, although there was concern about the implications of the absence of US military and naval intelligence organizations from among those invited.[9]

The conference was scheduled to take place on 5 January 1942, and Canadian and British delegates were making their preparations for attending when suddenly, on 1 January, the conference was cancelled. No reason was provided but it was most likely the result of the infighting occurring between the various US intelligence organizations, particularly during the confusing period immediately following the attack on Pearl Harbor. However, on 21 January, the Canadian Legation in Washington informed the DEA that the conference was rescheduled for the end of the month.[10]

The Hemispheric Intelligence Conference was held on 29 January 1942 in the office of the director of the FBI, J. Edgar Hoover. In addition to the FBI, the United States was represented by Adolf A. Berle Jr., a senior official of the State Department. Britain was represented by William Stephenson, who by this time headed British Security Coordination (BSC), the office housing all British security and intelligence services in the United States. The Canadian delegation was led by Hume Wrong, who at the time was the senior political officer at the Canadian Legation to the United States (the Canadian delegation included representatives of the RCMP).

Berle opened the meeting by explaining that the objective of the conference was to develop liaisons between the civilian intelligence services of the United States, the United Kingdom, and Canada, and that the discussion would be limited to civilian intelligence. It was underscored that the FBI had exclusive US jurisdiction in the civilian field in the western hemisphere.[11]

By the time of the conference, a line had already been drawn in the sand between Donovan of the Coordinator of Information office, strongly supported by Stephenson of BSC, and his rival, Hoover of the FBI. BSC had the protection of the White House, which was concerned with the greater geopolitical issues and wanted to assist Britain to the greatest extent possible, using the British intelligence service as an unofficial communications channel.[12] Hoover did not trust Stephenson. Obviously expressing a concern over the activities of BSC, Berle stated that "no country can be expected to be permitted to operate an intelligence service inside another country; that certain activities had been overlooked during peace-time, but now that the United States is at war it was logical that the FBI should take care of intelligence activities in this country and that the other representatives should take care of the intelligence activities in their own countries."[13] While sparring followed between Hoover and Stephenson, Wrong sought to remain isolated from the fray and stated that Canada wanted to co-operate and eliminate duplication of effort in intelligence matters.

Although the conference was marred by undercurrents of distrust between the FBI and BSC, it was not a failure. Very sound constructive work on the mechanics of intelligence liaison relationships emerged from the meeting. The FBI proposed to set up a radio transmitter in the US Legation in Ottawa to facilitate communications between the various parties, and there was a proposal to station an RCMP liaison officer in Washington. There was agreement to liaise further and to strengthen security. However, the constructive achievements of the conference tended to be in the area of security intelligence, with which the FBI probably felt more familiar. More might have been achieved had there not existed FBI distrust of what BSC was doing, which was probably exacerbated by the FBI's police security approach to intelligence co-operation. The conference ended on a note of admonition from Hoover not to ignore the Communist problem. Such a preoccupation with an enemy who was not then threatening any of the three nations participating in the conference is instructive of Hoover's thinking and likely did little to cement a foreign intelligence partnership with the British.

A follow-up meeting was held in Washington on 16 March. Apart from the RCMP and the FBI, it is uncertain who else participated.[14] By the time of this second meeting, discussions had clearly shifted to an entirely security-oriented agenda, an area with which the RCMP and the FBI were more comfortable and that fell within their respective areas of responsibility. A third conference followed in Ottawa on 3 August. This meeting had a more extensive agenda than the second meeting and was again focused on security issues, although discussions also covered the establishment of more formal liaison relations between the RCMP and the FBI, including securing radio communications between the two organizations.[15] Security matters relating to POWs were also discussed, although many sections of the released documents are blacked out so as not to permit interpretations of all the points that may have been raised.

Following the August conference, the DEA, which likely attended neither of the follow-up meetings, sought access to the RCMP's minutes of the meetings. The RCMP informed Norman Robertson, the under-secretary of state for External Affairs, that it felt "duty bound" to inform Director Hoover of the FBI of the request before copies were made available.[16] The response from External Affairs was swift and unequivocal. Robertson informed Commissioner S.T. Wood of the RCMP that he could not "agree that the views [blacked out, presumably Hoover's] should be solicited in this matter. The Secretary of State for External Affairs is responsible for the conduct of the international affairs of this country."[17] Robertson went on to suggest that the letter to Hoover should be recalled, something that was duly done.[18] What happened next is uncertain. Only one additional file entry was released under the Access to Information Program and it relates to the suspension of the Working Committee Meetings of the Western Hemisphere Conference about one year later.[19] The DEA's ire stemmed from the RCMP's wish to seek Hoover's agreement to share the conference minutes with Canada's foreign ministry. While External Affairs was indeed responsible for the conduct of Canada's international relations, the RCMP had the authority to deal with the FBI on matters relating to security intelligence, but this did not extend to seeking FBI permission for the RCMP to share its documents with External Affairs!

Shortly after the FBI launched its first Hemispheric Intelligence Conference, a United States-British Naval Intelligence and Security Conference was held in Kingston, Jamaica, from 26 February to 6 March 1942. The conference attempted to add structure to the existing naval co-operation among the three Anglo-Saxon powers by shifting to US control some of the Ottawa (Naval) Intelligence Area's responsibility of monitoring shipping in North America.

A more substantive inter-Allied intelligence conference followed with the British-Canadian-American Radio Intelligence Discussions, which took place in Washington on 6-17 April 1942.[20] The conference had been proposed in January by the British Government Code and Cipher School because of its correct perception that the United States and Canada did not possess extensive knowledge of wireless intelligence collection.[21] The conference gathered radio signals collectors, rather than individuals engaged in decryption, and was the most substantial of a series of Allied intelligence conferences attempting to bring organization and harmony to what was still an industry in its infancy. Because so much had been accomplished so quickly, there was great disarray, duplication, and overlapping of activities between the three partners and even between organizations within the three countries.

The British sinking of the German battleship *Bismarck* that previous May likely influenced the decision to improve the effectiveness of signals direction finding. A critical intelligence factor in the hunt for the *Bismarck* was direction finding and traffic analysis.[22] The lessons learned from the pursuit of the *Bismarck* underscored the greater effectiveness possible when all Allied resources were harnessed in a coherent and co-operative manner. The Canadian intercept stations "played an important part in mounting the successful attack on the Bismarck."[23]

The Washington conference began with the dispatch of a British Admiralty "Y" Commission (i.e., an organization engaged in activities pertaining to signals direction finding and collection) to North America to bring Canada and the United States up to date on the latest "Y" equipment and techniques, and to advance mutual co-operation.[24] At that time, Canada's three armed services were independently engaged in interception of "Y" material. On the west coast, the RCN concentrated on Japanese naval and diplomatic traffic and on direction finding. All the material collected was sent to the Admiralty intelligence division in London. The army's activities on the west coast duplicated those of the navy, although more attention was paid to Japanese army and air force traffic. All of the material collected by the army was sent directly to BSC in New York for transmittal to the Canadian Army intelligence division in Ottawa, to Britain's SIGINT service, and to the US military intelligence service. Discrimination of the material (i.e., interpretation of the traffic but not its decryption) was done by Canada's wireless intelligence section of the Army Intelligence branch. Material was also forwarded to the Examination Unit for decryption. At this phase of the war, the Canadian air force was only just becoming involved in SIGINT collection.[25]

Within Canada there was little coordination among the armed services on the collection of SIGINT; no single body oversaw the activities of the various monitoring operations or of collating the material for examination and analysis. This situation existed in large measure because of the different types of warfare and intelligence requirements with which each service was confronted. Before the Canadian delegation went to Washington, agreement was reached in Ottawa that something had to be done about an intolerable situation that was wasteful of resources and that accomplished less than could be achieved through even a moderately co-operative effort. Work to make improvements was already underway between individual officers within the armed services, but inter-services jealousies were significant factors in promoting the chaotic state of affairs that existed. Much of what was done, or not done, hearkened back to the lack of coordination among the armed services when they had initially embarked on foreign intelligence gathering.

The Washington conference was the most ambitious of inter-Allied discussions yet. The agenda was large. The conference was eventually constituted as an initial gathering that postulated the challenges, and was attended by a dozen separate subcommittees addressing various narrower issues (such as Wireless Telegraphy Interception and Aerial Systems Employed), and concluded with a final gathering that attempted to bring the findings together.[26] The number of delegates was not large. However, an actual count of the number of participants is difficult to establish since no master list exists and the names of some participants appear only as presenters associated with one subcommittee meeting. Canada probably had fewer than a dozen delegates drawn from the armed services.[27]

The April conference successfully imposed organization upon a chaotic state of Allied intelligence gathering. Divisions of labour were agreed upon, duplication of efforts was eliminated, technology exchanges took place, and, most importantly (not only for the war effort but also for the longer term), the conference framed the intelligence struggle then underway as a team effort in which all parties had roles to play and where no partner could easily return to a single autonomous national effort. The critical outcome of the April conference was recognition by all participants that the challenges were greater than could be met by the resources of a single nation. The conference established the principle that the sole path to success lay in co-operation among the Allies. In that sense, this conference marks the beginning of the intelligence-sharing club of the United States, the United Kingdom, and Canada – soon to be joined by Australia and New Zealand – that has lasted to the present day.

For Canada, one outcome of the Washington conference was that the co-operation of US and Canadian intercept stations would be arranged by a committee residing in Washington; the collection of Japanese naval intercepts would be directed by the US station at Bainbridge Island on the west coast working directly with the Canadian intercept station at Esquimalt. A clear decision of the conference was that Britain would leave to the United States and Canada the responsibility for all "Y" traffic over the Pacific Ocean. Canada was also to establish an ionosphere station at Churchill, Manitoba (listed erroneously in the final report as being in

Ontario). Many of the other deliberations related to technical matters and the transmittal of collected information. The conference was a meeting of technical experts, and it did not attempt to reach agreement on the distribution of the intelligence derived from collection efforts.[28]

US-Canadian success against Japanese communications would depend on both countries establishing "Y" committees based on the existing British model, and on the integration of the Canadian facilities with those of the United States. New communications means were organized for the rapid exchange of collected information, one of which involved the linkage of the existing BSC circuit between Ottawa–New York–Washington with another one between Bainbridge Island and Victoria, British Columbia (Esquimalt). Canadian raw intelligence was forwarded to the Americans; in return, Canada received whatever decrypted intelligence products resulted.

For Canada, an enduring outcome of the Washington conference was the creation of a Canadian "Y" committee. Canada's SIGINT collection facilities had by this time grown to such an extent that a unifying structure was required. A number of British delegates to the Washington conference, led by naval Captain H.R. Sandwith, the senior British representative, had stopped in Ottawa en route to Washington to explain the structure and mandate of the British "Y" committee and to suggest the creation of something similar in Canada. A "Y" committee, they explained, should include representatives of all of the armed services and related departments. Most importantly, it should coordinate all "Y" operations, allocate priorities in interception, and ensure that the monitored material was forwarded to appropriate recipients for decryption and discrimination. A "Y" committee would bring together and make available to the three services all the collected information of the individual services.[29]

The Canadian "Y" committee was created on 2 June 1942. Lieutenant Colonel W.W. Murray, director of military intelligence, was appointed chairman.[30] The committee reported to the Chiefs of Staff Committee and consisted of representatives of the service intelligence directorates and various technical units as well as representatives of the DEA and the Examination Unit.

The British-Canadian-American Radio Intelligence Discussions, taking place in Washington on 6-17 April 1942, were a watershed. For the Canadians, who had been working on the fringes, it was a revelation. The Canadians could do more, be more effective, and would derive greater benefit if their work was integrated with that of the United States and the United Kingdom.[31] In the months after the conference, there followed formal and informal intelligence meetings to work out the modalities of co-operation. One significant meeting was on 15 January 1943 at Arlington Hall Station, the home of the US Army SIGINT service, at which British, Canadian, and American representatives arranged for the exchange of intercepted diplomatic traffic.

The meeting clearly marked an expansion of the relationship. The participants agreed to make available schedules containing circuits coverage de-
sired by the three countries, which would allow all to identify resources and
request material.[32]

Regular subsequent meetings were normally held at the offices of BSC in
New York, probably selected because it was the midpoint between Ottawa
and Washington. One meeting on 12 April 1943 standardized preambles,
established formats, and solved routing problems, all of which were vital to
an enduring relationship in which each partner benefited from a standardized format.[33] Another meeting, on 3 September 1943, again at BSC, sought
to attain total coverage of Japanese weather station messages and avoid duplication in coverage, and established interdependence in the process.[34] Messages from Japanese weather stations were extremely important. Not only
did they provide meteorological information vital to operational tasks, but
also, because the information was often in a low-grade cipher, its decryption
was relatively easy and could provide important assistance in breaking more
complex codes that repeated the known text of the weather reports.

Another important intergovernmental meeting was held at Arlington Hall
that summer. On 16 June, representatives of the United States, the United
Kingdom, Canada, Australia, and India met to discuss coordination of effort in the exploitation of Japanese military and air force ciphers.[35] The
American host, Colonel W. Preston Corderman, of the US Army's Signal
Security Agency, offered to provide any information available that would
be helpful in their collective work. The Americans offered full and mutual
exchange of information on cryptanalysis and research work, and sought
the same from the others. Much of the discussions centred on traffic coordination of intercepted material to eliminate duplication of intercepts and
to fill gaps. Arlington Hall became a coordinating centre that would also
serve to provide comments and suggestions on incoming material.[36]

The various inter-Allied conferences began a process of formalizing the
co-operative inter-Allied arrangements that existed by this time. Signing of
the first formal SIGINT co-operation agreement took place in the midst of
the U-boat battle for the North Atlantic shipping lanes, and occurred on 2
October 1942 between Britain and the United States. The agreement provided for co-operation on naval SIGINT. This initiative was followed on 17
May 1943 by the signing of the British-United States Communications Intelligence Agreement (BRUSA), which provided for broader co-operation
between the US Army's Signal Security Agency, the US SIGINT organization,
and the British Government Code and Cipher School.[37]

The extent of co-operation between Britain and the United States went
beyond the potential for full participation by Canada. The agreements between the two principal Allies were taking into account Ultra intelligence,
the decryptions of German Enigma enciphered messages (on the part of the

British), and the Purple code, decryptions of Japanese communications (by the Americans). Although Canada had access to some of this material, Canada played no role in the attacks on these complex machine ciphers beyond providing some of the raw intercepted material. While not a full partner in the more sensitive SIGINT efforts, as a junior partner in the broader Anglo-American SIGINT alliance, Canada benefited from the emerging relationship, as did Australia and New Zealand.[38]

The date of Canadian access to Ultra material cannot be determined with precision. C.H. Little of Naval Intelligence states that he was the point of contact for Ultra material for three years during the war, likely beginning some time after May 1942.[39] He may have stumbled upon the existence of breaking Enigma messages while in London that May when he learned of an agreement between Britain and the United States *not* to share the "most significant German and Japanese decrypts with Canada."[40] As a result of this discovery, Little gained access to Purple messages – that is, US decrypts of Japanese traffic – through Commander Denniston of the Diplomatic and Commercial branch of the British Government Code and Cipher School, who authorized Little to pass the material to Norman Robertson at External Affairs. There is no evidence of whether this ad hoc exchange involved Ultra material. Nor is there any information on what authority Denniston used to provide Canada with what was US-produced and -owned SIGINT. Possibly emerging from Little's discovery, the Canadian Naval Operations Intelligence Centre began to receive "a full series of Enigma decrypts in May 1943, a year later."[41] From that time on, while Canada continued to play no direct role in decrypting Ultra messages, there was a "full service of Enigma decrypts" to Canada.[42]

Critical to the success of Canadian, American, and British intelligence cooperation during the early phase of the war was the effort made by the British to help the other two partners achieve their full potential. While British special intelligence liaison missions to Canada and the United States were a common occurrence (and always helpful), it was the daily link between the three partners, maintained by the office of BSC in New York, that proved vital. BSC was an amalgamation of all British security and intelligence organizations, headed by William Stephenson, who, although a Canadian, had lived in the United Kingdom before the war. Stephenson had arrived in New York on 21 June 1940 aboard the SS *Britannic*, and was assigned to the British Consulate there. He had made an earlier visit in the spring to meet with J. Edgar Hoover of the FBI, among others.[43]

Strong links between Canada and BSC were forged as early as 1941. At that time, the Special Operations Executive (SOE), a British covert action organization, secured agreement allowing them to recruit Canadians from military units already in Britain. Initially, the administrative link between Canada and the SOE was through the senior intelligence officer at Canada's

DND. This was very quickly reassigned to be conducted between BSC and External Affairs.[44] BSC had discussed the idea of establishing an office in Ottawa in 1941 but nothing came of it since the British government wanted relations to be dealt with by the British high commissioner. In addition, if any British intelligence representative was assigned to Ottawa, such a person had to come from the British Security Service (MI5), in accordance with the existing practice of assigning only MI5 personnel to Commonwealth nations.[45]

In the BSC history written at the end of the war, Stephenson acknowledged that the "goodwill of the Canadian authorities" was vital to his mission in the United States.[46] The relationship with Canadian policy makers like Norman Robertson of External Affairs became close. But the details of the ties between the two men is lost in history since Robertson did not have note-takers in the room during his many meetings with Stephenson, and BSC archives were destroyed.[47] While BSC had a very free hand in Canada, the Canadian government was kept fully informed.[48] Canada was also the major source of staffing for the BSC office in New York. External Affairs closely co-operated in this activity but eventually had to put a stop to that, since BSC was hiring so many Canadian stenographers that Canada's own war effort was diminishing.[49] During the summer of 1942, Stephenson also made an attempt to recruit Herbert Norman, the DEA's Japanese scholar who was in the process of being repatriated with the Canadian Legation staff from Tokyo. Canada was initially amenable to the idea, but in September 1942 assigned Norman as head of the DEA's special intelligence section attached to the Examination Unit.[50]

While books about Stephenson and BSC have focused on the more exciting elements of the BSC story, the reality of intelligence work often involved less dramatic endeavours. By far the greatest of BSC's resources was directed at the mechanics of security and intelligence; a core purpose of BSC was the physical protection of British interests and purchases in America and the provision of an intelligence link between the partners through communications and coordination activities. For Canada, BSC provided a vital service by making available a reliable, fast, and highly secure communications link between Canada and its allies.

In mid-February 1942, Lester B. Pearson made a visit to New York to discuss with Stephenson the creation of a Telekrypton (a new and more secure enciphered communication system) link between Ottawa and New York. A Telekrypton line was subsequently established between the Examination Unit on Laurier Avenue in Ottawa and the BSC offices in New York. Decrypted enemy communications collected by Canada were forwarded in "raw" format (i.e., unevaluated and undeciphered) to New York as they became available. In turn, Pearson asked that Stephenson send him "personally for my own information, and *not* for distribution, the material which you discussed with me in New York and which it was thought might be in the possession of some one person here." Pearson's letter to Stephenson does not disclose what the material was. Most likely, the cryptic reference was to Ultra intelligence material.[51] By May 1942, the Telekrypton line was in operation and by the following year, BSC had linked the Ottawa–New York–Washington Telekrypton connection to the BSC wireless station, code named Hydra, which was located at the special BSC training facility near Oshawa, Ontario.[52]

The Hydra wireless station was located at what has become popularly known as "Camp X," a British SOE special training school near Oshawa on the shores of Lake Ontario, which was administered by BSC. The facility was officially designated Special Training School (STS) 103, although the DND referred to it initially as "Project J" and eventually came to call it S25-1-1, the name of the DND file housing documents pertaining to the SOE school. Officials at External Affairs referred to it as "the country house."[53] The facility was managed by the Canadian Army, which publicly referred to the site as an adjunct facility to the District Depot, Military District No. 2. Normal liaison and consultation by BSC with Canada was through the DEA.

During the early history of Camp X, it was staffed by British instructors assisted by a Canadian subaltern as adjutant and quartermaster, and some twenty-six other Canadian ranks to run the camp.[54] T.G. Drew-Brook, a Canadian stockbroker in Toronto who had served with William Stephenson during the First World War, was the BSC representative in Canada who oversaw the selection of the farmland for the camp and its construction. Drew-Brook had approached J.L. Ralston, Minister of National Defence, through a common acquaintance to seek permission to establish the facility. Agreeing to the project, Ralston informed Drew-Brook that BSC need not advise Mackenzie King since it would suffice to inform various heads of departments that might be affected.[55] Mackenzie King probably did not know much, or anything, about Camp X during its early phase. After all, it was not a significant matter and hardly involved important national policy. Probably at some point during the war Mackenzie King became aware of the Camp X facility. Certainly, it was the practice of Norman Robertson, the undersecretary of state for External Affairs, to provide oral briefings to the Cabinet War Committee on different aspects of intelligence activities.[56]

Robertson was one of the first to be called by Ralston about establishing the British training facility. He quickly assented to the creation of the establishment, and was the primary policy point of contact on the Canadian side for all BSC activity in Canada, including preparation of Camp X, although responsibility for the daily Canada-BSC relationship was soon delegated to Pearson and ultimately to Stone.[57] The DND continued to act as the administrative overseer of Camp X.

Notwithstanding Robertson's ready accession to the British request to establish Camp X in Canada, he always retained some hesitation over playing host to a "spy school," and feared its disclosure and the resultant Canadian public response. Two of Robertson's close intelligence associates have both recalled that Camp X in Canada was the only part of the secret relationship between Canada and the United Kingdom over which Robertson is alleged to have hesitated.[58] At the time the construction of Camp X was being discussed, the sheer scale of the operation worried him. The decisions on Camp X also occurred only months after Robertson succeeded O.D. Skelton as under-secretary of state, and any hesitation may have reflected unfamiliarity with his new responsibilities. There can be no other obvious basis for Robertson's concerns except the recent elevation to his post, since the creation of Camp X posed no greater risk or potential adverse public attention than other intelligence activities in which Canada was engaged then or later.

David Stafford's book on Camp X provides a very complete picture of the creation and role of STS 103.[59] The school had been established as an SOE training centre for secret agents with a particular view to providing training to Americans in the fine arts of espionage and sabotage. This was at a time when the United States had not yet entered the war, and such a facility, staffed by British trainers, could not be established on American soil. The irony of Camp X is that the facility was finished and opened within only a few days of the Japanese attack on Pearl Harbor, after which there were few restrictions on where and how the Americans could prepare for the darker side of war.

More than 550 students passed through Camp X. Most were Canadian, American, or British, but there were also many immigrants to Canada among Camp X alumni; Yugoslavs were particularly well represented. Agents were trained for operations in every theatre of the war. For much of the war, Camp X continued not only to train secret agents, for covert action behind enemy lines under SOE auspices, but also to provide training of security personnel, intelligence officers, psychological warfare experts, and individuals engaged in less exotic pursuits.[60]

Camp X remained in operation as an SOE training site for about two years, until it closed in April 1944. Ironically, in the weeks before the closure of Camp X, the British approached Canada for co-operation in establishing a similar facility in British Columbia. Few details about the proposed new site have emerged. The British Columbia camp was for a temporary purpose only, ultimately involving only a small number of persons – a total of one officer and twelve other ranks, all of whom were Canadian – for an operation against the Japanese. Details about their mission have not emerged. Training for the small unit was completed in August 1944, and the participants probably departed for their jumping off point, Australia, in September.[61]

While Camp X ceased to function as a covert training facility in April 1944, it took until that fall before the arrangements to terminate all the training functions were in place. However, Camp X did not close down. Because of the earlier establishment of the Hydra communications station at the site, staffed largely by Canadian Army personnel, it was decided that the DND would continue to contribute to the facility, now renamed the No. 2 Military Research Centre.[62] Camp X, then, remained a joint British-Canadian communications establishment linking the Allied intelligence services until after the war when, in the reorganization that followed the end of hostilities, Canada entirely took over the communications responsibility. For a short time after the end of the war, Camp X also became home to Russian defector Igor Gouzenko.

Canada also maintained a relationship with the American OSS, led by the colourful "Wild Bill" Donovan. At times tenuous, the relationship had been formed to provide a resource for Herbert Norman's special intelligence section to exchange information with which to enhance the intelligence evaluations being prepared. As mentioned earlier, Norman and the special intelligence section had access to all intelligence material and prepared intelligence assessments based on the raw intercepts, supported by information available from other sources. By the fall of 1942, T.A. Stone had arranged for Norman to visit BSC in New York and the OSS in Washington to establish liaison arrangements on assessed intelligence.[63] The arrangement put in place with BSC worked well. So too did Canada's liaison with the American OSS, which valued Norman's reports on Japanese economic policy, particularly his evaluation of Japanese efforts at economic exploitation of conquered territory.

However, the relationship with the OSS was not smooth from the beginning. Security concerns, which are not articulated in the available archival documents, overshadowed the relationship with the OSS, which was not provided with copies of Canadian intelligence assessments. Instead, a designated OSS officer was permitted to read the Canadian reports in Lester B. Pearson's office in Washington, to which he was now posted.[64] In turn, Norman received considerable information from the OSS.

Possibly at the root of Canadian security concerns enveloping the relationship with the OSS was fear of its discovery by G2, the American army intelligence organization, which had its own turbulent relationship with the OSS. There was always an assumption that the Canadian ties to the OSS would not remain unknown to G2, which was "bitterly opposed to sharing its traffic in any way with O.S.S."[65] Canada's main exchange with G2 was raw intercept material that was critical to the work of the Examination Unit. Should G2 learn of the Canadian ties to the OSS, it was feared that supply of this material could cease. Sir Edward Travis of Britain's Government Code and Cipher

School who had recently been in Ottawa and was aware of Canada's links to the OSS, was urging Canada to end these ties. In exchange, he would intercede with G2 to ensure a flow of "high grade traffic" to which Canada had previously had no access. If Canada maintained the links with the OSS, Britain could do little to gain access to fresh traffic from G2 for Canada.[66] Canada was reluctant to break with the OSS, partly because the intelligence received from this source was valuable, and also because it was thought that G2 (or the US Navy's Office of Naval Intelligence) was not particularly interested in establishing a working relationship with Canada.

However, growing links between G2 and the Examination Unit seem to have forced a review on Canada's part: "We may have to consider the advantages in breaking off with O.S.S., although these relations have been most cordial and useful."[67] No details are available on the manner in which Canada curtailed its relationship with the OSS, or if it ceased altogether. As will be seen in the following chapter, Canada continued to maintain ties with the OSS on intelligence derived from POW censorship activities. One can surmise that the advice of Sir Edward Travis to cease ties with the OSS was accepted by Canada as far as it concerned exchanges of intelligence assessments derived from SIGINT material that was the bulk of the output of the special intelligence section. Having ceased an exchange of information with the OSS that was identified as problematic, it is likely that Canada continued to maintain other links with the OSS that had not been specifically labelled of concern.

While Canada developed complex intelligence relationships with the British and Americans, these were dominated by the central affiliation on SIGINT. In this area, the association was particularly robust. Canada's co-operation with the larger intelligence partners gave Canadian decision makers access to foreign intelligence material that the country could never have hoped to collect with its own resources. The extent of such additional material cannot be assessed, but Canada's foreign intelligence resources were modest throughout the war and one must assume that the Allies provided such additional information as Canada required to carry out its tasks. The impact of this material on Canadian decision making is more elusive. It is clear from Mackenzie King's diary and other documents that he received regular intelligence reports, including Ultra decrypts. However, policy making is sufficiently amorphous as to obfuscate much of the origins of inputs into decisions.

The demands of participation with more advanced partners also provided a framework for the Canadian intelligence actors to increasingly work together as a team. The DEA and DND had already achieved a certain synergy through the collection of raw SIGINT by the armed forces and the cryptanalysis of the material by the Examination Unit. Critical to the success of inter-Allied intelligence co-operation were the many Allied intelligence conferences that moved all three countries to eliminate duplication and ensured that limited resources were used where they could best contribute to the overall effort.

While Canada began its foreign intelligence collecting capability on its own, the contributions from its allies were critical to success. Canada did not possess the resources or skills to build a strong foreign intelligence capacity on its own. At every stage in the early wartime years, and in every type of endeavour, the contributions by Britain or the United States were vital to success. The knowledge and experience of Canada's two allies saved time and resources for Canada.

However, the help from Canada's allies came at a price. Canada was not a first-tier ally. While Canada's intelligence contribution to the Allied cause was valued for the size and resources of the country, Canada could not shake its position as a junior partner. While greater resources allotted to the intelligence task would have resulted in a more significant role for Canada in the early part of the war, it is doubtful that any realistic contribution could have significantly modified the Canadian position within the alliance.

At no time were Canadian foreign intelligence activities during the war viewed as operationally fully independent. However, had Canada acted entirely independently of its allies, it would not have enjoyed as significant an access to foreign intelligence with which to guide decision makers.

As mentioned earlier, Canada did not operate a clandestine HUMINT service during the war. Nevertheless, the country did not limit its intelligence collecting efforts solely to SIGINT. While resources continued to remain minimal, there were other opportunities for collecting information. Some of these were not dissimilar from non-clandestine forms of HUMINT. As always, the resources were meagre, but the effort and successes were surprisingly significant.

4
Canadian HUMINT Collection

As noted at the end of Chapter 3, Canada had no clandestine foreign service collecting HUMINT when war began, nor did it consider the creation of such a service in the midst of war. The Canadian situation was paralleled by the experience of the other British dominions, none of which had clandestine intelligence-gathering organizations before the outbreak of the Second World War, or created such establishments during the war. The question of setting up a covert intelligence service in Canada seems to have never arisen during the course of the war. Such an omission is understandable. Creating a clandestine HUMINT service is costly, risky, and resource draining. Heavy demands exist in time of war, and necessary skills and resources (financial and personnel) are in short supply.

While giving no consideration to the establishment of a covert HUMINT service, Canada did pursue overt forms of HUMINT collection activities, which were possible with the resources at hand. The value of HUMINT, whether collected overtly or through clandestine means, lies in the wealth of details it can supply from first-hand observations. The danger in using HUMINT rests in the subjectivity of individuals who have varying powers of observations and objectivity. Nevertheless, a great deal of intelligence that might not be attainable otherwise is available through HUMINT collection. Overt HUMINT collection is less dangerous than clandestine activities and can often be as fruitful. The ease and magnitude of overt HUMINT intelligence collection efforts should not diminish its contribution. Canada made a small but important contribution to the intelligence war effort through its very limited involvement in overt HUMINT collection.

An important Canadian HUMINT program during the war collected intelligence derived from censorship activity. Information was obtained from both incoming correspondence from enemy-occupied areas and a review of all letters sent by enemy POWs in Canada. Another HUMINT effort, which circumstances permitted to last only for a brief time, was the collection of intelligence through the debriefing of Canadians repatriated from enemy captivity. Debriefing of individuals is a classic example of low-tech, high-impact intelligence gathering that continues to be employed to the present day by most intelligence organizations. Both of these collection programs involved minimal risk and were easily achievable within Canada's limited wartime resources. A separate program debriefed and interrogated POWs and enemy civilian internees. Collectively, these efforts did not provide intelligence of dramatically actionable impact. However, they provided the building blocks that contributed to an understanding of life in occupied territories as well as some insights into enemy military tactics.

One of the few initiatives taken by the Canadian government in anticipation of the Second World War involved censorship preparation, which began with the appointment of an Interdepartmental Committee on Censorship in March 1938, to prepare operational guidelines. With the commencement of hostilities, censorship was to be applied to the mail and other forms of communications passing between Canada and foreign locations with a goal of preventing vital information from reaching the enemy, whether wittingly or unwittingly.

The general staff of the DND drew up regulations for censorship in September 1938, providing for an information section within the Directorate of Military Operations and Intelligence, with a mandate to circulate information affecting censorship and to compile for circulation a daily summary of information gleaned from censorship activities. The information section was also responsible for directing cable, radio, and postal censorship officers in the type of "information required or to which special attention is paid."[1] Initially, this was done to enhance the efficiency of censorship operations and was only later recognized for its potential intelligence value. The prime architect of the regulations for censorship was Colonel Maurice A. Pope, who was the army director of operations and intelligence.[2]

With the German attack on Poland, censorship was implemented by an order-in-council on 1 September 1939; the censorship function within the DND gradually became one of the most important tasks of the armed services' intelligence directorates. Incoming mail passing through the censors often contained significant intelligence insights of military and political value. This was particularly true when an effort was made to collect and collate all information from various pieces of correspondence that might relate to a common issue, such as food shortages in Germany or the experience of enemy sailors engaged in naval battle. While individual pieces of data contained in censored correspondence might have appeared innocuous, it was the collation and evaluation of many pieces of seemingly insignificant pieces of information that held the potential for shedding light on conditions in enemy territories or on details of enemy war fighting dogma. It was a failing on the part of the responsible military authorities that the value of this intelligence source was not recognized. The resources necessary for its full exploitation at the outset of the war were not accorded, and it took considerable time before the intelligence-gathering facet of the censorship process became effective.

The Censorship Coordination Committee was appointed on 3 September 1939 to ensure interdepartmental coordination on censorship matters. Members of this committee were drawn primarily from the DND, the Department of Transport, the Post Office Department, the Department of Secretary of State, and the DEA. The first chairman of the committee was Walter S. Thompson, who assumed the position of director of censorship. The National Defence participant was Colonel Pope, then the director of military intelligence. The involvement of the military intelligence service should not be misconstrued. Rather than implying proactive intent to exploit communications for their intelligence value, the department's participation was a defensive posture to prevent unauthorized revelations about military preparedness from reaching the enemy.

Upon Thompson's resignation in December 1939, Colonel Pope became chairman of the censorship committee.[3] He held the office until the spring of 1940 but was not replaced as chairman after his departure until the autumn of 1941. In the interim, meetings were held on an ad hoc basis, often convened by T.A. Stone of the DEA.[4] Stone was charged with overseeing foreign intelligence matters, and the meetings during this period reflect his efforts to direct Canada's censorship activities toward exploiting their foreign intelligence potential.[5]

Intelligence collection from censorship work grew slowly, although by early 1942 a system was in place for exploiting information of intelligence value. While limited intelligence collection was obtained by monitoring civilian mail, the censorship activity with the greatest potential was that tied to correspondence involving POWs. The families of enemy POWs wrote about family news, which gave the Allies insight on enemy knowledge, resources, morale, the availability of food stocks, the impact on industries of bombing campaigns, and, sometimes, the location of enemy military units. Extracting and collating shreds of knowledge from censored correspondence often held the possibility of supplying insights into conditions in enemy territory that might not otherwise have been available.

The censorship reports were compilations of extracts of potential intelligence value from individual letters. One such report, for example, related to the economic situation in Madagascar and the reaction of the population to the British occupation of the French colony.[6] Individual censorship reports were collated into thematic studies. For example, a report from March 1945 records comparative statistical shifts in attitudes in Germany from September to December of the previous year. A number of indicators were tracked, including expressions of anti-war sentiments (which went from 5 percent to 4 percent), faith in victory (which rose from 30 percent to 34 percent), and war weariness (which also rose from 33 percent to nearly 48 percent).[7]

German military prisoners captured in 1939 and early 1940 had been held in Britain until after the fall of France when Canada was asked to take the prisoners for reasons of security and because they were consuming precious food resources. The first shipment to Canada of enemy POWs consisted of 153 German officers and 323 enlisted men who arrived on 29 June 1940. By 1943, there were seventeen POW camps in Canada: nearly 25,000 inmates, mostly German fighting men, but also more than 3,000 merchant seamen and some 1,200 civilians.[8] Eventually, Canada was to hold close to 40,000 German POWs and civilian internees at twenty-five sites across the country.[9]

The scale of the intelligence-exploiting censorship operation quickly grew in size. By the end of 1942, at the Ottawa postal censorship office, the naval vetting table alone looked at 24,000 letters in a single month, from which 1,000 intelligence reports resulted. These were generally single-issue reports citing pieces of information of potential intelligence value. A month later, at the beginning of 1943, this same unit reviewed 21,000 letters (12,500 written in German to German naval POWs interned in Canada) and prepared about 420 intelligence reports. During February-March 1943, 45,034 letters (i.e., for two months) led to the preparation of 2,084 intelligence reports.[10]

In spite of the volume of material reviewed and the many intelligence reports generated, Canadian censorship activities were hampered by an absence of a central focus. No one seemed to be in charge. On the non-POW side of censorship activities, the army was responsible for telegraph censorship, the Post Office looked after postal censorship, and National War Services carried out press censorship. The thrust of censorship activities remained largely defensive rather than offensive. The DEA, a key contributor to the architecture of the censorship operation throughout the war, drawn into the planning and policy direction of censorship because of the potential intelligence benefits,[11] was not an enthusiastic participant in actual censorship operations. Often, they bristled at the cost of resources demanded by the rather mundane activities.[12] Of particular interest to the DEA was the analysis of the mail of enemy POWs and other internees in Canada, all of which was contrary to international protocols but potentially valuable from an intelligence perspective.

Stone introduced a system requiring censorship staff to sort interesting correspondence by subject matter for later analysis. Full intelligence value was not always drawn from censored material unless many minuscule pieces of a puzzle were placed side by side in context to provide a composite view. It fell to George Glazebrook, Stone's assistant, to carry out many of the daily tasks of assessing the intercepted material. Glazebrook, a well-published historian who had been recruited from the University of Toronto as one of the temporary war intakes, was a tall, lean, erudite, pipe-smoking academic with a penchant for the works of Dashiell Hammett and his fictional private detective, Sam Spade, whose dialogue he could quote at length. Glazebrook found the censorship task nearly impossible because of the volume of correspondence needing his review, and he often drew in junior officers to help him. On one occasion, copies of intercepted mail being burnt in a fireplace following analysis were sucked up through a chimney in the East Block, not entirely consumed by the fire, and landed on the grounds of Parliament Hill. Junior DEA officers were made to run across the expanses of grass on Parliament Hill to collect the incriminating charred documents.[13]

While the majority of the Canadian intelligence reports are missing – either destroyed, lost, or still locked in classified cabinets – sufficient administrative and operational memoranda have survived to permit a conclusion that Canadian HUMINT collection during the Second World War was limited and reflected the resources and skills available at the time. Within the existing confines of the program, and once the imposing administrative hurdles were overcome, Canada produced information from censorship operations that provided the building blocks to create composite views of socio-economic conditions within Germany and its occupied territories. The individual reports from censorship reviews suggest a tedious undertaking that bore fruit only when many reports were collated and analyzed to capture changes in attitudes and circumstances over time.

The intelligence products that eventually grew from these efforts were able to provide decision makers with detailed insights into life in Germany. The Germans exercised extensive censorship of correspondence sent to their POWs. One must assume that German censors were reasonably effective overall and removed most information that might be considered of potential use to the Allies. The fact that the Allies nevertheless extracted so much information from the correspondence attests to the tenacity and skills of the intelligence staff wading through mounds of letters, and explains why some intelligence reports were listed as representing material drawn from thousands of letters. It is unlikely that German censors were lax in compliance with some elaborate disinformation campaign. One must also assume that Canadian and other Allied censors, no matter how capable and conscientious, similarly allowed a significant amount of information of potential use to the enemy to slip through in letters to Allied service personnel.

An evaluation bridging the period of the Normandy landings covered a host of socio-economic indicators of well-being. It recorded that there was plenty of food, little mention of clothing shortages, indications that city dwellers were moving to the countryside, and that health topics were being censored by the enemy, suggesting that the population was not satisfied with existing health services.[14] Also included was military information, primarily on enemy losses. A similar report shortly thereafter covered much the same ground but also recorded a significant increase in coverage of air raids, usually in the form of telling a POW he would not recognize his hometown.[15]

An intelligence report from early 1945 that derived information from 51,447 letters written in November 1944 provided an evaluation on conditions in Germany covering air raids, amusements, commodities, crime and punishment, crops, education, food, health, housing, justice, labour, livestock, mail, and travel.[16] This report reflected a standard format that was regularly revised and updated. Toward the end of the war, as the Allies entered Germany, reports were also prepared on individual German regions, assessing local peculiarities and impacts of air raids, availability of food stocks and other commodities, labour, health, travel, acceptance of propaganda, faith in victory, military events, patriotism, the home front, anti-war sentiments, war weariness, and so forth. In other words, these were detailed assessments that provided significant insights. Each regional report was usually based on 500 to 800 individual letters.[17] More exceptional reports were also prepared. One that has survived covered political, social, and economic conditions in France *after* the war in Europe had ended. Ten pages in length and based on 183 specific items collected from 795 letters posted in France, it portrays the reaction of the French population to conditions in their country. Overall attitudes were described as gloomy and there was disappointment with the Provisional Government, the Allies, and the nation itself. Particularly insightful is the section on economics, which paints a picture of confusion as the country tried to reorganize itself.[18]

A major challenge to the exploitation of censorship material for intelligence value arose from the conflicting approaches to censorship requirements within the different military jurisdictions. It was an entirely uncoordinated operation; consequently, it was difficult and labour intensive to extract valuable intelligence from the effort.[19] By the beginning of 1942, the censorship-intelligence link was not functioning effectively; instructions to censorship officers were received verbally or in writing from each of the separate intelligence organizations of the three armed services. Confusion resulted. For example, Army Intelligence required all information and had no defined priorities. Conflicting instructions resulting from the absence of a clear and coherent mandate put a heavy burden on the censorship officers, and some found themselves fully occupied with collecting intelligence on behalf of the armed services.[20]

Following a review of censorship-related intelligence operations, Glazebrook advised his superiors that success in obtaining intelligence from censorship operations was unlikely to be possible in the absence of a central authority to provide a supervisory function. Norman Robertson, the undersecretary of state for External Affairs, agreed and drafted a memorandum for the prime minister on 5 March 1942, calling for a reorganization of censorship operations to remedy the lack of central coordination. Robertson stated that many of the challenges stemmed from the absence of a consistent policy, the lack of a central authority, and the conflict arising from separate censorship and intelligence functions. He proposed changes that allowed censorship to be better used to obtain intelligence information, and ended by voicing his view that wartime demands required a reorganization of censorship to permit the necessary "assistance to the intelligence departments."[21]

Robertson's concerns were addressed by a May 1942 order-in-council,[22] which removed the censorship function from the DND and brought it under the Minister of National War Service, provided for a director of censorship, and authorized the creation of censorship advisory committees, including one with responsibility for intelligence and security matters.[23] The first meeting of the Advisory Committee on Intelligence and Security was held on 16 July 1942 under the chairmanship of the new director of censorship, Colonel O.M. Biggar. Subsequent meetings were held fortnightly, and agenda items typically included discussions of censorship activities, providing support for Canada's intelligence efforts, and issuing appropriate directives in support of security and intelligence activities.[24]

A new dimension to intelligence collection from POW censorship activities was added at the end of 1942, when Britain's Political Warfare Executive, which was part of the Foreign Office, sought the DEA's assistance in obtaining information from POWs that could be of use in propaganda efforts against the Germans. Robertson did not favour the proposal and the momentum for the initiative seems to have come largely from Stone and Glazebrook.[25] Nevertheless, following consultations with David Bowes-Lyon, the British Political Warfare Executive representative in Washington, the Political Warfare Planning Committee was established within the DEA. Creation of a committee avoided the need for establishing a new division within External Affairs for which there were no resources. Instead, the committee drew upon existing skills and expertise distributed within several divisions by simply adding these new responsibilities.[26] T.A. Stone, E.M. Reid, S.F. Rae, and George Glazebrook initially formed the governing committee within the DEA's British Commonwealth and European Division.

By the early summer of 1943, Glazebrook sought to expand the role of the Political Warfare Planning Committee toward a broader government function. Following advice to the prime minister, the Cabinet War Committee approved creation of a political intelligence committee with a broader interdepartmental membership, to replace the Political Warfare Planning Committee.[27] The DEA provided the chairperson. Having been created only in June 1943, the Political Intelligence Committee recommended to the Chief of the General Staff in July that the DND establish a POW intelligence division to work with the Political Intelligence Committee to collect and collate intelligence, re-educate (i.e., politically influence) POWs, identify and segregate POWs according to political views, and establish a secret intelligence unit "charged with ... securing from inside the camps information by whatever means it might devise."[28] In a separate letter to Major General H.F.G. Letson, the adjutant general, Stone made it clear that the intent was to allow the Political Intelligence Committee to "extend its work into a much broader field than the one in which we are at present operating," indicating that this involved specially chosen full-time personnel dedicated to intelligence tasks.[29]

When the Chief of the General Staff had not agreed to the Political Intelligence Committee's proposal by September, Glazebrook took a new approach and wrote to suggest that the focus be on re-education to "break down the prejudices and Nazi convictions" of some of the POWs.[30] Glazebrook's new tactic probably reflected a change in thinking at the DEA since about the time of his letter the Political Intelligence Committee spawned the Psychological Warfare Committee, partly with the same membership but also including representatives of the Wartime Information Board and the intelligence organizations of the three armed services. The new committee was charged with planning and coordinating the efforts of the various departments that were directing propaganda to enemy and enemy-occupied countries, including propaganda to POWs in Canada. The Psychological Warfare Committee sought and received the approval of the Cabinet War Committee for its efforts both among POWs and against the enemy.[31]

The Cabinet War Committee approved the creation of the Psychological Warfare Committee on 12 October 1943, even though there was no significant support for the concept from the Cabinet War Committee or the undersecretary of state for External Affairs.[32] Psychological warfare, as Stone and Glazebrook understood the term, included all propaganda activities directed against the enemy and enemy-occupied countries, as well as propaganda directed at neutral and even Allied countries. Propaganda was not normally an intelligence function, but sought to influence existing perceptions in enemy-held territory. An intelligence-related link with propaganda efforts arose when psychological warfare (sometimes called political warfare) attempted to mislead and disturb the enemy. Although Canada became involved in psychological warfare under the direction of External Affairs, there was no evidence of success since clear targets and objectives were absent. The early efforts of psychological warfare were limited to recording radio programs for German merchant seamen, French-language programs from Quebec beamed to France, and programs for occupied and neutral countries.[33] These programs were aired by the BBC since Canada did not have a sufficiently strong short-wave transmitter to reach Europe.

In support of psychological warfare, hundreds of extracts from POW mail were collected for use in political intelligence broadcasts back to Germany. Many related to working on farms or ranches, which was universally enjoyed, according to the extracts. Two examples capture the essence of the messages. One POW wrote about how "the so much-talked [about] cowboys are at home in this region ... I am very, very comfortable with my farmer, an ENGLISHMAN" (from Brooks, Alberta). Another wrote, "Work is heavy but there is so much food here that sometimes one does not know where to start first" (from Cooksville Labour Camp).[34]

Meanwhile, the Chief of the General Staff had finally responded to Glazebrook's efforts to have the DND create a division responsible for POW intelligence matters. On 9 September 1943, the Chief of the General Staff directed that a review be conducted of the intelligence structure of the DND's Directorate of Prisoners of War "so that full advantage may be derived in all intelligence spheres from our custodianship of enemy P's/W [POWs]."[35] This was not a solution since the directorate was already overworked with administrative tasks and counter-intelligence; instead, it limited its foreign intelligence collection efforts to obtaining operational intelligence from POWs who had long been absent from theatres of war. However, a great deal of intelligence continued to be collected from POW incoming and outgoing mail. The intelligence collected in this manner focused on such subjects as the German army order of battle, leadership information, campaign conditions from a German perspective, civilian attitudes and responses to the war, and morale.[36]

By the beginning of October, still with no military intelligence POW directorate, Stone and Major General Letson met with British authorities in London on the subject of a special POW intelligence unit and underscored the importance for Canada of the establishment of a system for securing information through censorship activity.[37] Still, the senior Canadian military leadership was not prepared to act.

Colonel W.W. Murray,[38] director of military intelligence and acting on behalf of the intelligence chiefs of the three armed services, sought to advance the creation of a POW intelligence division in mid-November by interceding with the Chief of the General Staff, advising that the officers of the DND Directorate of Prisoners of War, charged with administering and controlling the POWs, could not do double duty by also acting as intelligence officers.[39] Colonel Murray claimed that the existing intelligence structure was inadequate. Although some 300 postal censorship examiners were active in the fall of 1943 in examining POW correspondence, this activity was limited to gathering intelligence from correspondence and ignored the potential that was available from interviewing the prisoners themselves.

An eventual Chief of the General Staff review suggested that greater benefits could be obtained if an intelligence officer was appointed to each camp, distinct from an interpreter officer, who also carried out intelligence tasks without appropriate training. The recommendation called for forty intelligence officers to monitor Canada's 24,494 POWs. Some intelligence officers could also combine positions with interpreter officers after necessary training.

While the intelligence officials at External Affairs were preoccupied with psychological warfare and propaganda initiatives, the prisoner of war intelligence division finally received approval from the Chiefs of Staff Committee on 14 January 1944, after the matter had been deferred for more than six months.[40] The new POW intelligence section would have responsibilities that differed from the "jailer" role of the adjutant general, who remained responsible for all other POW tasks.[41]

The authority from the Chiefs of Staff Committee to establish the POW intelligence division did not diminish the tension existing between the DND and the DEA, since the POW intelligence division was not immediately staffed. The Chiefs of Staff Committee sought the views of the DEA on POW intelligence and was informed by Robertson that the DEA was in full agreement with the 14 January decision to establish the POW intelligence division. The reiteration of DEA support from Robertson drew particular attention to the portion of the mandate requiring the POW intelligence division to support the Psychological Warfare Committee, headed by the DEA. With this in mind, Robertson reminded the DND that the Chiefs of Staff Committee had been aware of the Psychological Warfare Committee since its inception and had approved the participation of defence directors of intelligence in its work of gathering intelligence and preparing psychological warfare against Germany. He added that it was urgent that the DND establish the POW intelligence division, which would support psychological warfare activities.[42]

Two days later, Robertson informed the prime minister of his support for a POW intelligence division at the DND to complement the political activities of the Psychological Warfare Committee, as well as to collect foreign intelligence. He also berated the Chiefs of Staff Committee for its tardiness in taking action on the matter and expressed his hope that a POW intelligence division would soon be in place.[43] Mackenzie King's reaction is not recorded, although it may have stimulated the action that followed.

A DND memorandum to the ministers was prepared at the end of March recommending that the Directorate of Prisoners of War be staffed and organized to function under the Chief of the General Staff and that specially trained intelligence officers be assigned to POW camps for the purpose of collecting intelligence.[44] Again, no action was immediately taken and it was only on 9 May 1944, nearly one year after the idea had been launched by External Affairs and only one month before the Allied landings in Normandy, that the Minister of National Defence approved the submission for the establishment of a POW intelligence organization.[45]

The new unit was known as MI7 and was under the direction of the DND's Directorate of Military Intelligence. The designation provides a humorous insight into the continuing close ties to British intelligence organizations. In the DND nomenclature, the directorate should have been designated MI5, the next MI number to be used, but Britain informally objected over anticipated confusion with its own MI5, the British security service. For much the same reason, Canada also skipped the next number, MI6 (the British secret intelligence service).[46] Hence, the new unit became MI7.

Hampered from the moment of its creation because MI7 was subservient to the Directorate of Military Intelligence, it "had not the weight and prestige of a Directorate and because of this, its officers were handicapped in their work with other Directorates."[47] By the following September, there was a recommendation to reduce the activities of the Psychological Warfare Committee, which was supported by the work of MI7.[48] Canada's efforts in psychological warfare had not met with great success and the experiment was being wrapped up with a recommendation made that "we should not attempt anything [like it] towards the Far East."[49]

Creating an organization directed at exploiting intelligence from POWs had been an administrative nightmare. The DND was slow to recognize the intelligence benefits and even slower to allocate reasonable resources to allow the task to be successfully carried out. Exploiting POW intelligence through interviews and active measures was hopelessly inadequate, suffered from poor direction, had limited resources, and enjoyed no commitment to success from the leadership of the DND. Only one report, from March 1945, has been identified in the surviving archives as likely emerging from this program: it collated intelligence on the Marine Kriegsschule at Flensburg-Mürwik.[50] The detailed report listed staff, training at the naval academy, and the resources of the different engineering branches of the German navy, including its torpedo school. Although with limited actionable intelligence value so late in the war, this report was of benefit in postwar Allied exploitation of German military prowess.

The censorship activities directed against POWs in Canada paid a more significant dividend. This activity was directed at outgoing POW mail rather than the very valuable incoming correspondence to POWs. The nominal purpose of censorship activities was to hamper the disclosure of strategic information by the POWs to the Germans, and this was largely effective. However, a corollary of this activity was the counter-intelligence mandate of Canadian censors, since many of the POWs communicated with their superiors back home through clandestine means. The effort of POWs to communicate with their superiors gave rise to an attempt by captured submariners to escape and be retrieved by German U-boats off the shore of Canada. Though there were several endeavours, one by prisoners in Bowmanville counted for the largest group involved. The plans became known to Canadian authorities before the escape occurred and the RCMP was called in to assist in verifying the attempted breakout. Canada subsequently made preparations to seize the U-boat that was to recover the escapees. Soon, a U-boat did arrive off the coast of Canada to pick up prisoners. One escaped prisoner evaded recapture and came very close to the pickup point. Neither the Canadian side nor apparently the POWs were aware of how to contact the U-boat, and neither the escaped POW, still on the loose, nor the waiting Canadian navy ultimately made contact with the U-boat.[51]

In spite of the misgivings some Canadian officials had about the efficacy of Canada's censorship intelligence activities, by early 1943 Canada's reputation for censorship-derived intelligence, particularly with respect to POWs, was well established. For the purpose of studying the Canadian approach to intelligence gathering from censorship operations, the US Office of Strategic Services (OSS) sent two officers, Robert C. Tryon and James M. Minifee, first to Camp X, then to a POW internment camp near Bowmanville, Ontario, and finally to Ottawa for a few days. The visit was a clear success; Tryon wrote to Stone a week later that the Canadian censorship material constituted "a veritable gold mine for our work," and hoped that more formal collaboration could be established.[52]

Other OSS visits followed in May when three experts came to examine Canadian POW material. The three, Robert MacLeod, Dr. H.C. Deutsch, and Dr. Irving Sherman, did not impress their Canadian hosts. Stone and Glazebrook, as reported by Stone to Pearson in Washington in what must be one of the strongest letters present in Canadian intelligence records, found that the visitors had little appreciation for security and had a "very superficial knowledge of Europe and European problems." Stone complained that "not only are O.S.S. intelligence reports on Europe bad but if these men are a sample they must be read by people that have a tragically insufficient knowledge of their fields on which to base any critical study of the reports."[53] Stone added, "We are pretty discouraged to-day to think that these are the opposite numbers with whom our baby political warfare organization in Canada will have to deal in Washington. There isn't, I think, anything we can do about it except to hope that in the rapidly shifting sands which are O.S.S. some little grains of a higher calibre will eventually get up to the top."[54] Glazebrook recalled that he spent an evening at Stone's house with some visiting OSS officers, one of whom was a French expert by virtue of having been "a professor of something who had once had a holiday in France."[55]

With the exception of positive attitudes toward a few individual OSS officers, the intelligence community at the DEA had a low opinion of the OSS, at least during the early part of the war. They paid little attention to the organization and dismissed the value of any intelligence reports provided to Canada. Glazebrook viewed the OSS as "overwhelmed by size, inexperience and romanticism."[56] However, in fairness to the OSS, it was a newly established organization needing to affirm and develop areas of expertise. Indeed, many Americans also had "doubt[s] ... that OSS would get organized soon enough to be a productive organization."[57]

Nevertheless, OSS officers continued to visit Ottawa to review Canadian censorship-derived intelligence material. The OSS had no particular interest in the individual letters collected through censorship operations, but found the evaluated assessments on the impact of bomb damage, food shortages, and general morale to be valuable for its own analytical purposes.[58] Canada also established informal training programs for OSS officers. By late 1943, more than 800 Canadian intelligence reports, derived primarily from POW intercepts, were forwarded to the Americans per month. Regular liaison visits by OSS staff, primarily Rhoda Metraux who had been one of the early OSS visitors, continued throughout the war.[59]

Other Allied efforts to coordinate censorship activities and pool information collected from civilian correspondence and through the POW channel took place concurrently. A censorship conference was held early during the war to discuss the practical side of the task. A communications link was established between Ottawa and the British Security Coordination office in New York, dedicated in part to transferring information collected through censorship channels.[60] The Canadian department of postal censorship established a procedure in June 1943 for an expanded exchange of information on both intelligence and postal censorship to cope with the increasing number of POWs that both Canada and the United States were receiving.[61]

In August 1943, Allied heads of censorship programs met in Miami, Florida, together with representatives of various Allied intelligence organizations, to discuss counter-intelligence and intelligence gathering, as it was derived from censorship tasks. Canadian participants explained that all of the mail arriving in Canada was examined physically and in some cases through laboratory analysis. All the incoming mail for German POWs was physically checked, while all of the POW mail to Germany also received a laboratory examination to check for secret writing.[62] By that time, some 30,000-35,000 letters per week received laboratory examination.[63]

The Miami censorship conference led to changes in Canadian censorship practices. The conference had been called because there was general agreement that the intelligence collected had to be improved. As did the other Allies, Canada established a security section within the censorship bureau. This unit was to ensure that censorship officers became "collectors" of intelligence, leaving to others the analysis of the information. The censorship security officer acted not only in a counter-intelligence capacity, and liaised with the RCMP and the Allied counter-intelligence bodies, but also as the principal censorship liaison with the services intelligence organizations and the DEA.[64]

The results of censorship intelligence operations, which generated evaluations on the commercial activities of the neutrals, oil production and sales, shipping reports and cargoes, enemy commercial shipping, and morale in occupied countries, were circulated in weekly censorship intelligence bulletins to interested parties, including the British and the Americans. Sensitive reports were circulated on a more confidential basis to Canadian departments requiring access to the information. Counter-intelligence obviously played an important role, as did the prevention of innocent transmission of valuable information to the enemy.[65]

Although intelligence derived from censorship of POW correspondence was the prime Canadian HUMINT activity during the war, there was a fleeting opportunity to collect HUMINT from the credible observations of Canadians who had lived under enemy control. This entirely separate source of Canadian HUMINT collection occurred briefly early in the Second World War and involved the debriefing of Canadian civilians and diplomats repatriated primarily from Asia but also from Europe. There is little evidence that Canadian foreign intelligence programs fully exploited the knowledge possessed by those individuals being repatriated from occupied Europe at the beginning of the war. This reflects the early phase of Canada's foreign intelligence program, when the country did not yet possess the skilled resources or inclination to take advantage of such opportunities. Debriefings may also have been carried out by the British, since repatriation had likely been via the United Kingdom.

The first Canadian-conducted intelligence debriefing of repatriated Canadians took place in the early summer of 1942, and was carried out in the United States, involving nine Canadian women arriving on the Swedish ship SS *Drottningholm*.[66] Some of the women had been interned in Germany and others had survived the torpedoing of an Allied vessel. The women arrived in New York on 29 June 1942, and were met by a phalanx of five US and Canadian intelligence organizations before being permitted to disembark. In spite of an oversupply of intelligence officials, the process was handled expeditiously. The actionable intelligence derived from debriefing the women was limited. Nevertheless, insight was provided on the general dissatisfaction among German Christians toward the Nazi regime (some of the women had religious affiliations), the quality and availability of food in Germany, availability of commodity items for civilians, the impact of the early bombings on the German people, and the "impotent resignation" of the Germans.[67] Although the intelligence obtained was limited and anecdotal in nature, it provided a snapshot of the situation inside Germany at a time when such information was difficult to obtain. Coupled with debriefings that were taking place in Britain and information from neutral sources, relatively complex evaluations of life in Germany could be constructed by Allied intelligence.

Repatriations of Canadians interned by the Japanese in Asia began in the summer of 1942. The first group was made up of fifty-one Canadians arriving on the Swedish ship SS *Gripsholm* from North and South China, Hong Kong, Manchuria, Indochina, Japan, and Korea. Many were missionaries or diplomats. The group was met on arrival in New York by seven intelligence officers from the DND and Lester B. Pearson from the Canadian Legation in Washington, DC.[68] The intelligence officers had area expertise covering all the above regions. Their objective was to "secure any intelligence on Japan or Japanese occupied territories in the Orient which might be of benefit to our Military, Naval or Air operations in that sphere."[69] Not all the arriving Canadians appear to have been debriefed in detail. Only those who provided actionable intelligence had their debriefings recorded.

Pearson thought he had arranged for the Canadians to be handled as if in transit and thus outside normal US Customs protocols, such that debriefings would be conducted by Canadians on the New York docks before the returnees boarded a train for Canada. However, the US Customs authorities refused to honour any of the arrangements Pearson and the DEA in Ottawa had painstakingly put in place with the US Department of State before the arrival of the returnees. Full US Customs inspection was demanded, including that of Canada's returning chargé d'affaires in Tokyo, a breach of diplomatic protocol. The Canadian intelligence officers were denied access to the repatriates prior to their clearance by US Customs, and the debriefings could not begin until the whole group left New York for Canada by train at 4:00 a.m. The subsequent interviews were so hurried that information was not fully exploited.[70] Nevertheless, the final assessed debriefing report consisted of well over fifty pages of analysis containing a wealth of information about industrial production potentials, raw materials reserves, and transportation resources in Japanese-controlled Manchuria and Korea.[71] The interviews were clearly rushed and more might have been achieved if the process had been handled differently, including re-interviewing after the returnees had arrived in Canada. Even so, the individual reports reveal the extent of intelligence material available from untrained but observant civilians.

Interviews on Hong Kong provided details of the structures of Japanese convoys leaving the British colony, including normal departure direction, sizes of ships employed, and number of ships in convoys. Another report provided details of Hong Kong harbour including the location of minefields and anchorages for naval vessels. Other information included details of the Kai Tak aerodrome and runway enlargement that was underway, the military air base on San Chan Islands, and the location of oil storage facilities and POW encampments.[72]

Twenty-two Canadians were interviewed on Japan, twelve of them on Tokyo alone. Only three of those describing Tokyo provided information of operational intelligence value. Their information covered aircraft factories, airfields, anti-aircraft defences, air raid precautions, supply of gas, coal, and water, oil storage, radio communications, and transportation. Most of the information was provided with descriptions, directions, and local landmarks, and included any impediments to low-level bombing attacks.[73]

Herbert Norman, a Canadian diplomat being repatriated from the Canadian Legation in Tokyo, was an expert on Japan and a keen observer of that country. He was among the group that returned on the SS *Gripsholm*, although there is no clear evidence that he was debriefed at the time.[74] However, a postwar security file indicates that Norman was interviewed at the time of his repatriation about some of the other passengers aboard the SS *Gripsholm*. The document is ambivalent on whether this was a security interview he had at the time with the FBI or part of an intelligence debriefing by Canadian officials.[75] An intelligence interview capturing his knowledge and observations is inexplicably absent from the released files. A failure to interview Norman is hard to fathom; Pearson was present on the New York docks and he knew Norman. A possible explanation is that the chaos in New York resulting from US Customs intransigence led to a postponement of Norman's debriefing until he returned to Ottawa. If that was what happened, the resulting interview has been lost.

One debriefing warrants special attention. This covered information on Indochina secured from an eighteen-year-old student named Paul Jeffrey. No details are available on who he was or what he was doing at that age, seemingly by himself, in Indochina. However, one thing is certain. This young man had exceptional powers of observation and recall. His eleven-page debriefing covered the military, naval, and political-economic situation in Indochina. His information included details of recent Japanese troop movements from Saigon toward China for a "big drive." Information was also provided on Japanese preparations for a drive against India, after the end of the monsoon, which would include one division of Indian troops, specially trained and said to have been captured in Malaya. Details covered Korean, Formosa, Manchurian, and Chinese mercenary units led by Japanese officers. Young Jeffrey also had details on petrol and oil dumps in the Saigon area, including map locations, as well as airports in Indochina, with map locations and details of their infrastructure (and recent improvements), including one facility that was partly underground (presumably storage buildings). He provided details on the location of telephone and telegraph exchanges in Saigon, details of various Japanese military and naval headquarters, coastal defences, mine fields, the absence of submarine nets in Saigon harbour, and information on POW camps in Saigon. Lastly, he detailed Vichy co-operation with the Japanese, shifts in the sale of narcotics, and Japanese confiscation of foodstuffs.[76] This debriefing report, based on the observations of a very young man, contains such a wealth of specific and actionable intelligence as to make it exceptional by any standards for intelligence collection.

When the SS *Gripsholm* returned a second time in October 1943, with an additional 221 Canadians repatriated from Japanese control, arrangements were made for a Canadian military intelligence officer, posing as a member of the DEA, to join the ship in Rio de Janeiro en route from the Far East, to interview the returnees.[77] The detailed intelligence and political questionnaire used by the Canadian military officer was prepared by Herbert Norman, only recently returned from Japanese captivity, who was by now involved in intelligence matters at the DEA. There is some evidence that Norman joined the ship in Rio de Janeiro and participated in the debriefings. Minutes of a meeting of the Canadian Joint Intelligence Committee (CJIC) on 27 October 1943 states that Captain Archibald and Dr. Herbert Norman would be sent to Rio de Janeiro to meet the SS *Gripsholm*.[78] A later meeting of the CJIC records, after the fact, that Archibald and Norman had conducted debriefings on the SS *Gripsholm*.[79] No other record can be found to verify that Norman met the SS *Gripsholm* in Rio de Janeiro.

The debriefing of travellers with information of potential intelligence value might have been expected to cease with the return to Canada of the last repatriates. However, there is some evidence that a small ad hoc program continued to debrief foreign sailors visiting Canadian ports. The year following the *Gripsholm* debriefings, the OSS sought access to the crew members of Swedish relief ships that stopped at St. John, NB. The DEA was initially inclined to be helpful until the director of naval intelligence pointed out that this was counter to normal Canadian practices. The DEA quickly reversed itself and responded, in a letter signed by Robertson, that "it would be the view of this Department that the securing of information in any Canadian port from any sources should be the responsibility of the Canadian Intelligence Services who, no doubt, are prepared to make available to the Intelligence Services of the United States or the United Kingdom any information which was obtained."[80]

When the RCMP, whose security control service was tasked with intelligence collection at the ports, admitted to an existing debriefing arrangement with Donovan's OSS, they were reprimanded and informed that "the responsibility for security and intelligence in Canadian ports clearly rests with the Canadian authorities. Where, for some reason, they are unable or unwilling to do work which is recognized to be of importance from the point of view of security or intelligence, they may well allow interested agencies of other countries to do that work, provided that the Canadian authorities are kept informed ... Where, however, Canadian authorities are already functioning adequately, they should not hand over their proper functions to the agency of another government."[81]

The intelligence collected through debriefings of returning Canadians was well received by Canada's allies. The information contained specific details that assisted in determining war-making capabilities. Copies of the debriefs were provided (sometimes in response to specific requests) to the British War Office, the Ministry of Economic Warfare, and the British Political Warfare Mission in Washington.[82] The value of the material is recorded in one British response that stated, "Nearly all the matter in these reports is most helpful to us as providing background information. Of special value is the report on French Indo China which seems to add a great deal of concrete information on this country. Also most useful are the notes on Chinese, Japanese and German personalities scattered throughout the reports."[83]

Canada's involvement in HUMINT collection during the Second World War was limited and reflected the resources and skills available at the time. Nevertheless, within the existing confines, and once the administrative hurdles were overcome, Canada produced information from censorship operations that helped provide the building blocks to create a composite view of socio-economic conditions within Germany and its occupied territories. The individual reports from censorship reviews suggest a tedious undertaking that bore fruit only when many reports were collated and analyzed to capture changes in attitudes and circumstances over time within Germany and German-occupied nations. The efforts of the Psychological Warfare Committee were largely ineffectual for lack of an agreed national policy. However, the extracts from POW correspondence suggest that there was ample material for a credible propaganda effort, had that been possible.

The debriefing of repatriated Canadians provided substantial and credible intelligence of possible use to Allied war-making plans. Much of the information was specific and in sufficient detail to provide actionable intelligence. Although Canada successfully adapted to the challenges confronting the program (e.g., joining the *SS Gripsholm* mid-voyage), the program was limited since the supply of repatriated Canadians was quickly exhausted. Canada was remiss in not pursuing more extensive debriefings of individuals who travelled to or from neutral states, a potential source of significant intelligence.

In summary, Canada's wartime forays into overt HUMINT collection were successful but limited. Too little was done in either program to create an appetite in Canada for HUMINT. The material available in released files demonstrates that sufficient HUMINT was collected from POW correspondence and debriefings of repatriates to result in a considerable number of seemingly valuable intelligence reports. The sheer volume and acknowledged welcome the reports received from the OSS also suggest the Canadian effort was successful. It is therefore baffling that HUMINT in Canada drew so little positive attention at home. One can speculate that the closely held knowledge about HUMINT activity did not create a significant constituency in support of continuing such activity at the end of the war. Another possibility is that Canada did not fully possess the military and political infrastructure to benefit from such an intelligence resource, and thus did not value the products sufficiently to expand or continue the activity.

The limited successes of both the censorship intelligence program and the debriefing program did not influence Canada's postwar decision on a clandestine HUMINT collection program. However, had the wartime efforts been more significant in meeting a national need, the results might have been different.

There was one known interesting departure from the limits on Canadian HUMINT collection. This departure merged both the SIGINT and HUMINT dimensions in a unique operation that lasted for about one year during the middle of the war; one element of the project involved the posting of a Canadian to the United States for the express purpose of securing telegraph messages of intelligence value that reached the United States. This was not a clandestine operation unknown to the US government, but it did involve some clandestine activity and was of importance to British and Canadian intelligence collection efforts while it lasted. This project was code-named Mousetrap.

5
The Mousetrap Operation, 1942-43

For just over a year, between August 1942 and September 1943, Canada played a key role in securing copies of telegraphic communications in the United States for SIGINT exploitation by Britain and Canada. The operation was confidential but not clandestine; the US government knew. While most SIGINT tasks involved passive listening to communications transmitted by radio waves, the Mousetrap operation also collected landline telegraphic messages accessible only within the United States. This was all done by Canadian personnel stationed in the United States.

The entire Mousetrap operation involved the collection of foreign diplomatic and economic communication – *en clair* and encrypted commercial cable, wireless, telephone, and radio traffic – for the purpose of analysis by a small British intelligence unit. In the United States, the intercepted material consisted of telegraphic traffic subject to censorship vetting, while in Canada the Mousetrap operation was more multi-faceted and also included intercepted wireless communications. This was Canada's first foreign intelligence operation. While the Examination Unit also benefited from the Mousetrap material collected in the United States, Canada's role in the operation was primarily as a facilitator for British access to the raw material.

There is little publicly available information about the Mousetrap operation, or on Canada's role therein. *A History of the Examination Unit 1941-45*, prepared at the end of the war by one of the organization's key staffers and available in an Access to Information Act vetted format, contains partially excised segments that relate to Mousetrap.[1] A portion of the applicable text reads, "In late August or early September, Denniston made a certain proposal to Kendrick which put Stone in something of a quandary," at which point the text has been removed on national security grounds. It continues, "Mr. Denniston reassured Canada in the following terms," after which the text is again cut out for security reasons. Removal of the text indicates that at the time of the release of *A History of the Examination Unit 1941-45*, there remained concerns about revealing the Mousetrap operation.[2] Over time, however, various individual documents, including several containing the code word Mousetrap, have surfaced in Library and Archives Canada, the US National Archives and Records Administration, and the British Public Record Office.

When the British approached T.A. Stone about Mousetrap collection in the United States, they had suggested that the DEA scrap its newly created special intelligence section, charged with intelligence analysis under Herbert Norman, in favour of concentrating on work for the British Ministry of Economic Warfare (MEW).[3] There is no rational explanation for Denniston's request. Norman's newly created section did not overlap with the interests of Mousetrap, nor was the special intelligence section in competition or conflict with the Mousetrap operation. But the special intelligence section did draw some limited resources that could have been directed elsewhere. Or Denniston's request could simply have reflected the British penchant for retaining the dominions as suppliers of raw material with little autonomous analysis or assessment activity.

When Alastair G. Denniston, the man referred to in the text, approached Stone, he had been replaced as head of the British Government Code and Cipher School at Bletchley Park by Edward Travis and now headed a branch in London that handled all diplomatic and economic traffic.[4] Denniston's organization was located on Berkeley Street, behind the marquee of a women's hat shop.[5] The organization does not appear to have had a formal name and numbered about 500 people, small in comparison with the resources available to the Government Code and Cipher School proper. Denniston had left Bletchley Park in February 1942, probably because his management style and skills no longer served the needs of the SIGINT organization, which had grown substantially and required stronger leadership. Denniston moved sideways, retaining his title of deputy director (Travis received the same title), but he had more limited responsibilities.[6] The organization he led in Berkeley Street supported the MEW, which was tasked with bolstering Britain's economic warfare operations (including the economic blockade of Germany) and which evaluated economic conditions in Germany and its economic capacity to conduct war. In support of MEW's mandate, the Government Code and Cipher School had established a small unit in 1938 to supply the ministry's Industrial Intelligence Centre with foreign commercial intercepts for analysis. Using the collected SIGINT and other sources of information, the intelligence unit of the MEW could "collect, collate, appreciate and present ... information about the enemy's economic strength, dispositions and intentions."[7]

The Mousetrap designation was probably the code name for the North American collection program (it was used in both Canada and the United States) conducted by Denniston's unit at Berkeley Street. The name Mousetrap could also have referred to the wireless address for Denniston's organization.[8] The few available details about the term Mousetrap are unclear. However, in North America, Mousetrap was only one source of intercepted communications used by Denniston's unit. In addition to commercial traffic sent by commercial carriers, Mousetrap also collected encrypted diplomatic communications sent by commercial carriers in the United States and by radio signals intercepted in Canada.

Much of the target raw intelligence used by Mousetrap was already collected in both Canada and the United States under existing intelligence programs associated with censorship or SIGINT activities. Unique to Mousetrap was the exploitation of the main commercial wireless stations in the western hemisphere, which were readily intercepted in Canada.[9] Commercial code and *en clair* wireless and cable messages on the Buenos Aires–Santiago–Tokyo–Indochina circuits were easily read in Canada because of special atmospheric conditions.[10] The telegraphic material was already being exploited by Canada through existing intelligence collection programs.

The Mousetrap operation had its genesis in early 1942. Denniston wanted a steady supply of intercepted communications, particularly commercial decrypted messages from North America.[11] Denniston already had access to the Canadian material through existing intelligence-sharing arrangements, but sought access to telegraphic communications not accessible from Canada. In late February 1942, Lester B. Pearson (in Ottawa) wrote to the Canadian Legation in Washington to seek its views about "a highly confidential matter," which involved the establishment of a section of the Examination Unit in New York. This was almost certainly a suggestion that the Examination Unit wanted to assign someone to New York to process material for the Mousetrap collection operation.[12] The timing of Pearson's message suggests that Denniston's initial petition to Canada for assistance occurred immediately after he moved to Berkeley Street. Canada's collection of telegraphic communication in the United States was likely opportunistic. Pearson's letter indicated that Mousetrap collection was already taking place in Canada, and he proposed that the Canadian telegraph censor, working with the United States telegraph censor in New York, supply an Examination Unit subunit in New York with access to raw material for local processing. Pearson also indicated that US censorship authorities were aware of the collection project and were in full co-operation,[13] and added that Canada was willing to exchange the decrypted intercepted messages with the Americans.[14]

Hume Wrong, at the Canadian Legation in Washington, informed Pearson that he was reluctant to put the proposal to the Americans, citing the strong views of the state department's Adolf Berle about foreign states, whether Canadian or others, engaging in intelligence collection within the United States. Instead, Wrong proposed that a teletype link recently installed between Ottawa and New York for the use of the telegraph censorship office be employed by the Canadian telegraph censor stationed in New York to transmit selected messages to Canada for decryption. This would eliminate the need for an Examination Unit presence in the United States.[15] The Canadian telegraph censor in New York already forwarded messages to Canada as part of his liaison duties, and additional collection priorities were presumed capable of being subsumed within the existing traffic. Telegraphic communications collected in the United States by Canadian officials for exploitation under Mousetrap began in the spring or summer of 1942 and by July collection was well underway in New York. However, the change proposed by Wrong altered the project from an essentially overt presence by an Examination Unit office to a clandestine collection operation conducted under the guise of routine censorship liaison. It should be underscored, however, that the collection activity was always known to select members of the US SIGINT community.

The Mousetrap operation took time to get underway. That May, while C.H. Little of Naval Intelligence was in London for meetings with British SIGINT authorities, Denniston approached him with an offer to provide high-grade decrypts of Japanese diplomatic traffic, to be given to Norman Robertson at the DEA in exchange for raw diplomatic and commercial traffic intercepted by Canadian stations. Denniston's offer involved only material collected in Canada, and thus involved only one element of Mousetrap. However, the approach underscored the confusion that still existed in the Allied SIGINT community since Canadian material was already routinely forwarded to the Government Code and Cipher School at Bletchley Park as part of existing arrangements.[16]

By August 1942, Mousetrap was working well in New York. It was managed by E.A. Martin, from Canada's Directorate of Censorship in the Department of National War Services, who was assigned as a liaison officer to the US cable censorship office in New York.[17] No satisfactory explanation exists for using a Canadian as opposed to a British national to select the material in New York, considering SIGINT exploitation of the communications was not clandestine but known to senior American officials. However, the US State Department, particularly Adolf Berle, had strong views on activities by foreign intelligence services in the United States and it may have been thought that such activities by a Canadian censorship liaison officer would be more palatable than if carried out by a British official. The Canadian also had existing access to the material and could carry out the task without any need to indoctrinate US cable censorship officials at a working level (the US director of censorship was one of those aware of the program). Martin's ostensible function was genuine censorship liaison duties, but he had also been given a list of countries of Mousetrap interest, and selected between 300 and 400 intercepted messages per day in New York for handling under the Mousetrap operation.[18]

All messages were copied by Martin to the US Army's SIGINT service in Washington and to the Examination Unit in Ottawa; priority messages went by teletype. The priority category included messages in code (commercial code, most likely) and ciphered diplomatic cables.[19] For messages of a lower priority, Martin arranged for copies to be prepared, which were shipped by diplomatic bag to Ottawa. Corresponding copies were sent by air mail to Washington. No record exists of the volume of lower priority messages, although the preparation of the copies of these required six to ten hours a day.[20] Copies of the material identified by Martin were also forwarded to British Security Coordination (BSC) in New York for transmission to London. But the record is unclear whether this was ever done by Martin or, as was certainly later the norm, was carried out by Ottawa. The deciphered material prepared by the Examination Unit was forwarded to both London and Washington.

Great care was paid to the means of communication throughout the duration of the Mousetrap operation in the United States. Even though the US government was aware of the project, sensitivity existed about the method of collecting Mousetrap material. While communications that went from the New York censorship office to the chief telegraph censor in Ottawa before being forwarded to the intelligence organizations may not have been efficient, a more direct routing would have drawn attention to Martin's expanded duties. The transmission mode was cumbersome but Stone opted for taking no action, stating, "This seems to be a clumsy and long way round route but it may be the only system under which our present relations with United States Telegraph Censorship are not interfered with (if the policy of allowing the sleeping dog to sleep still seems desirable) and the best one for ensuring that copies of all material reach Ottawa."[21]

Mousetrap collection within Canada was operationally less complicated, and subsumed within other collection activities. By November 1942, Mousetrap was a component of the collection programs carried out by the SIGINT stations in Ottawa (Army No. 1 Wireless), in Grande Prairie (Army No. 2 Wireless), and in Victoria/Esquimalt (Army No. 3 Wireless).[22] While all of the traffic was of interest to the Mousetrap operation, only that portion of the traffic which contained commercial or diplomatic material and passed a cable censor was designated Mousetrap.

As early as the end of August 1942, a proposal was made to change elements of the Mousetrap operation in New York. One suggestion was to have Martin send selected intercepts directly to BSC in New York instead of forwarding the material to Ottawa. When the proposal was made by BSC in late August, Stone had Colonel O.M. Biggar, the director of censorship, respond that any change in the operational procedures could jeopardize the status of Martin and should not be attempted. Biggar proposed that a new teletype circuit between Martin in New York and the chief telegraph censor in Ottawa would eliminate any problem since Canadian Pacific Telegraphs had already made special arrangements to carry the traffic.[23] BSC ultimately accepted continuation of the existing procedure for handling the traffic. Ironically, Martin, writing separately to Wilfrid Eggleston, the chief telegraph censor in Ottawa, had doubts that the proposed improvements for forwarding material to Ottawa were sufficient to handle the growing volume.[24]

By December, Martin had been indirectly proven right when the Telekrypton (encrypted Canadian-British telegraph link) from Ottawa back to BSC in New York was unable to carry the volume of Mousetrap information. Martin was in Ottawa for discussions when the problem was raised during an evening at Stone's house in the company of a BSC representative and various Canadian intelligence and censorship officials. Martin opposed any changes being made to the manner in which he got the intercepted material out of the New York cable office. It was agreed that Stone would inform BSC in New York that Canada was opposed to any change occurring that jeopardized Martin's status at the American cable censorship office. Stone proposed that, if necessary, a second Telekrypton line to BSC be put in place to carry the voluminous cable traffic.[25]

Stone's support for Martin's position was based on his view "that there might be some competition between various agencies un [sic] the United States to be let in on information, and it was said that if information was got from certain US agencies it was only on terms that it should not be passed on to other US agencies, so that it was necessary to walk very warily." Stone was of the opinion that the continued success of the operation was contingent on keeping some US agencies in the dark.[26]

BSC agreed that it was unwise to disturb the existing arrangements for passing cable censorship material to London via Ottawa, and that nothing should be done that might weaken Martin's position. In the meantime, however, it became apparent that there was confusion about what material should be sent to Denniston in London and what should be forwarded to the Government Code and Cipher School proper. BSC was forwarding raw material to both. Canada was forwarding Mousetrap material to Denniston in London. A copy went to BSC, which in turn sent it to the Government Code and Cipher School at Bletchley Park. The Examination Unit was also forwarding to BSC additional diplomatic and commercial material that was not Mousetrap related. Confusion and duplication ensued. A solution was found in having BSC in New York act as the single transmission point from which all material was relayed to Bletchley Park using Telekrypton.[27]

Meanwhile, the Mousetrap operation within Canada continued to be successful in its collection efforts, although its success resulted in a continuous demand for ever more raw material. On 29 September 1942, the

Canadian "Y" committee discussed the growing requests from the DEA, the Examination Unit, and the British MEW for interception of commercial and diplomatic traffic. As a member of the committee, Stone proposed an extension of facilities to meet the rising demand. The committee felt that this could only be accommodated at the cost of a decrease in operational intelligence, something that could not be justified. A proposal to build a new collection facility under the jurisdiction of the Department of Transport, working exclusively with assignments from the DEA and the British MEW, was held in abeyance in the hope that some pressure would be alleviated by the opening of a new Canadian naval intelligence intercept station at Coverdale, New Brunswick, early in the new year.[28] Although under tremendous pressure to do more, by the end of 1942 Mousetrap was already collecting SIGINT within Canada from Monte Grande (Argentina), Saigon, Hanoi, Dakar, Lyons, St. Denis, Reunion, Fort-de-France, Shanghai-Zikawai, Bamako (French Sudan), Djibouti, Tokyo, Indochina, Afghanistan, Italy, France, Sweden, Switzerland, Russia, Chile, and Germany.[29]

The Canadian side of the operation was neither seamless nor without administrative concerns. The naval and army intercept stations, sometimes using Department of Transport resources, were subject to different protocols for processing and forwarding the collected wireless intercepts. This made the Canadian Mousetrap operation more complicated than was necessary. For example, naval intelligence intercepts were cabled to Britain from the intercept stations. Copies went to the director of naval intelligence in Ottawa, who in turn passed the diplomatic encrypted traffic to the Examination Unit and the commercial plain text and coded messages to a MEW liaison unit in Washington. However, intercepts from army stations were forwarded to the Discrimination Unit in Ottawa under Major E.M. Drake. Copies of the diplomatic traffic were sent to the Examination Unit. All commercial intercepts, plain text and encoded, travelled to the MEW liaison officer in Washington by mail. In addition, all army intercepts were also sent to the chief telegraph censor, who sent the diplomatic traffic by telegram and the commercial traffic by bomber mail to Britain.[30] The complexity and duplication of the process resulted in no one ever being certain whether all material had been correctly forwarded.

Confusion extended to the distribution of intercepted material within Ottawa. Stone, the director of censorship, and Jock de Marbois met on 27 October 1942 to seek a solution. Stone expressed his criticism of the "unnecessary division at Ottawa" between the Examination Unit and the chief telegraph censor.[31] As Biggar complained, "To have it gone over twice seems to be a waste of time."[32]

Stone found that with the collected material sometimes being sent twice to the United Kingdom, apparently some to the Government Code and

Cipher School and some to Denniston in London, there was duplication in wireless interception. He concluded, "The origin of these confusions is in the duplication of assignments to Canadian intercepting agencies by various United Kingdom authorities."[33] Even as Stone was attempting to impose order and structure over the Canadian Mousetrap operation, there was evidence by August 1943 of discomfort in the United States with the Canadian presence in New York for transparent intelligence collection purposes. The US cable censorship office was anxious to eliminate the transmission of raw Mousetrap telegraphic traffic to London and Ottawa.[34] The obstacle to the existing arrangement in which Martin collected telegraphic raw material in New York was Byron Price, the US director of censorship.

With the potential of Canada no longer able to directly obtain telegraphic communications in New York, the question arose of how Canada would have access to this material in the future. Under a new Anglo-American agreement, it was proposed that the British, who could now gain secure access to the telegraphic communications from American intelligence authorities in Washington, would forward the material to Canada.[35] In proposing the new arrangement for supplying Canada with US telegraphic material via the United Kingdom, the British pointed out that the new scheme might fall apart if knowledge of the plan to send copies to Canada reached the US director of censorship. Consequently, the British recommended that Canada seek a separate formal bilateral arrangement with the Americans to forward US telegraphic material to Ottawa from Washington.[36]

In the midst of confusion, the Mousetrap operation in New York was coming to an end. The Canadians were informed that the operation in the United States was to terminate on 12 September 1943; it would become part of the normal exchange of raw communications that moved between Britain, the United States, and Canada to meet specific national interests and decryption capabilities. However, what precipitated the end of the American segment of Mousetrap is murkier. Beginning at least in August, there was an effort made to limit Martin's access to raw traffic in the Office of Censorship in New York and to direct the exchange of intercepted material through the US SIGINT authorities in Arlington.[37] The cause of American concern is evident in a message from Stone to Pearson in Washington: "For your own very private information the complication seems to be that the United Kingdom are [sic] no longer willing to maintain an arrangement with the United States under which there is full exchange of terminal traffic between the two countries."[38]

Contributing to the American efforts to close down the Canadian operation in New York was action by the British to achieve efficiencies in the manner in which Mousetrap material from the US reached Denniston's unit in London. Both BSC in New York and the DEA were wary of proposed British changes for greater direct access to Mousetrap material, knowing full well "the possible dangers of putting forward proposals for changes which might affect the present very satisfactory position of Martin in the Office of the U.S. Cable Censorship in New York. I [Stone writing to William Stephenson of BSC] feel that at the moment any such proposals would be extremely risky in that they might bring about a reconsideration by the U.S. people of Martin's present position, which might result in changes of a kind disadvantageous both to Ottawa and London."[39]

Stone proposed that efficiencies in Mousetrap transmissions from the United States to the United Kingdom could be achieved by faster communications facilities for Martin in New York.[40] The British attempt to gain direct access to US Mousetrap material stimulated the Americans to seek a reciprocal arrangement in the United Kingdom equal to what Britain and Canada enjoyed in New York through Martin. The British had anticipated since the spring an American request for reciprocal access to censorship material in the United Kingdom but had decided not to grant such access but instead negotiate an exchange of censorship material through the respective British and American SIGINT agencies.[41] As a result, the British Government Code and Cipher School and the US G2 (Military Intelligence) reached agreement that the British and American liaison officers, in each other's capital, would exchange *en clair* Mousetrap-related material. This eliminated American acquiescence in US raw cable material being collected by Canada in New York and transmitted via Ottawa to London without knowledge or control by American intelligence authorities.[42] It also suddenly left Canada out in the cold.

The United States, rebuffed by the British over reciprocal direct American access to British censorship material, ended the Canadian Mousetrap operation in New York as the only way of ceasing British access to raw telegraphic communications without clearance by US authorities. On 10 September 1943, BSC in New York informed Biggar at the Canadian censorship office that London had instructed that "traffic may cease" for Mousetrap material collected by Canada in New York.[43] The Mousetrap intercepts nevertheless continued to reach Ottawa for about another week, the suspension having been delayed "until alternative arrangements [were] made for the Department of External Affairs to get the messages it require[d] through some other channel, and negotiations to that end were undertaken in Washington on Monday."[44] Canada was not pleased with the turn of events, and Biggar made this clear to BSC in New York. Biggar wrote, "It might do no harm if you indicated in the proper quarters that we feel here as if we had been let down rather badly after having undertaken quite a heavy job on London's behalf for a long time."[45]

Informed by BSC at the end of August about the new arrangements, Stone had received assurance that Canadian requirements would somehow be addressed.[46] He knew that there was a risk that Canadian access to the US

Mousetrap material through the British-US arrangement with the US Corps of Signals at Arlington could collapse. Fearful that access to US censorship raw material could be jeopardized, Stone requested that Pearson approach the US Corps of Signals for direct access to the US material.[47] Although the Mousetrap operation in New York had been launched to assist the British in gaining access to telegraphic material transiting the United States, the Examination Unit had also made use of the collected material, and an end to the New York Mousetrap operation had direct implications for Canadian SIGINT activities.

Biggar entered into discussions with his US counterpart Byron Price on 1 September. Canada wanted to ensure continued access to "liberated French" and Spanish traffic.[48] Biggar was not aware of how fragile the British-American arrangement might be and limited his intervention to the horrendous delays Canada experienced in gaining access to the material provided under the arrangements the British had made with the US Army Signal Corps.[49] Biggar suggested that there was no point in having Martin in New York, even for liaison purposes, if the cables had to be routed through Washington before going to Canada. Price responded by agreeing that the processing time had to be improved, but declined to commit to anything other than "exploring the possibility of continuing to send messages from New York direct to Ottawa."[50]

In spite of a reluctance to reach any concrete agreement, the US director of censorship nevertheless reversed his earlier position and agreed to expand Martin's role as a Canadian liaison officer by arranging for copies of non-governmental messages (i.e., only commercial traffic) to be provided to him. US censors selected for Canada all messages "which in their opinion [came] under Canadian requirements" and made available for Martin's review all other messages.[51] For all intents and purposes, access to the Mousetrap material would briefly return to the status quo ante, although the material received by Canada was no longer forwarded to the British but used exclusively for Canadian SIGINT purposes.

On 24 September, the Canadian director of censorship informed his American counterpart that Canada's participation in the Mousetrap operation in the United States would cease at 00:01 hours on 26 September 1943.[52] At that moment, all foreign government communications that had been made available to Canada under Mousetrap ceased. In the weeks that followed, Martin, by now the chief telegraph officer in Ottawa, made arrangements for a new Canadian liaison officer to be stationed at the New York offices of the chief censor, reports division, to identify messages of interest to Canada. The reports division was a separate entity from the US cable censorship office in New York, where Martin had previously operated. Copies of all non-government messages (i.e., only commercial) were made available to the new Canadian liaison officer. Messages of exceptional importance, selected by US intelligence staff, were sent to Washington, while copies were given to the Canadian liaison officer for transmittal to Ottawa by teletype or mail, as he chose.[53] The available documentary material is unclear about the genesis of this arrangement, and it is possible that this procedure reflected the guidelines put in place after the US director of censorship reversed his stand on supplying material to Canada. Mousetrap collection within Canada continued as part of the ongoing intercept operation; copies of the material were forwarded to Britain.

Mousetrap was Canada's first offshore intelligence collection effort. Although it began as an opportunistic attempt to use an existing Canadian resource (Martin in New York) to collect raw material for use by Denniston's unit in London, it was not long before the Examination Unit made use of the material, which significantly augmented Canada's limited collection efforts. At the end of the operation, Mousetrap information collected in New York was solely for the use of the Examination Unit since the British had made alternative plans for accessing the material. No documents have survived to facilitate an evaluation of the value of Mousetrap for Canadian interests. Likely, the information made available through this resource was helpful but not critical in meeting Canadian collection objectives. Mousetrap material collected in New York included French traffic, all of which has been released through Library and Archives Canada. However, the material is not arranged according to collection site or method and is indistinguishable from French material collected within Canada.

The value of Mousetrap rested with Canada collecting the material for Britain and thereby garnering some unquantifiable debt that could be collected. Canada was a minor actor in the greater Allied intelligence efforts and as such had little control over the manner of making a contribution. It was being seen as making a contribution that was of value to Canada in terms of gaining access to raw material or finished intelligence from its allies. As such, Mousetrap served its purpose. However, Canada appears to have viewed Mousetrap solely in terms of facilitating British access to the material for the purpose of meeting MEW information requirements. The operation was never seen as an opportunity for Canada to develop offshore collection experience in a safe environment.

By now, the war had reached its midway point. After fits and starts and lack of clarity of direction, particularly with respect to the start of SIGINT activity, Canada had served its intelligence apprenticeship well and was launched on the path to making a valuable, albeit proportional, contribution to the Allied war effort. The tools of intelligence were largely in place and Canada now had the opportunity to play its part.

6
Canadian Intelligence at War

With no substantial intelligence infrastructure when war began, the first years of the Second World War saw Canada create its limited foreign intelligence capacity. Although there were clear successes, such as the creation of the Examination Unit and the establishment of SIGINT intercept stations, the impact of Canada's foreign intelligence effort on the war was limited, peripheral, and beset by early administrative hurdles. The censorship operations ultimately became beneficial but did not function seamlessly in the earliest phase. Debriefing repatriated Canadians was successful but ended almost as quickly as it had begun. At its core, the Mousetrap operation was a support function of British intelligence. Nevertheless, by mid-war Canadian efforts at intelligence capacity building were having an impact. Because it was Canada's premier foreign intelligence collecting vehicle, SIGINT was at the core of almost all intelligence activities in which the country was involved for the remainder of the war.

Nowhere was the impact of Canada's maturing foreign intelligence efforts more apparent than in the battle for the North Atlantic. Here, perhaps more than anywhere else at the midpoint in the war, Canadian SIGINT efforts, as part of the greater Allied effort, contributed to an Allied victory. As Christopher Andrew has written, "ULTRA made a major, possibly decisive, contribution to the allied victory" in the Atlantic.[1] While Andrew was referring only to the Ultra interceptions, the overall and broader SIGINT effort was significant.

Until the midpoint in the war, the response to the U-boat threat had been one of evasion. The British had used intelligence to steer convoys away from threatening German U-boats. Initially, the tool was direction finding, which was not always very precise in the early days. Subsequent successes in cryptanalysis permitted the Allies to learn not only the number of U-boats at sea but also their specific instructions.[2] By reading the Enigma signals between the U-boats and their headquarters, it was possible to plot U-boat deployments and to direct convoys away from the threats.[3] However, the tactic was not always successful; until 1942, the evasion strategy was often defeated by British shortages of bunker fuel, which necessitated that ships be routed on the most direct route to minimize diversions.[4]

Until the middle of 1943, the British and Canadians adhered to the British doctrine of emphasizing safe and timely arrival of convoys. By then, they were acting upon a principle of "defence by offensive measures," defined by Canadian acting captain J.D. "Chummy" Prentice early in the war but only introduced in 1943. Prentice vowed adherence to the existing British rules on protecting convoys but suggested that assaults on U-boats by escort vessels ensured the safe arrival of the convoys.[5] Prentice's timing for introducing his interpretation of the British doctrine was also a critical factor, since by 1943 the Battle of the Atlantic had turned in favour of the Allies.

Allied shipping losses caused by German U-boats reached 807,754 tons in November 1942, a wartime high.[6] Thereafter, the tonnage losses declined dramatically as a result of Allied naval and air action. Although the Allies had inadequate sea and air fighting resources to successfully meet all potential challenges in the struggle with German U-boats, the use of intelligence to pinpoint where danger to shipping was greatest and where none existed allowed limited resources to be used with greatest impact.[7]

The U-boat war in the North Atlantic reached its zenith in early 1943. Hunting in "wolf packs," the U-boats were ferocious and hardly a single convoy escaped attack. However, the German naval vessels operating on the high seas left an ether signature trail, which led to pursuit by Allied forces. The volume of communications between the U-boats and their home bases in their search for Allied prey ultimately contributed to the demise of the threat. Indeed, the number of messages threatened to overwhelm the capabilities of the Allied "Y" intercept centres.

A network of radio intercept stations built by the Allies, aided by close cooperation and a sharing of the workload, could triangulate on any communication in the North Atlantic. By late 1942, a worldwide Allied "Y" network (i.e., wireless direction finding) worked together to pinpoint the location of all enemy and neutral vessels in the Atlantic that used their radios. There were ten intercept stations in Canada and Newfoundland engaged in "Y" work, another ten stations in the United States, thirteen stations in the United Kingdom, two in South Africa, and five stations elsewhere in the world.[8] Canada had "Y" intercept stations at Harbour Grace, Botwood, Hartlen Point, Cap d'Espoir, Pennfield, St. Hubert, Ottawa, Strathburn, Portage la Prairie, and Rivers, Manitoba, which were primarily tasked with monitoring of U-boat frequencies.[9] By feeding intelligence about U-boat locations to special Allied attack groups, it was possible to maintain relentless pressure on the U-boats and ensure a high mortality rate among them.

The intelligence war against the U-boats had begun slowly. Occasional early wireless direction-finding efforts and high-frequency radio intercepts had provided locations of U-boats and identifiers for the boats and crews. By the beginning of 1942, however, extensive use of radio communications by the U-boats allowed the Allies to follow their paths by monitoring the constant messages to track individual U-boats throughout their cruises.[10] Communications channels that were established during 1942 allowed the Allies to quickly share the information on U-boats as it became available.[11]

The radio direction-finding efforts were augmented by an additional study of enemy high-frequency radio transmissions called "Z" work, more correctly described as "radio fingerprinting." "Z" work was the identification of wireless transmitters by the idiosyncratic characteristics of the signals emitted and the individual radio operators according to the rhythm of their Morse transmissions.[12] Although introduced into Canada in early 1942 by Britain and initially carried out at three locations in Ottawa because of excellent local wireless reception, "Z" work had a slow start and was only extensively used after May 1943. "Z" work was eventually introduced at a number of Canadian intercept stations, including Harbour Grace, Newfoundland.[13]

In spite of initial problems, Canada so successfully mastered "Z" work that the US Navy adopted the "Ottawa system" of classification after a 1942 meeting in Washington. However, the Royal Canadian Navy (RCN) did not benefit as significantly as it might have from the identification tool that "Z" work provided; a postwar assessment called it "at worst a failure, at best a limited success."[14] The German U-boat radio transmitters were highly standardized with too few faults to make individual transmitters identifiable. Problems were also traceable to initial poor staff selection for "Z" work, although this improved when greater reliance on the Women's Royal Canadian Naval Service began in 1943. Most telling, however, was the great success of "Y" work, which had reduced U-boat activity to low levels by the time "Z" work had reached a high level of efficiency.[15] Nevertheless, "Z" work was instrumental on some occasions in estimating the number of U-boats involved in an attack on a convoy.[16]

While both sides were aided in the battle of the North Atlantic by their abilities to read the low-level encrypted communications of the other side, it was not until the British Government Code and Cipher School broke the German naval Triton code (code-named Shark by the Allies) at the end of 1942 that the Allies gained an insight into the strategy and tactics of the enemy, which strongly aided the Allies in turning the battle against the German U-boats.[17] The breach of the Triton code (an Enigma code employing four rotor settings) was followed by successive Allied decryption of other German naval codes.

The Allies' decryption of German U-boat communications was important in winning the battle of the North Atlantic, but should not detract from direction finding, "Y" work, having been a determinant to the outcome. Code breaking was vital for the longer-term strategy, but was too slow to help locate and sink an enemy submarine. Direction finding was often the only intelligence that operated in real time and could pinpoint the locations of individual U-boats in time for Allied forces to launch attacks.[18]

Canada's intelligence role in the North Atlantic submarine war was advanced by the work of Commander Jock de Marbois. He was the flamboyant language teacher from Upper Canada College who had been placed in charge of Canada's naval "Y" work and the RCN's foreign intelligence section, which passed information to the British Admiralty. De Marbois successfully headed the RCN's signals intercept and triangulation operations, supported by a forceful personality and access to scientific resources that could identify naturally occurring atmospheric phenomena that enhanced signals interception.[19] By 1942, de Marbois was the deputy director of signals "Y," a constituent unit of the larger signals division at naval headquarters, which had a total staff of about 450 people.

British, American, and Canadian representatives convened in Washington at the beginning of March 1943 at the Escort and Convoy Conference to discuss enhanced co-operation in battling the German U-boats.[20] De Marbois' "Y" organization had sought permission from senior Canadian naval authorities to participate in the conference when the meeting had first been broached. His position was that "no diversions or defensive or offensive anti-U-boat operations in any area can be carried out without having a sound and efficient shore 'Y' organization to advise the authorities responsible for operational control in that area and, secondly, by the fact that the R.C.N. already had in being an efficient 'Y' organization in close contact with similar organizations in R.N. and U.S.N."[21]

Although senior Canadian naval officers had rejected de Marbois' request to attend the conference, once it began, his presence quickly became necessary since the British and American participants were adamant that the RCN "could not be given operational control of any area" unless it had the services of an effective "Y" organization available.[22] Commander de Marbois and a colleague were immediately ordered to Washington to explain what Canada had already achieved and to work out inter-Allied co-operation among three operational intelligence centres (OICs) that were to be established, to coordinate the intelligence war against the U-boats.

From de Marbois' presentation about Canadian capabilities, the conference concluded that Canada's "Y" and direction-finding organization was adequate enough to form an OIC, although improved communications with British and American counterparts would be required. After the conference, de Marbois was given the job of establishing the Canadian OIC and responsibility for providing intelligence coverage for the area north of 40°N and west of 28°W.[23] With some reluctance, Canadian naval authorities came to accept the value of what de Marbois and others had been advocating for the past year or more; Canadian operational intelligence would now begin to play a critical role in pursuit of enemy submarines.[24]

A Canadian OIC was established by June by severing the necessary resources and responsibilities from the RCN's signals division. The objective was to have the OIC responsible for setting the intelligence requirements, while the signals division remained in charge of the equipment and personnel needed to collect the signals data. However, the navy was perennially short of qualified radio operators and sent the best of those who were available to sea, while placing less skilled operators at "Y" stations. Because much of the success of SIGINT rested with the experience and exhaustive training of the operators, this competition for resources contributed to an inconsistent quality of "Y" products, which plagued the RCN "Y" intercept stations for most of 1943 to the extent that some were "practically useless."[25] Indeed, it was often the work of the very effective Department of Transport "Y" intercept stations that saved the day.[26] The demand for continuous availability of high-quality signals intercepts was only relieved by the expansion of Canada's overall collection capacity, particularly the establishment of the Coverdale SIGINT collection station in 1943, the largest "Y" operation in the Canadian network up until then.[27]

By the time the OIC was fully functioning it consisted of nine sections. The operational side of the OIC was divided into German (OIC1), neutral (OIC2), Japanese (OIC3), direction-finding analysis (OIC4), U-boat room (OIC5), and "Z" classification (OIC7). Handled as administrative centres were Ionosphere (OIC6) and "Y" traffic (OIC8). An editor of publications was listed as OIC9.[28] The OIC did not collect the intelligence but merely acted on the material collected at stations operated by the armed services and the Department of Transport. The operation had become so efficient that "fixes" on enemy vessels through direction finding could be attained within ten to twenty minutes. Each day, beginning in June, a top secret message codenamed Otter was issued to Canadian air and naval operational groups charged with protecting Allied convoys. The messages gave the known, probable, and possible U-boat locations.[29] This was eventually augmented in September by daily sighting and attack summaries listing all activity occurring in the North Atlantic during the previous twenty-four hours.[30]

The RCN's operational intelligence centre, the key unit in Canada's intelligence war against the U-boats, located at naval headquarters in Ottawa, was at its peak of efficiency by the beginning of 1944. Special intelligence work was not performed by Canada's naval service headquarters, and all decrypted Enigma traffic, code named Ultra, was provided to Canada by the Interservice "Y" Centre in England.[31] The decision to provide Canada with decrypted Ultra intercepts, instead of the tools with which to conduct the process itself, was made for practical and policy reasons. The complexity of breaking the Enigma codes was such that Canada probably could never have put together the necessary resources. In addition, the British never showed any inclination to part with exceptionally sensitive intelligence skills unless it was in their best interest to do so. There was no particular reason why Canada should decrypt Enigma traffic.[32]

Canada possessed one unique advantage over the British and American operational centres. Because of the much smaller sizes of the components making up the Canadian OIC, it was possible to house the U-boat tracking, high frequency and direction-finding plotting and promulgation, the discrimination section, and other support entities in adjoining rooms.[33] Consequently, the Canadian operation gained a measure of efficiency from the proximity of information or advice available from a variety of technical experts who were readily accessible. This horizontal integration of all constituent elements in the intelligence battle against the U-boats gave the Canadian operation a marked advantage in speed and efficiency.

The OIC was under constant threat by Canadian naval operational commands that urged that part or parts of the operational intelligence organization be moved to Halifax to be closer to those finding and destroying the German submarines on the basis of intelligence furnished by the OIC. However, the British Admiralty pointed out to the Canadian naval command the importance of centralization of intelligence coordination at headquarters and the danger inherent in dispersing limited resources; the OIC must operate as the sole advisor in directing pursuit of enemy U-boats. The British made a similar intervention at about the same time in the United States, where an analogous initiative was made to move the intelligence function closer to the operational side.[34]

By 1944, the Germans had acknowledged Allied radio direction finding as a key factor in their own heavy U-boat losses and had introduced greater radio security. By the end of 1944, operational U-boat radio traffic dropped to nearly nothing as enemy sailors became cautious and preoccupied with their own survival. The diminished U-boat threat was attributable to the contribution made by intelligence. Germany continued to produce U-boats for the remainder of the war, but the new crews lacked the experience and daring of their predecessors; their tactics changed from one of mass attack to more limited and cautious thrusts against the Allies.[35]

Although significant, Canada's role in the U-boat intelligence war never deviated from that of a junior partner. Canada did not decrypt the messages originating from the U-boats, but Canadian intercept stations and direction-finding organizations were indispensable in locating the U-boats in the North Atlantic.

Throughout the same period, the SIGINT focus on Canada's west coast was on the war with Japan, but the United States had made it clear that this was their war.[36] Nevertheless, Canada was concerned with protecting its west coast, and an intercept network was slowly built, although the east coast received priority for equipment. Dè Marbois' OIC established a presence on the west coast as part of its "Y" work. By the time resources had been identified for SIGINT collection on Canada's east coast and equipment had become available, Canada was finding it hard to carve out a role for itself in the Pacific war. The small RCN SIGINT operations at Gordon Head, British Columbia, worked closely with and under the direction of the US facility at Bainbridge, Washington, to provide coverage of the west coast of North America. A Canadian liaison officer had been stationed at Bainbridge since September 1943.[37]

While Canadian SIGINT efforts on the west coast quietly assumed a subservient position to the US Navy, British intelligence was attempting to create a new role for Canada in the Pacific war. In fact, directing some of their SIGINT resources at the Japanese codes, the British were finding the American Navy reticent about co-operating against Japanese ciphers.[38] British intelligence contacted T.A. Stone at the DEA in September or October 1943 to seek his views on Canadian agreement to collecting Japanese meteorological intelligence for operational use in the Pacific. A formal British proposal followed in November and called for the creation of a unit of about 100 cryptographic staff using twenty-five interception sets, plus various ancillary support and administrative staff. An instructor for cryptographic staff as well as ten cryptographers would be provided by Britain, all to arrive at a later, unspecified time.[39]

Japanese meteorological communications were relatively easily intercepted in British Columbia, and the British wanted this information collected, decrypted, and provided to the Allied forces in the southwest Pacific. Collection of meteorological communications was a secondary intelligence task, but vitally important for code breaking. The original meteorological messages were generally transmitted in less secure codes, but were then often repeated unchanged to Japanese fleet commands in more complex operational codes. By providing a known text, or "crib," it was possible to break more difficult codes that were not yet fully accessible. The "crib" was tested against messages corresponding to the anticipated time of a follow-up meteorological report until a match was found in a higher-grade code.

The ad hoc committee of the wireless intelligence board, the current designation for the Canadian inter-agency committee overseeing SIGINT matters, sometimes referred to as the "Y" committee, met in the East Block of Parliament on 14 December under the chairmanship of Stone. Also present were representatives of the service intelligence units, the DEA, and the Examination Unit. The meeting was to assess whether Canada had the resources to establish a meteorological-cryptographic unit along the lines of the British proposal. Because of a presumed urgency to begin collecting meteorological intelligence, it was decided that the RCN's intercept facility at Esquimalt would initially be used for the project, with an RCAF station elsewhere in British Columbia serving as an alternative station. For more permanent quarters the committee looked at various alternatives before settling on the Gordon Head, British Columbia, naval station for housing both the intercept and the cryptographic units.[40] On 6 January 1944, Stone informed the Minister of National Defence, J.L. Ralston, of the proposal. Although the personnel burden for the project had to be borne by the DND, the operation would not be responsible to it. Stone skirted the issue of what department had responsibility for the meteorological-cryptographic unit, although he explained that the Examination Unit was in charge of the project. He emphasized that the proposal constituted a significant contribution to the operational intelligence available for military, naval, and air operations in the Pacific theatre of war, and reassured the minister that sufficient equipment and personnel were available.[41]

Stone also informed the Minister of National Defence that the project broadened Canadian intelligence connections with the other Allied intelligence services, particularly in the Far Eastern field, and added that Canada's contribution ensured that Canada would be on the receiving end for much intelligence that otherwise might not be made available to Canada.[42] Stone was already looking toward the end of the war, and he recognized that Canada did not have the resources to meet its national intelligence requirements in a postwar world, and that the simplest solution was to build links to the Allies to ensure a continued free flow of intelligence. This point was underscored by the British a month later, after the decision had been made in favour of the project. A message from British Security Coordination (BSC) in New York, which discussed the need for ensuring a high level of security by restricting the knowledge of the sensitive project to a small number of people, ended with the statement, "It is obviously desirable from a long time political view that this [Meteorological-Cryptographic Unit (MET)] unit be rather regarded as the thin edge of the wedge if Canada is going to take her proper place in this field in the future to the benefit of the U.K. and Canada."[43]

Authority from the Minister of National Defence to proceed was granted on 18 January. Stone informed British intelligence that Canada would begin building up the MET Unit. Canada faced the challenge of finding the qualified staff among the Canadian services, and considerable discussion followed within the "Y" committee about approaching the Americans for cryptographic people and using Canadian Women's Army Corps (CWAC) to carry out the clerical work.[44] The Examination Unit would eventually seek seventy-five CWACs from the DND, to act as typists, IBM operators, and clerks.[45] Norman Robertson informed the Deputy Minister of National Defence of the request from the Examination Unit for the CWACs and proposed that a senior military officer be seconded to the National Research

Council, the nominal home of the Examination Unit, to oversee the west coast collection operation. Robertson stressed that this was the first instance of a joint service-civilian establishment in the SIGINT field in Canada and that all sides had to ensure its successful operation.[46]

Stone also attempted to obtain staff from de Marbois' naval SIGINT facilities on the west coast, although there is no evidence that he was successful.[47] At the time, de Marbois' naval SIGINT facility in British Columbia was already understaffed and acted primarily as a junior partner to the larger American facility in Bainbridge, Washington.

Robertson briefed Prime Minister King on 4 March, outlining the case for the MET Unit, and established a responsibility framework for managing foreign intelligence matters in Canada. The prime minister was already aware of the proposal, having granted approval in principle in the Cabinet War Committee on 12 January 1944.[48] Robertson masterfully outlined the importance of collecting meteorological intelligence and placed the task in the context of the greater intelligence links with the United Kingdom and the United States, explaining the chain of authority and concluding with a statement that "authority and policy guidance in these matters [intelligence collection] should come from the Prime Minister [who was also the secretary of state for External Affairs], the Minister of National Defence and the Acting President of the National Research Council." He concluded with a recommendation that the authority and guidance for foreign intelligence matters operate effectively through the under-secretary of state for External Affairs and the Deputy Minister of National Defence.[49] Approval of the proposal to create a political authority for intelligence matters was granted within two days. However, there is no record that this authority structure came into being during the war.

Then, in early 1944, within days of the Canadian commitment to the establishment of the MET Unit on the west coast, the Americans announced that they intended to do the meteorological job themselves. This was a surprise to the Canadians. There was little Canada could do in the face of American opposition to its participation. The prime minister was informed on 28 March that the US Navy would take over the work proposed for the MET Unit. Robertson told Prime Minister King that the sudden change in direction should not affect the recommendation that a higher direction needed to be given to Canadian participation in cryptography and secret intelligence.[50] While ending what might have been a new chapter in Canada's foreign intelligence activities, the failure to establish a MET Unit did achieve Cabinet acceptance for the introduction of a more formal political authority for intelligence matters in Canada than had previously existed.

The event that triggered an end to Canada's nascent MET Unit on the west coast had taken place nearly two weeks earlier, on 17 March, when the US Navy issued its trans-Pacific coverage plan under the auspices of Op 20-G, the US Navy's SIGINT collecting body.[51] Op 20-G was much larger than the US Army SIGINT operation, and although Op 20-G was active in the Atlantic theatre of war, it was the Pacific theatre that received its priority. The change in attitude of the US Navy to the Canadian MET Unit resulted from the capture in February of Japanese cipher tables that permitted Op 20-G to easily read some of the Japanese meteorological reports.[52] This convinced the Americans that they could easily collect meteorological reports them-selves, and any interest in having the Canadians meet this operational need quickly evaporated. The US Navy was set on providing a central control point for all intercepted intelligence.[53] Op 20-G's plan, also known as BRUSA,[54] would maintain an hourly record of all intercepted enciphered material, in-cluding meteorological messages, covered by the contributing networks lo-cated on the North American west coast, Washington, DC, Honolulu, Melbourne, Flowerdown (UK), and Colombo. This included Gordon Head, British Columbia, as the key Canadian intercept station involved. Op 20-G would know at all times what each collecting station was monitoring, and would have available all of the intercepted material.[55]

The Examination Unit, having been unsuccessful in establishing its MET Unit, did not participate in the Op 20-G plan. It fell to the RCN to provide the Canadian contribution, but RCN headquarters in Ottawa remained ex-cluded as one of the processing centres. Subsequent attempts by Ottawa navy headquarters to obtain other discrimination (i.e., interpretation) as-signments in support of the Op 20-G plan were not successful. Canada's OIC did continue discrimination assignments for the US Navy that pre-dated the Op 20-G plan.

However it may seem, Canada was not excluded from the Allied intelli-gence war in the Pacific out of spite, in an American determination to con-trol all aspects of what they saw as "their" war. The RCN had only one intercept station of note centred on the Pacific. While important as a col-lection centre, Gordon Head was overshadowed by the Bainbridge facility in neighbouring Washington, which had better reception potential, better-trained staff, and faster communication facilities to Washington.[56] By ac-cepting a role commensurate with its resources and reception potential, Gordon Head guaranteed access for Canada to intercepted material on the Pacific theatre of operation available to the major Allies from their stations ringing the Pacific Ocean. Nevertheless, if the Examination Unit's MET Unit had survived, Canada would have undoubtedly played a more important intelligence role in the Pacific.

A division of decryption labour had been negotiated between the United States, Britain, Australia, India, and Canada at the end of 1942 and the begin-ning of 1943, launching a redirection of Examination Unit interest toward the Pacific war. Unrelated to the subsequent grief surrounding the aborted creation of the MET Unit on the west coast, the new focus merged well with the recent creation of the special intelligence section under E.H. Norman, part of the DEA but co-located with the Examination Unit, to summarize and interpret the increasing volume of Japanese decrypted material.[57]

By the following year, the Examination Unit, now located at a National Research Council annex at Laurier and Chapel Street in Ottawa but still under the direction of F.A. Kendrick, had developed a substantial Japanese section comprising twenty-eight people.[58] Japanese diplomatic traffic was handled by fourteen cryptanalysts, translators, and clerks, under the direction of Lieutenant Commander Earl Hope. Japanese military text was looked after by eight people under the guidance of F.E. Bartlett. Although it provided intelligence for Canadian clients, some of this unit's work was done on assignment for the US Army's Signal Security Agency. Japanese military addresses (i.e., identifying call signs and locations) were performed by six staff members under D.M. Hayne in a condominium arrangement with the Discrimination Unit. The Japanese diplomatic section decrypted about thirty-five low-grade ciphered messages per week in addition to deciphering about 3,500 code groups (individual segments of four to five numbers each identifying a letter/number or a specific word) per day using a current "keybook" to the Japanese cipher. After assessing the value of each communication, up to 200 deciphered, high-grade, coded Japanese messages were translated and disseminated each month.[59] Only the shortage of expert translators prevented the issuance of a greater number of intelligence reports.

While by 1944 the Examination Unit had consciously shifted many of its resources to work on Japanese communications, it maintained a separate unit of nineteen people under G. de B. Robinson to decrypt French diplomatic communications.[60] Canadian interest in French secret communications began after the fall of France when the Department of Transport's monitoring station at Forrest, Manitoba, had begun to intercept French naval wireless traffic on behalf of the British naval intelligence department.[61] The first Canadian-decrypted Vichy intercept occurred on 1 October 1941, involving a message that had been sent on 12 September.[62] By the time Canada ceased working on Vichy traffic on 7 August 1944, some 5,490 reports had been prepared. The Examination Unit could initially only handle traffic that was in code rather than in more complicated ciphers. That changed by late 1943 when the four highest-grade and four lower-grade ciphers for North African Vichy diplomatic traffic were readable (100 percent of the Ottawa traffic and 75 percent of the Washington traffic). However, most of the naval and military traffic remained unreadable.[63]

Both Ottawa and Washington traffic had priority, although Vichy communications out of Tokyo also had a high priority.[64] The DEA, the principal client, was primarily interested in the Washington traffic as well as all political reporting. In a message to Kendrick, Stone expressed low interest in the movement and salaries of Vichy personnel, except in a few individual cases. Unfortunately, administrative, travel, media, and cultural messages constituted the bulk of the traffic. The Vichy traffic is noteworthy for the near absence of analysis in political reporting. The bulk of traffic constituting political communications was media coverage or exchanges between Vichy diplomats and Canadian or American officials.[65] Little traffic contained actionable intelligence, although it provided insight into Vichy thinking for Allied officials engaged in a daily discourse with them.

One Vichy official, Cosme, the head of mission in Shanghai, is the only individual whose reporting consistently reflected insight and good political analysis of local events. While most Vichy political reporting was banal, Cosme begins one message, "It would appear to me that a rupture between France [Vichy] and the [Chinese] government at Chungking is being considered."[66] He analyzes Franco-Chinese relations, French political relations, and the Chinese-Indochinese relationship to conclude that the Chinese will not continue to recognize Vichy. Political evaluations of this nature – and he also wrote on Japanese attitudes toward Vichy[67] – were highly valuable to Allied intelligence analysts seeking to determine relationships between adversaries. This kind of information provided insight into political relations, alluded to the importance of political players, and gave details of active policy options under consideration. Collated with other material, complex assessments on areas of denied access could be prepared.

The invasion of North Africa in November 1942 severed diplomatic relations between Vichy and Canada, resulting in the closure of the Vichy legation in Ottawa, and thus ending a prime reason for reading Vichy traffic. This left the French section of the Examination Unit largely unemployed, although decryption of Vichy traffic to Latin America and the Far East continued.[68] The Examination Unit maintained a good window on events in Asia by intercepting and decrypting Vichy inter-colonial communication and Vichy reports from Tokyo.[69] But the significance of the Vichy traffic declined after the German occupation of the French "free zone" after the Allied landings in North Africa. To avoid disbanding, a decision was made to work on Free French material.[70] By late 1944, two-thirds of the French unit was working on Free French diplomatic intercepts. Virtually no cipher was unbreakable.[71] The earliest Free French message decrypted by the Examination Unit was dated 19 February 1943[72] but it was not actually decrypted until June; some later messages were decrypted already in late March. By the time the last Free French message was read on 26 July 1945, more than 6,500 decrypts had been solved.[73]

Although the Free French communications contained a high volume of administrative, financial, media, travel, and personal messages,[74] there was a greater proportion of political information. A considerable amount of the traffic related to the internecine French struggles involving Vichy, Gaullists, and Giraudists. The Washington traffic received the highest priority, and the Examination Unit was the Allied SIGINT centre with prime responsibility for all Free French traffic.

Decrypted Free French messages were sent to the American army SIGINT agency, which reciprocated with Vichy French messages. The specialization avoided duplication from decryption of the same messages. No single theme can be drawn from the decrypted traffic; messages ran the gamut of relations with the Free French. There is higher-quality political analysis in the Free French political messages over those of Vichy.

While many messages out of thousands were decrypted, a few warrant recounting. One message from Washington to Algiers reports on Lend-Lease bases negotiations. The author set out his negotiating strategy with the Americans, the arguments to be made, and the underlying principle that France could not enter into discussions about granting bases to an international entity until its sovereignty has been integrally and unconditionally re-established in all parts of the French empire that existed before the German and Japanese aggression.[75] This message, in the hands of the American officials, would provide vital information on how to frame negotiations and marshal countering arguments.

The longest Free French political report (ten single-spaced pages) decrypted by the Examination Unit was that of a French delegation to Lublin reporting on the Polish Provisional Government, known as the Lublin Committee. The report described the new government as having no credibility, no ties to the internal resistance, and resting on the strength of Russian arms. There is information on the estimated 3 million Polish Jews massacred by the Germans as well as a detailed evaluation of conditions in Lublin. Most significantly, it provides insight into the new Soviet frontier on the Oder-Neisse line.[76] At a time of limited insights into eastern Europe, a report containing this wealth of detail would have provided highly valuable intelligence and insight into a rapidly evolving postwar situation.

Toward the end of the war, Canada became involved in a unique deployment of a SIGINT collection unit outside the country. Individual SIGINTers had been lent or seconded to other countries before, but this was a self-contained unit sent outside Canada for SIGINT collection purposes. The unit was specially formed as Canada's No. 1 Special Wireless Group (1SWG), and was despatched to Australia during the first weeks of January 1945 to assume SIGINT responsibilities directed against Japan in the north of Australia. 1SWG was the only Canadian Army unit to see service in the Pacific theatre. Planning for 1SWG had already begun in April 1944 when the commander-in-chief in India had requested a Canadian SIGINT unit to play an intercept role for which the Indian army did not have sufficient skilled staff.[77] No existing resources were available in Canada, but it was decided that a new unit could be formed within months to meet the need.[78] Cabinet approved the idea of sending two units (a special wireless unit and an intelligence group) at the end of May, and planning was begun.[79] 1SWG was formed by July but by August the British War Office asked that dispatch of the unit be deferred. A request from Australia for assistance had arisen and a tug-of-war ensued as to who would receive 1SWG. Australia won.[80] On 20 January 1944, 1SWG, made up of nearly 340 men under the command of Lieutenant Colonel Harry D.W. Wethey, an electrical engineer and regular army officer, and accompanied by fifty-one trucks and tons of specialized equipment, sailed out of San Francisco aboard the *USAT Monterey*. After a circuitous journey across the Pacific, they reached Brisbane on 16 February.[81] Wethey had been one of the early heads of the SIGINT station at Rockcliffe Airport in Ottawa, where Drake had been his second-in-command.

After a long and hot trek across Australia, 1SWG reached McMillan's Road Camp near Darwin in the Northern Territories and set up a wireless station that became operational on 30 April 1945. The station took over from the Australian Special Wireless Group.[82] Although Japan surrendered only a few months later, 1SWG remained active in northern Australia until long after the war had ended. Little information is available about the work of 1SWG. By all accounts, the unit was proficient and well regarded, performing to a high standard and handling 1,000-1,200 messages a day.[83] 1SWG monitored all Japanese traffic in the Darwin area, concentrating on Japanese naval communications and radio stations from the Dutch East Indies to the central Pacific, piecing together the Japanese communications network between Tokyo, Singapore, Rabaul, and the Pacific islands, many of which had been bypassed by US General Douglas MacArthur in his drive to Japan.[84] The work seemed dreary and consisted of routine tasks: "The first [task] is to clear all traffic as rapidly as possible and to give every assistance to the operators. Then all traffic is edited and tabulated and the results signaled to Central Bureau. A detailed tabulation is made of all traffic here, and this is analysed in the light of past experience and data from other sources. Then daily bulletins and signals are sent out to the operational units here and to CB."[85]

After Japan's surrender, 1SWG became a disseminator of communications from the Allies to Japanese units among the islands of the south Pacific, dispensing surrender instructions to ensure the peaceful laying down of arms of the thousands of Japanese troops who remained in isolated detachments in much of the southern Pacific.[86]

1SWG concluded its mission in Australia on 24 October. The long journey home began, first by crossing 2,885 miles of Australia, and then going by ship from Sydney back to Canada. They landed in Vancouver on 26 February 1946.[87] After disembarking, all members of 1SWG were cautioned not to discuss anything about their experiences for thirty years.[88] Little information about 1SWG slipped out until well after that date. In 1948, C.P. Stacey published *The Canadian Army 1939-45, An Official Historical Summary*. Without going into great detail, Stacey clearly stated that 1SWG "did useful work in intercepting enemy wireless messages" in Australia.[89] Years later, he published *Six Years of War: The Army in Canada, Britain and the Pacific, Vol. 1,* by which time the only reference to 1SWG was that it had been in Australia.[90] No one had vetted the first book, but the second was reviewed by Canada's intelligence authorities, who vetoed any reference to 1SWG. When Stacey explained that he was only copying what he had already published, a short compromise passage on 1SWG was crafted.[91]

By war's end, Canada had made a distinct and important intelligence contribution, particularly in the SIGINT field. Canadian SIGINT was a small but significant element in the Allied SIGINT effort in terms of the collection of material and in the decryption of some messages. Canada's contribution in the battle of the North Atlantic was vital. Similarly, Canada carried much of the weight on French decryption. However, the Canadian contribution must also be viewed objectively. Canada was not a SIGINT leader but a nation contributing according to its abilities and resources.

Although the Examination Unit was making an important contribution to Allied intelligence achievements by this point in the war, it was never more than a small organization and there were limits to what it could undertake. In 1943, the staff had totalled in the forties[92] and had grown to about fifty by June 1944.[93] The Cabinet War Committee approved an expansion of the Examination Unit to an aggregate of 200 personnel in January 1944 (this may have included some who were only nominally counted within the Examination Unit structure, such as intercept staff at stations).[94] The budget for the organization was a mere $220,000 in 1944, up from about $108,000 in 1943.[95] While not of the magnitude of the intelligence effort of Britain or the United States, Canada's contribution was significant and respected by the Allies. None of Canada's efforts were unique or self-sustaining but Canada was seen as part of a team, carrying some of the weight and filling in where the country's resources and capabilities could best be of assistance. Canada's effort did not affect the ultimate outcome of the war but it lightened the burden of others.

For Canada, the wartime intelligence contribution created expertise and formed the core of an intelligence organization that might be used in the postwar world. But long before the guns were silenced in Europe and Asia, thoughts were turned to how Canada would conduct foreign intelligence collection in a postwar world where threats might still exist but would be of an entirely different nature.

7
Planning for Postwar SIGINT

Collection and decryption of foreign communications proved its value to the Canadian foreign intelligence community during the Second World War. With war drawing to a close, Canada faced a decision on whether to continue foreign intelligence collection in peacetime or return to the situation that existed on the eve of the outbreak of war. The choice for the Canadian intelligence community was not an obvious one.

No tradition of foreign intelligence collection existed in Canada and no substantial constituency was present in support of continuing in peacetime what had been created in the midst of war. Before the war, there was no perceived external threat to Canada except potentially from the United States, and that had long since disappeared. Surrounded by oceans on three sides and the friendly United States on the fourth, there were reasons to favour Canada returning to a prewar safe haven. But the world had changed in many other ways and there followed in Canada, as in the United States and to a lesser extent in Britain, a debate on the merits of collecting foreign intelligence in peacetime. Canadian policy makers, far from being naive, did not view the beginnings of Soviet intransigence and lack of co-operation as something that would translate into a potential threat to Canada. Pearson, in Washington during this period, recalls in his memoirs that it was only "in 1946 and 1947, that there was such a thing as Kremlin-directed communist subversion ... and that the safety of the state was involved."[1]

Canadian decision makers' recognition that Canada's role in the world had changed governed Canadian thinking on reorganizing the intelligence community. The county's position between two large oceans and the border of its protective neighbour to the south could no longer be seen as guarantors of protection. Foreign and national security policies had to be developed from a vantage point of knowledge. The discussion did not initially focus on any perceived Soviet threat but was broader in scope, looking at geopolitical considerations rather than ideologically based threats, and envisioned foreign intelligence collection as a tool to protect Canada in general and to augment the foreign policy-making process.

More than one debate was waged in Canada's small foreign intelligence community over how postwar intelligence might look. The most important discussion centred on the future of SIGINT collection by Canada. This debate was community-wide since the Examination Unit, housed at the National Research Council (NRC), was under the policy direction of the DEA but required the active participation of the armed services, which managed "Y" activities, the interception of radio communications, which provided the raw material for the Examination Unit. The debate over whether Canada would continue a SIGINT capability after the conclusion of the war was the most important issue confronting the intelligence community.

A move to place foreign intelligence on a peacetime footing had been made at the end of November 1943, when F.A. Kendrick, head of the Examination Unit, had written to T.A. Stone suggesting some initiatives for a smoother transition of the SIGINT unit to a postwar existence.[2] Kendrick proposed that the Examination Unit be a civilian organization under the control of the DEA as the chief client of the intelligence gathered, adding that the Examination Unit needed sophisticated cryptographers who had the ability to attack and solve a wide range of ciphers. During the war, too much reliance had been placed on Allied assistance, particularly from the British. While building the organization in the midst of war, the administrative leadership of the Examination Unit had been synonymous with the cryptographic leadership. However, a peacetime organization would be better served by capable administrative management that was divorced from the technical side of the house.

In anticipation of developing a Canadian position, George Glazebrook of the DEA, who had succeeded Stone on foreign intelligence matters, asked Kendrick for information about the workings of the British Government Code and Cipher School before the war and what might happen to it after the war. In addition, Glazebrook asked why the SIGINT organization was under the British foreign office, suggesting that a member of the DEA seconded to the Examination Unit "might have to act as an officer of External rather than as an officer of the National Research Council."[3]

Separately, Stone discussed the future of the Examination Unit with representatives of British intelligence that December when passing through London en route to Ottawa after a mission to North Africa: he now wanted "to make out a case which he [could] put before the higher authorities."[4] However, no decision on the future of the Examination Unit was made before the spring of 1944, and by then there had been a change in attitudes at the DEA. During this phase of the debate, from late 1943 until early summer 1944, the question in all sectors of the Canadian intelligence community was what kind of postwar SIGINT program was required, and how big, not whether any SIGINT capacity was indeed required.

At the beginning of May 1944, the "Y" committee discussed the future of SIGINT and whether the work should be carried out by two separate organizations.[5] The Examination Unit, under the direction of the associate committee of the National Research Council, led by the DEA, was concerned with diplomatic codes and depended on Canadian, British, and American intercept facilities for its raw material. The Discrimination Unit, under the authority of the "Y" committee, led by the military services, was concerned with communications traffic analysis. Canada was now a member of a large communications network linking Ottawa with London, Washington, Delhi, and Canberra for the transmission of secret intelligence and raw intercept material. The committee reiterated the earlier call for the prime minister (who was also secretary of state for External Affairs), the Minister of National Defence, and the president of the NRC to constitute an overall national authority for secret intelligence. It then proposed that the associate committee of the National Research Council and the "Y" committee be abolished, to be replaced by a new SIGINT committee responsible for all units operating in the field of cryptography and traffic analysis. The composition of the new committee would be the same as that of the two committees it replaced, and the Deputy Minister of National Defence would act as chairman.[6]

Within the DEA, Hume Wrong, having returned from his post in Washington and being charged with the daily management of the department, sought the views of the under-secretary on 9 June 1944, only days after the Allied landings in Normandy, about the future of the Examination Unit. Prompting the discussion was the departure of Stone for London to take up a position involving psychological warfare. Wrong stated, "There is no one left in the Department who is nearly as intimately acquainted as he was" with the Examination Unit.[7]

Wrong wondered whether the Examination Unit warranted the support of the DEA, what its value was to other departments in Ottawa, and how important was it to the Allied effort. Newly arrived from Washington, he did not share the perception of the importance of foreign intelligence that prevailed within the DEA, nor did he view the SIGINT from the Examination Unit as particularly valuable to External Affairs. Yet he acknowledged that intelligence, particularly SIGINT, seemed to have acquired a high reputation with the British and American agencies, both for the volume of output and for its quality. Although with little knowledge of the product of the Examination Unit, Wrong was inclined not to support its continuance, in part because so much of the output was derived from an Allied source (the raw intercepts). Furthermore, he doubted that the product was of any value to other departments in Ottawa.[8] Wrong saw the Examination Unit as a "side-show" and predicted that it would, in any event, likely be wrapped up after the end of the war.[9] His impact on the intelligence debate is significant and serves to underscore the small size of the Canadian intelligence community in that the views of single influential individuals could sway decisions.

Wrong is unlikely to have had access to significant amounts of intelligence while in Washington, although policy advice was often influenced by intelligence, as appropriate. No archival material records an evolution of views at the DEA on foreign intelligence collection. The change in attitudes happened quickly and probably reflects a confluence of factors: the arrival of Wrong, the departure of Stone, and the preoccupations of Norman Robertson, increasingly directing his attention to the conclusion of the war.

That September, Gilbert Robinson, a senior director at the Examination Unit, voiced his concerns to Glazebrook about the possible closure of the organization. Robinson thought that the future of the Examination Unit should be determined by the value of SIGINT to the DEA, including not only what was produced in Canada but also what was available from Canada's intelligence partners. Glazebrook worried that the Examination Unit was seen by the DEA as an expensive wartime expedient such that, with the war coming to an end, "there was a natural argument for stopping it."[10] Robinson suggested that Lester B. Pearson's difficult efforts early in the war to obtain decodes of Vichy intercepts in London be recalled. He added that if the DEA cut its ties to SIGINT, the work would be taken over by the armed services, which had not proven satisfactory in the United States.[11] Robinson did not expand on this theme but may have been referring to the rivalry between US Army and Navy intelligence, which contributed to the confusion during the lead up to Pearl Harbor.

During a discussion at the DEA of Robinson's intervention, Norman Robertson informed Glazebrook that he did not want the Examination Unit connected with the military, but nor did he want it as part of the DEA.[12] However, Robertson was not forceful in articulating precisely what he did want.

In a meeting of the Examination Unit Committee, Colonel W.W. Murray (army) and Commander C.H. Little (navy), the services' intelligence chiefs, favoured a continuance of the Examination Unit since, in their view, the British would be less ready to share SIGINT material with Canada if there was no possibility of a reciprocal exchange. Murray "was firmly of the opinion that we could never expect to obtain the close cooperation of the Services either during or after the war, unless such a single [SIGINT] authority were appointed in Canada." Little supported Murray, who extolled the intelligence value of the Examination Unit. Both were "emphatic that ... Canada's position in world affairs requires the existence of a cryptographic organization."[13]

The DND supported the appointment of a senior officer from the DEA to be responsible for all secret intelligence activities (i.e., SIGINT). Murray and Little were less concerned with who would control Canadian postwar SIGINT than fearful of abandoning a valuable tool for providing the country with a unique and autonomous insight into world events. The DND proposed that the Examination Unit be under the direction of a DEA officer, although housed with the NRC because of the difficulty of keeping the covert funding hidden. In addition, Murray and Little recommended that the Examination Unit be merged with the armed services' Discrimination Units. Both DND officers acknowledged that the ultimate decision on the future of SIGINT in Canada rested with the DEA and the value it placed on this information source. They accepted that the advice to the government had to come from External Affairs and would accept the government's decision, but "because of the lack of operational intelligence would not be persuaded in any other way."[14] This placed the onus on the DEA, which had to "decide ... on whether the material would be of sufficient value to justify the maintenance of a Unit."[15] When the Advisory Committee on the Examination Unit met on 4 October, Murray reiterated his earlier position "that some general policy must be adopted by the Department of External Affairs for dealing with the intelligence aspects of the various problems faced by the services in their interception activities."[16]

Briefing Robertson on the Examination Unit committee meeting, Glazebrook advised that Sir Edward Travis, head of the British Government Code and Cipher School, would be in Canada within about ten days and that the prime minister might want to seek his views on the matter.[17] Before Travis arrived in Canada, however, Murray and Little requested a meeting with Robertson "to place before [him] the views of the two Services on the general question of interception and cryptanalysis arising out of the recent discussions on the future of the Examination Unit."[18]

Travis likely did not meet with Mackenzie King; such a meeting would have been unusual. But on 10 October, Travis did meet with Wrong, in the absence of Robertson. Prior to the meeting, Travis had been asked for his views on the future of the Examination Unit and had been told that although the unit had "provided valuable intelligence ... it is doubtful whether the Canadian Government would wish to maintain it in time of peace."[19]

Travis began the meeting with Wrong by informing him that Benjamin deForest Bayly, a Canadian engineer with the British Security Coordination (BSC) office in New York, had invented a new communications device named the "Rockex" (for the Rockefeller Exchange, the office location of BSC), which had the security of a one-time cipher pad. Bayly would come to Ottawa to explain the new communications system. Wrong then asked what role the Examination Unit might play in intelligence exchanges with the British. Cautioning that he was expressing his own view, Travis led Wrong to believe that a scaled-down version of the Examination Unit would be inadequate for gaining access to intelligence of much importance. He suggested instead that Canada might focus on intercepting messages to be forwarded to the United Kingdom for processing, not unlike what the Royal Canadian Navy had done for the British Admiralty before the war. Britain would probably be ready to supply Canada with deciphered material for which an interest existed. Travis added that, in his view, SIGINT collection ought to be under the policy direction of the DEA.[20]

Travis was not speaking as a representative of the British government, but was senior enough within the British establishment to understand the prevailing views toward the dominions. His suggestion that Canada revert to a role of supplier of raw intelligence material for the "mother country" reflected an attitude that had not evolved much since the war began. To an individual of his background and experience, it may have seemed quite natural for Canada to return to a prewar role in matters of intelligence. That Travis met with Wrong rather than another senior DEA officer more favourably disposed toward intelligence matters is unfortunate. With little appreciation for an independent role of foreign intelligence for Canada, Wrong did not see much benefit in the intelligence product, and was not an advocate of an autonomous intelligence capability.

After Travis returned to London, he met with "C," Stewart Menzies, the head of the British Secret Intelligence Service, to discuss his conversation with Wrong about the future of the Examination Unit. From BSC in New York, Bayly arrived in Ottawa shortly thereafter to make a presentation on the new Rockex communications system, and brought further comments on British consideration of the discussions between Wrong and Travis. The British, likely reflecting a cautious perspective imposed by Menzies, now advocated a more nuanced view of the role of the dominions and recommended a wait-and-see attitude while Britain decided on the postwar role for its own SIGINT service. Glazebrook, who met with Bayly, informed Robertson of the exchange, adding that perhaps Canada need *not* maintain a cryptographic unit in peacetime but should accept the confining arrangement proposed by Travis.[21]

The rumour of a possible closure of the Examination Unit circulated quickly within the intelligence community in Ottawa. The day after Glazebrook met with Bayly, Gilbert Robinson of the Examination Unit wrote directly to Robertson to argue in favour of maintaining a nucleus of the Examination Unit as an adjunct to the cipher office in the DEA. The gist of his argument was that Canada would need some sort of organization for cryptographic work; in the absence of the Examination Unit, some of this activity would be assumed by the armed services or the RCMP, both of which had had limited involvement in this field before the war. Robinson wondered "whether certain quarters could wish for the closing of the Examination Unit on the larger ground that being in the cryptographic field Canada might sometimes have access to information of significance which might or might not concern her."[22] This suggests that Robinson was aware of the Travis proposal for Canada to provide raw intercepts for the British. Robinson added that, whatever was decided with respect to the Examination Unit, most other countries would continue to carry out cryptographic work after the war had ended.

In the meantime, the meeting between Travis and Wrong in Ottawa on 10 October had given rise to communications from Glazebrook to T.A. Stone in London to inform him of events and to seek his views. Stone responded a month later, reporting that he had met with Travis as well as a representative of the British foreign office, almost certainly a representative of the British Secret Intelligence Service. Stone had stated that with the Examination Unit being shut down as unable to meet future requirements, Canada's SIGINT contribution might be in the field of signals interception, and that Canada might contribute staff to the British Government Code and Cipher School as part of a burden-sharing arrangement.[23] Stone met with Menzies shortly thereafter and found that the British were receptive to a proposal along the lines Stone had discussed with Travis, and encouraged Canada in this direction. Stone reported to Glazebrook that the following March, when Kendrick was scheduled to return to the Government Code and Cipher School, was a good time to close down the Examination Unit. He added that a Canadian be specifically nominated as a liaison officer between Menzies and the under-secretary of state for External Affairs to select the SIGINT to be passed to Canada by the British. Stone discounted any vision of a Commonwealth Government Code and Cipher School, and ended his letter by categorically stating that Australia and India intended to continue their own interception and, probably, cryptographic activities. He added his own personal and growing unease with closing the Examination Unit in the absence of any vision of "subsequent [Canadian] participation in and contribution to this work."[24]

In his book *Best Kept Secret: Canadian Secret Intelligence in the Second World War*, John Bryden suggests that Stone's discussions with "C" were quickly dubbed the "UK/Canada plan," although the available archives do not portray the discussions in such terms.[25] Kendrick discussed the proposal with the under-secretary of state for External Affairs on 8 December, referring to the proposal to rely on Britain for future SIGINT as the "Travis Plan" and stating that Canada expected to receive Ultra intelligence, the highly classified deciphered machine-encrypted SIGINT, in return for providing Britain with intercepted raw material. Kendrick claimed that the plan did not require an end to Canadian cryptographic work, although a goal of the plan was to make it unnecessary. He briefly outlined how and when the Examination

Unit might be closed down, implying that Canada could lose access to some intelligence.[26] He added that his recommendations were based on a presumption that the Travis Plan would be approved, and suggested that the appearance of a lack of interest in the Japanese war should be avoided.

Robertson and Glazebrook met with Bayly that December and were told that the Examination Unit was regarded as efficient, within its limits, but that "no important contribution had been made to allied work in this field by the Unit because of its small size and limited equipment." Bayly added that Canada's intercept facilities were out of date, inadequate, and would have to be replaced if collection continued.

By now the debate in Ottawa on the future of the Examination Unit was reaching a feverish pitch as the DEA remained adamant about its closure, while the DND intelligence chiefs fought long and hard to preserve Canada's small but autonomous SIGINT capacity. Clearly, two fundamentally different visions existed. At least for the moment, the DEA acknowledged no significant benefit for itself or Canada from postwar SIGINT collection. The armed forces, perhaps acknowledging their fear of a postwar world whose complexities had begun to manifest themselves, were vocally reluctant to surrender a tool that had demonstrated its worth in the conflict just drawing to a close. The two solitudes overshadowed the intelligence debate in Canada for some time. Had it not been for the fortitude of the intelligence chiefs at the DND and some other individuals, things may have been much different.

At a meeting of the Advisory Committee on the Examination Unit on 14 December 1944, which seems to have lasted to a late hour, Murray and Little raised the issue of the future of Canadian SIGINT, suggesting that the cost of cabling decodes to Canada from the British Government Code and Cipher School would be almost as great as that of supporting a Canadian cryptographic organization. Kendrick dissented, noting that small-scale collection and decryption was unlikely to yield much information of interest to Canada. Little expressed his unwillingness to return to Canada's prewar state of cryptographic ignorance.[27]

By January, in the final year of the war, concrete plans within the DEA were set for closing the Examination Unit at the end of July. The Japanese section would be transferred to the Discrimination Unit for ongoing work in the war against Japan. It was proposed that the department support abolishing the existing "Y" committee in favour of a new advisory committee in its place. In addition, the DEA recommended the promotion of E.M. Drake, head of the Discrimination Unit, to full colonel.[28]

In mid-February, Glazebrook sought Major General M.A. Pope's agreement regarding the DND assuming responsibility for the Japanese section of the Discrimination Unit.[29] No response had yet been received two months later in April when Robertson repeated the message to the Chief of the General Staff, stating that "it is evident that we cannot contemplate the maintenance in peace-time of a Unit on a sufficiently large scale to give adequate coverage of diplomatic traffic." Lieutenant General J.C. Murchie quickly agreed to the more urgent appeal from Robertson for the transfer of the Japanese section.[30]

When Glazebrook briefed Drake at the end of February about the proposal to close the Examination Unit, the latter was discouraged by the continuing confusion and was reluctant to assume control of a joint Discrimination and Examination Unit unless it was on a proper basis. He preferred the future entity to be linked with the DEA and suggested that his nomination as director of the Examination Unit, in addition to MI2 (the Discrimination Unit), would give him the stature to facilitate the workings of a joint organization.[31]

Meanwhile, Robertson had informed the British Government Code and Cipher School that a decision had been made to close the Examination Unit in early August and that Canada hoped to retain Kendrick, who was due to leave in March, until the work was completed.[32] As the senior officer in the DEA, Robertson accepted the implication of the Travis Plan to downgrade Canada's role in SIGINT. A month later, he wrote to Lester B. Pearson, by now Canada's ambassador to the United States, to inform him of the decision to shut down the Canadian SIGINT organization, and to explain that the country could not afford an Examination Unit large enough to be adequate to the task. Robertson asked Pearson to take on the delicate task of informing the Americans of Canada's decision. Kendrick and Stone, the latter now back in Canada, were to join Pearson in Washington to explain Canada's decision and work out some of the practical considerations, such as the continuing joint effort directed against the Japanese. Interestingly, Robertson informed Pearson about the plans to supply Britain with raw intercepts after the war in exchange for decrypted messages. He added, "At the present time, however, I have not felt it possible to raise a question with such large implications with the Prime Minister, and any arrangement of that sort will have, therefore, to be left in abeyance."[33] While Mackenzie King would have been aware of the decision to close the Examination Unit, Robertson's statement makes it clear that the prime minister may not have been aware of the full implications of the decision.

Toward the end of April, Colonel W.W. Murray, the director of military intelligence, obtained a copy of Robertson's letter to Murchie. A meeting of the "Y" committee had been scheduled for the end of the month. No agenda had been circulated beforehand and the meeting occurred at a time when Robertson and Murchie were both away from Ottawa and could not be easily contacted. Although the "Y" committee was not responsible for the Examination Unit, its membership and that of the Advisory Committee on the Examination Unit largely overlapped. When the "Y" committee met, Murray read Robertson's letter to the group. Herbert Norman, still a junior officer, represented the DEA at the meeting. Glazebrook was inexplicably unavailable. Norman's strong objections to the substance of Robertson's letter being discussed in the "Y" committee were dismissed and the meeting proceeded, resulting in recommendations on the future of SIGINT in Canada.[34] It is uncertain whether there was co-operation between the service intelligence directors, as suggested by Bryden in *Best Kept Secret;*[35] whatever the extent of any inter-service agreement, Murray, the chairman, proposed a recommendation to the Chiefs of Staff that the "Y" committee be abolished and replaced by a SIGINT board to constitute the policy-making body for Canadian "Y" activities (i.e., SIGINT activities). The meeting was impassioned; one participant described it as involving "some fairly violent scenes."[36] Also discussed was the amalgamation of the remnant of the Examination Unit (the Japanese section) with the Discrimination Unit to form the Joint Discrimination Unit (JDU). The committee "was dead-opposed" to a permanent director (likely Drake) being appointed.

George Glazebrook had advised Norman Robertson, away in San Francisco for the preparatory meeting of the United Nations, about the merger of the Examination Unit with the Discrimination Unit. He had recommended that the Chiefs of Staff Committee abolish the "Y" committee and the Examination Unit committee in favour of a new SIGINT board, which would constitute a policy-making body for Canadian SIGINT activities. Glazebrook pointed out:

> The game then is painfully obvious as the Intelligence Officers, particularly Murray, are concerned about their post-war empires and are trying to create them. You may remember that when they came to you some months ago they urged that the Department of External Affairs should support post-war discrimination and cryptography since National Defence would not otherwise do it. They have now got from us a suggestion that this should be carried on at least throughout the Japanese war and now propose to go back to the Sig Int Board which would bring control of the Discrimination Unit and Examination Unit once more under the Intelligence Officers.[37]

There was great concern that the Americans be reassured about Canada's SIGINT commitment until the end of the Japanese war. Shortly after the meeting of the "Y" committee, Gilbert Robinson was dispatched to Washington to inform the US Army's Signal Security Agency, the SIGINT service, about the Canadian decision to terminate the activities of the Examination Unit. Some confusion had arisen when Pearson, assisted by Kendrick and Stone, had briefed the Americans in March and implied that Canada was planning to drop decryption of Japanese diplomatic traffic provided that the

Americans would make this available in exchange for Canadian-provided military and commercial traffic.[38] Robinson explained to the Americans that the plans were for the Examination Unit to cease operations by 31 July 1945; the cryptographic work on Japanese diplomatic activities undertaken by Ottawa would be transferred to a new JDU, while work on French diplomatic communications would be ended entirely. The American reaction was one of shock; at the time no one knew how long the war with Japan would last and at what cost. The United States was anxious for continued Canadian assistance on Japanese commercial traffic and considered it "vitally important just now that Canada present a united front [with the US]."[39] The Americans requested all code books, traffic, and other material from Canada that were not forwarded to the British.[40] When Drake visited Arlington Hall some days later, the United States was anxious to assure Canada that there would be "no lack of jobs for a continuing unit in Canada, and jobs of considerable importance." Americans also extended many compliments on the work of the Examination Unit.[41]

The reaction by the Americans to being informed about Canada's decision to end its SIGINT capability was the exact opposite to the attitude expressed by the British. The Americans encouraged continued Canadian engagement in SIGINT activity, whereas Britain had denigrated Canada's wartime effort and recommended a return to the dependent role of the interwar period. Herein, perhaps, lay the seed of postwar intelligence co-operation that saw Canada gradually drift from connectivity with Britain toward closer links with the Americans.

Discussions between the DEA and the DND over postwar intelligence remained tense, and the strong opposition of the DEA forced the "Y" committee to drop the idea of a SIGINT board under the control of the armed services intelligence chiefs.[42] In May 1945, the "Y" committee proposed that the Canadian Joint Intelligence Committee (CJIC) take over the function of managing SIGINT.[43] The CJIC, created in November 1942 by the Chiefs of Staff Committee to "conduct intelligence studies and to prepare such special information as may be required by higher authority" as well as to liaise with the corresponding Allied services,[44] did not have the same mandate as the British Joint Intelligence Committee (BJIC), from which it took its name. During the war years, the CJIC was a DND administrative committee with little power outside that possessed by its individual members, the intelligence directors of the armed services. The BJIC was already a powerful committee of all the chiefs of the intelligence units meeting weekly to reach common assessments of events and to resolve administrative difficulties.

The CJIC had served as the administrative coordinating centre for the armed services intelligence directorates, as a platform for the exchange of information, and as a clearing house for matters of joint interest. The CJIC was a low-key committee primarily serving as a venue for the service intelligence directors to communicate with each other, and had no responsibilities for SIGINT matters. The proposal would make the CJIC responsible for Canadian SIGINT, and sought to achieve the same objective as had been proposed through creation of a SIGINT board. Although seen by the DEA as a ploy to gain control over SIGINT, the action of the DND intelligence chiefs was merely a response to the DEA's desire to see the demise of Canada's limited SIGINT capacity.

The CJIC had proposed that assumption of SIGINT responsibility would be accompanied by External Affairs and the RCMP joining the committee. Gilbert Robinson, representing the Examination Unit on the CJIC, thought this was unlikely to be acceptable to the DEA since the original SIGINT board proposal had provided for two DEA representatives, while its CJIC replacement would include only one additional representative for each of the new members.[45] Nevertheless, the Chiefs of Staff Committee proposed to Robertson that the DEA appoint a representative to the CJIC and that the functions of the "Y" committee be transferred to the CJIC.[46]

Robertson agreed to the committee's proposal for the transfer of SIGINT responsibility to the CJIC, but pointed out that the expanded JDU would now be engaged in work involving cryptographic policy for which External Affairs remained responsible. He then suggested that "this situation would best be met by having the J.D.U. under the direction, for policy purposes, of a sub-committee of the C.J.I.C., of which sub-committee an officer of this Department would be Chairman."[47]

Robertson added that the CJIC subcommittee should be composed of Herbert Norman for External Affairs, the head of the JDU (who was Lieutenant Colonel E.M. Drake, a staunch External Affairs ally), and one other member of the CJIC. Robertson's proposal was reasonable, agreed to everything proposed by the services intelligence directors through the Chiefs of Staff Committee, and made one minor modification. The critical direction of SIGINT would remain in the DEA's hands through a subcommittee that controlled policy.

The outcome of the contest over postwar SIGINT direction reflected entrenched attitudes within the Canadian intelligence community. The DEA feared that SIGINT managed by the military intelligence establishment would be inefficient and, perhaps more importantly, that control by the military would cause Drake, the head of the Discrimination Unit, to quit. Glazebrook informed Robertson, "Drake, who is the only expert we have available [Kendrick, at the Examination Unit, was returning to the British Government Code and Cipher School], will try to get out. He is thoroughly fed up with the whole business and I gather disgusted with the present antics."[48] The armed forces rightly feared the demise of Canada's SIGINT facility, an organization that had proven its worth and that the intelligence chiefs viewed as providing Canada with an autonomous source of insight into international events.

Back from Britain and now at the Canadian Embassy in Washington, T.A. Stone was having second thoughts about the SIGINT debate in Ottawa, and voiced his concerns to Glazebrook:

> External Affairs must control all cryptographic work and all activities in the high levels of political intelligence. If External Affairs isn't prepared to undertake this responsibility, I would advocate recommending to the Prime Minister that immediately at the conclusion of the war with Japan all active operations in cryptography in Canada should cease. For what it wants by way of top secret intelligence our Department could then depend on the connections made from Canada having been engaged in this field. My own view is that these connections would only last as long as the present personalities remain active on both sides. I refer particularly, of course, to Herbert Norman and to you and to me as we are what might be called 'known names' ... Security measures in both London and Washington, post-war, will be tightened rather than in any way relaxed ...
>
> It is up to External Affairs to make up its mind whether from its point of view the game is worth the candle. If it isn't worth the candle we certainly cannot afford the risk, and I would regard it as a very grave one, of allowing another agency or Department, military or civilian, of the Canadian Government to muck about in the fields of high, top secret political intelligence. Unless External Affairs steps in very soon with a firm decision either one way or the other, people like Chiefs of Staff and W.W. Murray [director of military intelligence] are going to confront us with a fait accompli which will be very difficult to undo.
>
> I am advocating, of course, the British system after having examined them both at fairly close range over some years. The Americans, I think, are running grave risks with the complete control of high intelligence now as it is in the hands of G.2 [US Military Intelligence] and O.N.I. [US Office of Naval Intelligence], and with the State Department (as far as I know) getting what it pleases the military and naval authorities to hand out to them. In London, as you know, 'C' is an employee of the Foreign Office and he runs the show.[49]

Glazebrook also stated that he was "getting more and more despondent about the possibility of reaching any agreement with National Defence and am now mentally designing a continuing Examination Unit."[50] The chief impediment to maintaining the Examination Unit, he thought, was the difficulty of finding someone to run it following the departure of F.A. Kendrick, who had been seconded from the British Government Code and Cipher School and was returning there. Glazebrook sought Stone's thinking on his views and concluded "that we must do the work and that we cannot be bothered by J.I.C. [CJIC] control. How would it be to abolish the Examination Unit Committee, run the Unit in conjunction with National Research, and make our own arrangements with Washington? This is perhaps a wild idea, but one which I think we shall have to consider."[51]

In the final weeks of the war with Japan, what remained of the Examination Unit left its quarters at 345 Laurier Avenue, next door to the prime minister's residence, to move to the JDU facility on Guigues Street. The JDU formally came into being on 1 August 1945, two weeks before the collapse of Japan. The Examination Unit was expected to consume a budget of $87,000 for 1945.[52] The organization was now down to twenty-three civilians and one officer each from the army and navy. The rest of the JDU was not much bigger, with twelve officers and seventy-eight other ranks. At war's end, Canada's wireless intercept stations consisted of three army stations (Ottawa/Leitrim, Grande Prairie, Alberta, and Victoria, British Columbia), three navy stations (Coverdale, New Brunswick; Gloucester, Ontario; and Gordon Head, British Columbia), and two Department of Transport stations (Point Grey and Lulu Island, British Columbia).[53]

The Japanese surrender revived the question within the DEA of whether Canada should carry out peacetime foreign intelligence collection and, particularly, whether the department agreed to any sort of postwar SIGINT capability being lodged with the armed services, even if policy direction was decided by a subcommittee controlled by the DEA. While there was agreement to the JDU becoming responsible for the Japanese section of the Examination Unit while the war in the Pacific continued, it was an entirely different matter whether to support a DND-controlled SIGINT organization for the postwar world. Drake favoured a small postwar SIGINT unit, which he thought could be effective and would raise few concerns about costs.[54] A second constraint was uncertainty over where Canada would fit in with its British and American intelligence allies. The British were also ambivalent during the early postwar period over whether Canada should continue cryptographic work. However, both Allies had expressed interest in postwar collaboration, although only the Americans assumed that a Canadian cryptographic capability would exist after the end of hostilities.

A decision by Canada on postwar cryptographic work was not eased by an agreement among the Allies for the wartime SIGINT arrangements to carry over into peacetime, and nothing compelled Canada to reach a conclusion on the desirability of a postwar SIGINT organization. The DEA was unwilling to act in the absence of knowledge on costs, inter-Allied relationships, and whether only collection or collection plus decryption work was to be undertaken. However, the DEA was firm about its reluctance to hand over SIGINT to the armed services intelligence directors, who were viewed as "know[ing] exactly nothing about it and any recommendation they would make would have to be taken with several pounds of salt because of their desire to maintain their own positions."[55] This dramatic statement underscores the confining interdepartmental distrust in which Canada had to reach difficult decisions. Such strongly held views permeated many DEA documents of the period; less evidence suggested that the sentiments were reciprocated by the DND. In fact, CJIC discussions had clearly recorded that the army would not carry out cryptography in peacetime, believing that only the NRC seemed structured to accommodate a cryptographic organization.[56]

Discussions between the DEA and the DND continued throughout August 1945, with a gradual acknowledgment that a solution addressing Canada's national interests had to be reached. By the end of the month, the CJIC had prepared an extensive study outlining the history of SIGINT collection in Canada, how it assisted various national objectives, and what constituted the existing Canadian resources.[57] One of the telling sentences in the study underscored the reality of intelligence sharing brought home by the experiences during the Second World War. After suggesting that SIGINT was possibly the most important source of secret information available to Canada, it continued, "It is inconsistent with our national position that we should be dependent upon others for those things that we are capable of doing for ourselves. At all events, any such dependency could and should be elevated to the basis of 'quid pro quo.' In the 'Y' sphere the advantage of this approach was clearly impressed during the early war years. When our contribution was nil, we received nothing from either Bletchley [the British Government Code and Cipher School] or Washington ... By making our contribution, our dividend will vastly exceed our investment."[58] In essence, by doing just enough to be accepted as a partner, Canada would gain access to most or all of the SIGINT collected by its allies.

Nothing would be free. If Canada did not engage in intelligence collection, there was a presumption that it would not have significant access to material from its allies. While an exchange need not be between equals, it was imperative that each contributed according to its abilities. Without being stated, it seemed implicit that the service intelligence chiefs acknowledged the need to be a producing partner in order to reap the benefits of extensive access to the wealth of intelligence collectively available. This reality was intuitively recognized by the intelligence people at the DND but was not being acknowledged by those at the DEA. That the views of the DND intelligence chiefs ultimately prevailed was to Canada's long-term benefit.

In essence, this was the brilliance and failure of Canadian foreign intelligence activities. Access to Allied material was substantial, but Canada did not do enough by itself to be confident of its resources and access or to have assurance that its sovereign interests were addressed. The CJIC study went on to recommend that wireless interception continue during peacetime as "a requirement essential for adequate national defence," but it was unclear whether SIGINT would be under military or civilian authority: the study also recommended "that the Joint Discrimination Unit, including the cryptanalysis section, be continued as a joint services responsibility, or as a civilian establishment financially administered by the National Research Council, with services personnel seconded thereto as requirements warrant."[59]

The selection of the NRC as the possible home of the postwar SIGINT organization stemmed from its administration of secret budget votes throughout the war, something it was hoped would endure.

Meanwhile, Gilbert Robinson, who had assumed responsibility for the Examination Unit after the departure of Kendrick in May, had been asked to prepare a blueprint for a peacetime SIGINT organization. He presented this in September 1945, stating that he "would not like to see such work revived unless the highest officials in the Department of External Affairs were anxious for it and were prepared to take responsibility for making the changes in the existing structure which would be necessary for its success."[60] Robinson did not object to the SIGINT organization reporting to the CJIC, but thought it vital that an intelligence and security committee within the DEA be responsible for all collection assignments. He was also adamant that Canada supply all of the personnel resources required. While he proposed that the Japanese assignments might slowly be phased out, Robinson advocated a revival of French decryption (he recommended that the section be headed by Sonja Morawetz, one of many competent women in cryptography). Lastly, Robinson thought it advisable and expedient that the SIGINT organization be housed with the NRC.

Common ground had been reached between the DEA and the DND by late September 1945. SIGINT collection in peacetime was to be a combined military and civilian organization; interception would be under military direction and cryptography would be housed with the NRC. The CJIC was the administering organization, but policy was to be directed by External Affairs.[61]

No decision on a foreign intelligence organization had been reached by the early fall, when a visit to Ottawa by Sir Edward Travis of the British Government Code and Cipher School was scheduled. This visit on 22 and 23 October helped Canada move toward a decision. Travis attended a meeting of the CJIC, where he outlined Britain's expected postwar SIGINT organization of some 1,150 people and hoped to reach agreement for co-operation between Britain, the United States, and Canada.[62] He explained that London and Washington were reaching an understanding on postwar SIGINT collection and sharing, and "would like [Canada] to fit into [the] general plan by accepting defined responsibilities in all aspects of [the] work."[63] The new framework for agreement was not to be arrangements between specific departments but, rather, government to government. For unclear reasons, the minutes of the CJIC meeting with Travis indicate that there was no representative from the DEA present. However, the discussions were clear that the DEA's support was required for any co-operation between the three powers, even though the minutes record that "the interchange of diplomatic intelligence is *NOT* contemplated although service stations were used for diplomatic traffic."[64]

No commitment was made during Travis' visit, since both the prime minister and his under-secretary of state for External Affairs were in London briefing Prime Minister Attlee and the British government on the revelations of Igor Gouzenko, the Soviet cipher clerk who had defected the previous month. By early November, when it was clear that Britain and the United States would soon reach agreement on SIGINT sharing, Canada had accepted that it had to be a partner with direct links to both Allied SIGINT centres. However, Canada had still not decided how foreign intelligence matters should be arranged. The DEA wanted responsibility to be lodged with a Cabinet committee on defence questions, possibly with an advisory committee made up of the Chiefs of Staff, the under-secretary of state for External Affairs, and perhaps the president of the NRC.[65] Glazebrook recalled that the DEA favoured placing intelligence matters under the authority of the Privy Council Office, whose civil service head had undefined powers but great authority and very close links to the DEA.[66]

In the months following the conclusion of the war, as the debate continued over capacity versus a sense of Canadian national requirements and autonomous access to foreign intelligence, the decision on the future structure of postwar foreign intelligence was finally settled. On the afternoon of 29 December 1945, the DEA's Norman Robertson, with Hume Wrong and George Glazebrook, met with the DND's Lieutenant General Charles Foulkes and the NRC's Dean Mackenzie to agree to the establishment of a civilian SIGINT organization that would operate in peacetime.[67] The decision provided firm direction on the future of a postwar foreign intelligence capability, and set the Canadian government on a defined path that allowed other outcomes to follow more easily on the development of the nation's foreign intelligence community.

Responding to the December decision, Lieutenant Colonel E.M. Drake, the chief of the JDU, prepared a lengthy report for the CJIC in the middle of January on proposed Canadian postwar intercept facilities. Drake, an electrical engineer with degrees from the Universities of Saskatchewan and McGill, had worked for Northern Electric before the war[68] and had started in SIGINT in March 1940 as a lieutenant and second-in-command of the "experimental section" of the Rockcliffe intercept station. Drake believed that six stations with 100 intercept positions manned by 450 staff operating new equipment were sufficient for initial Canadian needs.[69] An important consideration in his mind was the requirement for a SIGINT effort capable of making a sufficient contribution to ensure Canadian participation in the postwar co-operative alliance being negotiated between Britain and the United States. This agenda was subsequently articulated in the minutes of the CJIC, which recorded: "1. That approval be given to maintain adequate Canadian post-war intercept facilities on a scale sufficient to ensure a fair Canadian contribution to the general pool of wireless intelligence set up between Canada and other Empire countries and the United States."[70]

The DEA had also recorded its commitment to postwar SIGINT collection: on 2 February, at a meeting of the CJIC, G.G. Crean stated that "his department was firmly of the opinion that wireless interception must be continued."[71] G.G. Crean, known to everyone as Bill, had come to the DEA in 1945 after wartime service in the British army's intelligence corps, and was charged with establishing a proper security regime within the department for the protection of classified material.

British-American negotiations for postwar SIGINT collaboration had been started the previous October with Sir Edward Travis' visit to Washington, followed by bilateral discussions that culminated in the BRUSA Agreement of 5 March 1946.[72] A Commonwealth SIGINT conference of Britain and the dominions took place in London from 22 February to 8 March 1946.[73] The Commonwealth conference had been called by the London Signal Intelligence Board for the purpose of discussing and recommending SIGINT co-operation between Britain, Canada, Australia, New Zealand, and India.[74] Canada was represented by Drake, soon to be appointed head of Canada's postwar SIGINT organization, and George Glazebrook and Bill Crean, of the DEA.[75] The meeting of the Commonwealth partners acknowledged that Canada had "a special position vis-à-vis the United States," permitting Canada to work on intelligence assignments agreed upon with either the United States or Britain, as long as all parties were informed.[76] It would take several more years before all the agreements and protocols governing SIGINT co-operation between the United States and the Commonwealth countries were concluded.

Canada's political evolution had accelerated during the war with closer ties being drawn with the United States, while the relationship with Britain remained stable or loosened slightly. This was reflected in the intelligence realm, in which the United States viewed Canada as a possible junior partner, whereas Britain continued to perceive a dominion that should be supportive of imperial needs.

Following the London conference, the Chiefs of Staff approved the continuation of SIGINT collection on 26 March.[77] The Chiefs of Staff met with Robertson and Arnold Heeney, of the Privy Council Office, on 28 March to approve "the conduct of wireless intercept work under the auspices of the Services on the scale proposed."[78] No additional personnel would initially be sought. An order-in-council was signed on 13 April for the creation of the Communications Research Centre. The order-in-council, signed by C.D.

Howe as chairman of the Privy Council on Scientific and Industrial Research, Louis St. Laurent, the acting secretary of state for External Affairs, and D.C. Abbott, Minister of National Defence, did not state the purpose of the organization, but only that a wartime activity "of great value" should be continued on a postwar basis.[79] As it turned out, the order-in-council never reached the Privy Council and was never considered by the Cabinet as a whole. Howe had signed the original submission and received the verbal concurrence of the other two ministers. Robertson sent a copy to Mackenzie King, who signed a carbon copy and asked that St. Laurent and Abbott sign the original (he likely did not know that verbal concurrence had already been given). Copies of the order-in-council were forwarded the following month to the Department of Finance and the Treasury Board for financial authority and support.[80]

The Communications Research Centre was tasked with SIGINT policy, discrimination and traffic analysis, cryptanalysis, code and cipher making, and cipher security. It was administered by the NRC and directed by an officer from the DEA who was assisted by a committee consisting of representatives from the NRC, each of the three armed services directors of signals and directors of intelligence, and a second representative of the DEA. The cipher making and cipher security would provide "cover" for the covert activities.[81]

The Communications Research Centre held its inaugural meeting on 20 June under the name of the Communications Research Centre Committee, and became the SIGINT policy authority, replacing the CJIC, which retained responsibility for setting overall foreign intelligence requirements. Meanwhile, the JDU formally folded at the end of the month; its staff and individual members of the old Examination Unit assimilated into the Communications Research Centre over the summer.[82] The original name of the centre was also dropped during the transition in favour of Communications Branch, since a blander description, devoid of intelligence associations, was required. The Communications Research Centre Committee was renamed to become the Communications Research Committee.[83] The branch became operational on 3 September 1946 as the Communications Branch of the National Research Council, and became Canada's first self-contained intelligence agency. Drake was its first director.[84]

The decision on whether to continue postwar SIGINT collection had consumed an inordinate amount of time. From roughly the time of the Allied landings in Normandy until almost the last day of 1945, approximately one and a half years, Canada was beset by the question of whether SIGINT collection would survive the end of the war. The DEA saw little value in continued SIGINT collection, while the DND viewed this activity as an important national resource that should not be impeded. The DND was correct; the position of the DEA was more complex. An important change in attitude at

External Affairs occurred with the arrival in Ottawa of Hume Wrong and the departure of T.A. Stone. However, it would be too easy to attribute such a significant shift in attitudes entirely to personalities. Norman Robertson, Wrong's superior, shared his views on the Examination Unit as did, if not consistently, the other officers at the DEA who were engaged in intelligence matters. Perhaps there was no strong support for the SIGINT product at the DEA. However, in the absence of clear archival evidence to the contrary, it may be safer to assume that the position of the DEA, whose minister was Mackenzie King, may have been influenced by perennial Canadian policy drivers of the time: caution and resources. It is to the credit of committed officers at both the DND and the DEA that the correct decision ultimately prevailed.

Hard as it may have been to make a decision in favour of continuing SIGINT collection in the postwar world, it was a simple task compared to the discussions and manoeuvring that accompanied the establishment of the remaining elements of foreign intelligence collection and the machinery of government that would oversee the tasks. SIGINT, limited as it may have been, had achieved some very clear successes during the war. The degree of success for other foreign intelligence activities was more ambivalent, although this did not detract from the intensity of debate that surrounded the question of their postwar structure.

8
Postwar Intelligence Structures

Preparations for Canada's postwar foreign intelligence architecture, apart from SIGINT, did not begin until almost the end of 1945 – that is, sometime after discussions on the future of the Examination Unit were well underway. Postwar foreign intelligence architecture was not a high policy priority. Wartime foreign intelligence activity, other than that associated with SIGINT, had been very limited and often fraught with problems and inefficiencies. Actually initiating a discussion of what would exist after hostilities ceased was a positive reflection on intelligence.

Discussions on the framework for postwar foreign intelligence were launched by a March 1944 call by senior civil servants to place all intelligence policy authority and guidance with the prime minister (and secretary of state for External Affairs), the Minister of National Defence, and the acting president of the National Research Council (NRC), which was host to the Examination Unit. With the war ending, the civil servants were relinquishing powers they had exercised by proxy. This initiative may have signalled a new orientation but accomplished little else at the time.[1]

Organizing for a postwar intelligence structure got underway with a September 1945 Canadian Joint Intelligence Committee (CJIC) proposal to the Chiefs of Staff Committee calling for the creation of a joint coordinating bureau of intelligence as a central agency, and inviting assistance and participation by other government departments. The proposal acknowledged a need for foreign intelligence, but tied this to scientific research and the acquisition of ethnographic, topographic, social, and industrial information. The proposed bureau was to acquire intelligence relating to the war potential of foreign countries, to analyze and correlate the information, and to disseminate such intelligence to policy makers as necessary.[2] The proposal also circulated within the DEA with a suggestion that a coordinating bureau of intelligence be jointly responsible to the Chiefs of the Staff Committee and to the under-secretary of state for External Affairs. The bureau would be a government agency under civilian direction and financed by a secret vote. There was uncertainty whether the RCMP, as home to the security intelligence organization, wanted to be tied to the bureau, or whether Ultra intelligence should be included, something favoured by the CJIC, but on which officers at the DEA were ambivalent.[3]

The architect of the proposal was probably Dr. Diamond Jenness, the DND's chief of the inter-service topographical section, who wanted to save the resource he had developed during the war. Jenness had sought an earlier partnership with the DEA, suggesting to Glazebrook that it seek the co-operation of the Chiefs of Staff to permit the inter-service topographical section to expand and serve as a topographical centre for other government departments.[4] The inter-service topographical section had been formed in 1944 by the Chiefs of Staff as an extension of the Naval Photographic Library and some minor similar units, and was a repository of topographical, geographical, and economic information available to all the armed services.[5] Although modelled on the British inter-service topographical section and the US JANIS organization, it had no topographical research capability and was largely a library of 1,000 books, some 100,000 photographs, and 4,000 maps of foreign countries, plus a further 10,000 maps in a separate RCAF collection.[6] Although such an establishment played an important in intelligence gathering by providing operational information to armed forces operating in unfamiliar environments, the thrust was distant from political intelligence and unlikely to benefit the DEA.

The proposal for a joint coordinating bureau of intelligence had merit and governed debate on foreign intelligence for the remainder of the year. Interdepartmental negotiations reshaped the ideas in a search for a formula acceptable to the key intelligence departments. The idea of such a unit was still in play in November when Glazebrook proposed to Wrong, in charge of the DEA during the absence of Norman Robertson in San Francisco, that the DEA support the concept but insist that the director be an officer from the department, and that the deputy director come from either a civilian or service department. The focus of the bureau would be to collect, assess, and disseminate intelligence relating to war plans and preparations for war by foreign states.[7]

The DND followed one month later with an expanded and more comprehensive vision of postwar foreign intelligence activities prepared by Lieutenant General Charles Foulkes, Chief of the General Staff. Born in England, Foulkes had joined the militia after briefly attending university and had transferred to the Canadian permanent force in 1926 where he was still a captain on the outbreak of war in 1939. Foulkes' plan called for the establishment of a national intelligence organization. The DND correctly stressed that Canada would gain access to Allied intelligence only on the basis of reciprocity. Intelligence collecting, Foulkes continued, must be done from a national perspective. He stated, "Any system whereby the appraisal is made from incomplete intelligence acquired from other countries, or the acceptance of another nation's appraisal insofar as it relates to itself, can not possibly satisfy the Canadian requirement. Such a system would presuppose a degree of political, economic and military dependence incommensurate with the national outlook."[8]

Foulkes believed that the government must make the most efficient use of the intelligence resources already existing in departments, but it must also resolve the problem of departments approaching foreign intelligence from their own spheres of interest. This could be overcome through liaison officers in the departments or, Foulkes' preferred option, through a joint coordinating bureau to examine and appraise intelligence and be responsible for its dissemination to all interested parties.

Whether "Canada should enter the field of active secret intelligence [clandestine HUMINT collection] is a matter of high policy," on which the DND paper did not elaborate. Foulkes' proposal, a reasonable blueprint for a Canadian postwar intelligence organization, concluded with a recommendation that a joint coordinating bureau of intelligence be responsible to the secretary of state for External Affairs.[9] Although Foulkes' plan reached the Cabinet Defence Committee the following March, there is no recorded decision on the submission.

Overshadowing the debate on the Foulkes plan was a British proposal that had reached the DEA in November, one month before Foulkes made his proposal. The British Joint Intelligence Committee asked that Canada establish a joint intelligence bureau as part of an interconnected string of Commonwealth units for the evaluation and assessment of all-source intelligence:

> We have for some time past been considering the postwar organization of intelligence, which we feel should be set up in the closest possible cooperation with the Dominions and India. Part of our proposals concern the establishment in London of a JIB, which would be a permanent body, mainly civilian, dealing with the overt collection, collation and where appropriate, the appreciation of all intelligence material of inter-service significance ... The main sub-divisions in the London JIB will be: (a) topographical; (b) economic; (c) airfields; (d) defences ... We feel that if similar organizations were set up in Canada and Australia, the most advantageous study of the defence resources and topography of all areas of the world would be assured.[10]

No decision on creating a Canadian joint intelligence bureau was made during the remainder of 1945. However, the British proposal dominated the discussion on a postwar intelligence organization.

In early May, Norman Robertson, the under-secretary of state for External Affairs, presented his view to the Chiefs of Staff Committee on a proposal for a Canadian joint intelligence bureau, in effect setting aside the Foulkes plan.[11] The DND approved the DEA proposal, recognizing that National Defence would be able to gain access to intelligence material that "would be difficult to obtain through the military intelligence organization." Likely, the DND was referring to the intelligence that was regularly gathered by a foreign ministry engaged in economic, political, and multilateral activities, and with an ability to debrief international travellers.[12] Agreement to establish the bureau chaired by an officer from the DEA "to give freedom of access with other government departments"[13] was reached on 14 May at a CJIC meeting, at which time it was also agreed that the CJIC would continue to function as a subcommittee of the Chiefs of Staff Committee.[14]

The head of the Canadian Joint Intelligence Bureau[15] became a member of the CJIC.[16] George Glazebrook assumed the chairmanship of the CJIC on 21 June. Shortly thereafter, the RCMP and the Directorate General of Defence Research (soon to become the Defence Research Board) became full members of the CJIC.[17]

The need for the Canadian Joint Intelligence Bureau to carry out the many tasks associated with intelligence activities had been evident for some time. The CJIC served as a coordinating body, but had neither the staff nor the expertise to carry out intelligence analysis. This failing had made itself dramatically clear by early 1946 when Canada and the United States began their joint assessment of the Soviet threat to North America. The CJIC had been requested by the Canadian Joint Planning Committee "to prepare an appreciation outlining the war potential of Soviet Russia and her ability to embark on a program of aggression, either directly or indirectly, against the North American continent."[18] The report prepared by the CJIC stated that "adequate information concerning Russia is not available through Canadian sources and the appreciation therefore is of little value."[19]

The Canadian Joint Planning Committee pointed out that the failure of the CJIC rested with an absence of intelligence about the Soviet Union, whether obtained directly by Canada or through intelligence sharing with the United States and Britain. The failure of the CJIC served to highlight the lack of resources within the Canadian intelligence community for screening intelligence, classifying and distributing the material, and for foreign intelligence collection. In addition to suggesting strengthening intelligence collection by assigning more service attachés to the task, the Canadian Joint Planning Committee also proposed that the CJIC review the intelligence organization within each of the armed services and present proposals for remedial action.[20] The obvious response was the creation of a dedicated operational intelligence body with the expertise to collect, maintain, and evaluate intelligence whenever it was required by Canadian military and foreign policy decision makers.

Under the direction of the CJIC, the Canadian Joint Intelligence Bureau would be "responsible for the collection, collation, study, and dissemination of certain types of intelligence."[21] It was to use the existing machinery to obtain secret intelligence, and through its own channels gain overt intelligence. The Canadian Joint Intelligence Bureau would be housed with the DND and administered by the Defence Research Board, but guided by a committee also representing "two civil departments."[22]

During the summer, the idea of an officer from the DEA as chairperson of the Canadian Joint Intelligence Bureau evaporated. Why this happened is unclear. During July, each of the armed services proposed one of its own people as a candidate for the position of director. George Glazebrook, who consistently demonstrated a low opinion of the armed forces, recalled that the attitude at the DND was that "the Chiefs of Staff found they were surrounded by retired admirals and generals who all thought this would be a cushy job."[23] Since each candidate received one vote from his own service, the DEA was placed in the position of casting the deciding ballot. However, none of the service candidates were acceptable. The DEA wrote to the CJIC:

It is the opinion of the Department of External Affairs that the Director of the Joint Intelligence Bureau should possess administrative experience and ability to make contacts with the heads of comparable intelligence organizations and of institutions from which information might be drawn. He would also require a thorough knowledge of the techniques necessary for research. Since the Joint Intelligence Bureau will be organized primarily for the purpose of serving the interests of the Services, the Director should also be a man with some knowledge of the organization of the Services and their special needs.

In the light of these qualifications the informal ballot taken in the Joint Intelligence Committee on the names proposed for the Director of the Joint Intelligence Bureau has been considered in the Department of External Affairs. It is the opinion of this Department that ... [none of the candidates were ideal and] ... that the field may not have been thoroughly canvassed as yet, and that further efforts might be made to discover additional names.[24]

No decision on a director for the Canadian Joint Intelligence Bureau was made for the remainder of 1946. The proposal for the creation of the bureau was sent to the Cabinet Defence Committee on 16 July, 24 July, and 18 September, only to be deferred each time. It was only on 31 January 1947 that the Cabinet Defence Committee finally approved the formation of the Canadian Joint Intelligence Bureau.[25] Triggering the decision of the Cabinet Defence Committee was information from the DEA that the US representative of the joint planners preparing the US-Canada joint defence plans had indicated that there was a requirement for a "compilation of topographical information, in its widest sense, concerning northern Canada." This information was needed if the two countries were successfully to defend North America against an attack by the Soviet Union across the north pole. Thus, the requirement for topographical information of military significance on the Canadian North beyond the limits of settlement provided the catalyst for the creation of the Canadian Joint Intelligence Bureau.[26] Two weeks after authority was granted by the Cabinet Defence Committee to create the bureau, the CJIC proposed that the latter be constituted as the body to coordinate all foreign intelligence for the Chiefs of Staff Committee, in conformity with the CJIC reorganization of July 1946, with formal and broad oversight for many of the elements of the Canadian intelligence community.

Following the decision to establish the Canadian Joint Intelligence Bureau, the inter-service topographical section from the DND was deployed as the nucleus of the bureau. Additional resources were made available as required.[27] The Canadian Joint Intelligence Bureau's first priority was to fulfill the information requirement on Canada's North, as well as on Newfoundland and Labrador, for the Canada-US Basic Security Plan, a task to be completed by 1948. The Department of Mines and Resources, organizing its own geographical bureau, volunteered to assist the Canadian Joint Intelligence Bureau with information, from a non-military perspective, on airfield facilities, rail, road and sea communications, inland waterways, cable and wireless facilities, and a study of the terrain, coast, anchorages, tides, currents, beaches, climate, population, health and sanitation, and natural and manmade resources in the area. Additional information came from the Departments of Transport and Health and Welfare, as well as from provincial governments, the Bureau of Statistics, the Arctic Institute, and the Social Science Research Council.[28] The reports were issued as Canadian Intelligence Surveys and were analogous in design and content to similar surveys prepared by the British Joint Intelligence Bureau and the American Central Intelligence Agency (CIA), itself created only in 1947.[29]

Even before a decision to establish the Canadian Joint Intelligence Bureau had been made in the first weeks of 1947, the CJIC proposed the creation of another organization, to be named the Canadian Joint Intelligence Staff, charged with preparing intelligence assessments.[30] The CJIC recommended that resources be identified to create a capacity for preparing coordinated intelligence assessments that could harness the resources of all departments and agencies. The Canadian Joint Intelligence Staff was to reflect the membership of the CJIC and its subordinate staff, but would be a fluid organization, periodically gathering area experts from departments and agencies for the specific purpose of preparing an intelligence evaluation under the guidance of an ad hoc chairperson appointed for the purpose.

In addition, the Canadian Joint Intelligence Staff was to prepare joint strategic intelligence assessments for the Canada-United States Permanent Joint Board on Defence, which could contribute to the annual revisions of the common defence plans for North America. Colonel W.A.B. Anderson, replacing Murray as the director of military intelligence in February 1946, thought it vital that the intelligence basis for the revision of the Joint Hemisphere Defence Plan contain a Canadian contribution, and he proposed a formal link between the Canadian and American Joint Intelligence Committees.[31] During the spring, when joint intelligence appreciations were first put forward, the military still thought that these would be done by the CJIC, which proved to have neither the resources nor the expertise for such work. The first Canadian Joint Intelligence Staff report was a credible fifteen-page assessment of Russian industrial war potential, the strength and role of each of the Red military services, and ice conditions in the Arctic. It concluded that there was no threat of a full-scale air attack against North America in the immediate future, although risks of Soviet mischief existed elsewhere in the world.[32]

In October, Hume Wrong wrote to Lester B. Pearson, incoming undersecretary of state for External Affairs, advising him to look at the postwar intelligence structure and reminding him that Canada had conducted its "most secret operations with the vague general blessing of the Prime Minister and under his authority."[33] Wrong now thought that the newly appointed secretary of state for External Affairs, Louis St. Laurent, would have to sanction the continuing activities and be brought fully into the picture. Wrong stated, "Unless the circle of Ministerial knowledge is widened and we carry the judgment of Mr. St. Laurent and Mr. Abbott [the Minister of National Defence], we shall find ourselves in difficulties that might lead to the cutting off of our receipts from other sources."[34] Wrong did not expand on his statement, but it suggests that intelligence from Canada's allies was provided under an assumption that an intelligence relationship was sanctioned by Canada's senior political leadership. He also gave Pearson an update of the Canadian intelligence community.

George Glazebrook had been chairing meetings of the CJIC since 21 June 1946, and continued to do so until his departure from the DEA late in 1946 to resume his career as a historian at the University of Toronto. At that time, the chairmanship rotated between R.G. Riddell, D.M. Johnson, and Bill Crean, all from the DEA.[35] The absence of a consistent and strong chairperson for the CJIC hindered the creation of robust foreign intelligence institutions. Postwar intelligence policy and activities were being conducted by a series of committees and small units, including the Communications Research Committee, chaired by the DEA, which oversaw the activities of the Communications Branch of the National Research Council (the postwar SIGINT service), the CJIC, the Joint Intelligence Staff, which prepared intelligence appreciations, the Joint Intelligence Bureau, which was not yet functioning, and the security panel set up to deal with all security questions of concern to more than a single department.[36]

The CJIC was now under a more permanent chairmanship of Riddell and efforts were being made to raise the level of what had hitherto been an ineffective body. The committee lacked the resources and skills to operate as an intelligence organization. The DEA hoped that the creation of the Canadian Joint Intelligence Bureau would establish a resource for conducting intelligence research while appreciations, or intelligence assessments, prepared by the Joint Intelligence Staff would give the CJIC something meaningful to consider.

The immediate challenge facing the Canadian foreign intelligence community in early 1947 was leadership of the Canadian Joint Intelligence Bureau. The Chiefs of Staff wanted the bureau to proceed, although they were concerned that the poor performance of the CJIC jeopardized success.[37] Too much CJIC time was spent on procedural and organizational matters, and few resources were devoted to the consideration of intelligence. Having established and partly manned the Canadian Joint Intelligence Bureau, the CJIC still experienced difficulty in identifying a candidate with the skills and availability to direct the new organization. The matter had been discussed with the head of the British Joint Intelligence Bureau, General Kenneth Strong, General Dwight Eisenhower's wartime intelligence chief, who was anxious to have a functional Canadian organization with which to collaborate. Strong offered to lend Canada someone to head the Canadian Joint Intelligence Bureau.[38] The CJIC declined the British offer and eventually settled on Lieutenant Colonel G.W. Rowley of the DND's Directorate General of Defence Research. Appointed in an acting capacity, Rowley was unpopular with the navy, which complained that he was a geographer with no intelligence experience, who leaned too heavily on the Department of Mines and Resources' geographical bureau, and who was unlikely to focus on the foreign intelligence function of the Canadian Joint Intelligence Bureau.[39] Unable to identify and gain broad support of a strong constituency within the armed services, Rowley faced an uphill battle but remained the acting director of bureau until the summer of 1948, when he tendered his resignation.

The Canadian Joint Intelligence Bureau collected and collated a great deal of intelligence from open sources as well as from diplomatic and intelligence sources. Once a month, a "Summary of Intelligence on J.I.B. Subjects Received from Canadian Sources" was circulated among readers in Ottawa. No distribution list has survived but the readership may be presumed to have included senior mandarins at the DEA in addition to appropriate divisional officers, the Chiefs of Staff and other senior armed services personnel, and selected other officials at the Privy Council Office and departments with particular interest in an issue. The topics covered in the "Summary" tended to focus on economic and social infrastructure. Only a small number were geopolitical in nature. There was little differentiation in coverage between Soviet bloc adversaries and the soon-to-be NATO allies.[40]

The Canadian Joint Intelligence Bureau sought funding of $107,000 for its first year, about half of which was for salaries. Authority was also requested to staff twenty-four positions, half officers and half support personnel; several of the officer positions were initially filled by personnel from the geographical bureau of the Department of Mines and Resources.[41] The organization was never envisaged as large, and probably never amounted to more than seventy-five people. By 1950, the total staff complement stood at nineteen research officers, ten technical officers, and thirteen support staff.[42] The Canadian Joint Intelligence Bureau was effective, and if one can gauge its value by a single indicator, it is worth noting that it produced eleven intelligence appreciations (intelligence assessments of between fifty and one hundred pages or more in length) during the period between January 1949 and January 1951, a respectable output.[43] Some other reports, of less significant length, were also prepared.

Although under the policy direction of the CJIC, the Canadian Joint Intelligence Bureau was housed with the Defence Research Board for administrative purposes, in part because the latter enjoyed a secret vote (unvouchered funds that did not appear in the annual budget). However, it was not long before the Defence Research Board balked at this arrangement. After a year of administrative responsibility for the Canadian Joint Intelligence Bureau, the board complained to the CJIC that the situation was untenable, and proposed that it be relieved of its administrative responsibility or that it assume full authority for the Canadian Joint Intelligence Bureau.[44] Military members of the CJIC reacted negatively to the recommendation. Colonel W.A.B. Anderson, the director of military intelligence, pointed out that coordination of foreign intelligence was vested in the CJIC; the Canadian Joint Intelligence Bureau had been created to "assume responsibility for all Intelligence work in such fields as could be demonstrated to be common to more than one agency."[45] Since intelligence work remained within the responsibilities of the service directorates and the DEA, which Anderson argued constituted the CJIC, the latter remained responsible for the Canadian Joint Intelligence Bureau.[46] The squabbling continued as no short-term solution was found.

Sensing the discord and lack of direction confronting the Canadian Joint Intelligence Bureau, the Chiefs of Staff Committee took the opportunity on 1 June 1948 to restate the tasks and organization of the Canadian Joint Intelligence Bureau. The duties were fourfold:

A. To collect and collate the information required for defence purposes on Canada, Newfoundland (including Labrador), St. Pierre and Miquelon to meet the requirements of the Strategic Information Appendix to the Canada-US Basic Security Plan.

B. To provide, in greater detail than the Canadian Intelligence Surveys, the
   basic information necessary for planning the movement of forces by sea,
   land and air in Canada and adjacent territory ...
C. To collect, collate and provide information on the topography, communications, economic and industrial war potential of foreign countries as
   required by the various intelligence and planning staffs.
D. To exploit all available Canadian sources of overt information on foreign countries, not already under the control of the other Intelligence
   Agencies.[47]

The Chiefs of Staff also reiterated that the Defence Research Board remained
responsible for the administration of the Canadian Joint Intelligence Bureau.

Although Rowley's resignation occurred three days after the restatement
of the Canadian Joint Intelligence Bureau responsibilities, the two events
were not related.[48] Rowley had been uncomfortable for some time with the
lack of support he received and decided independently to retire.[49] Each of
the armed services proposed its own candidate as his successor. By this time,
however, the DEA was losing patience with the prolonged organizational
struggles of the unit, and by October 1948, George Glazebrook, the former
DEA officer, agreed to have his name considered for appointment as director of the Canadian Joint Intelligence Bureau.[50]

Glazebrook had resumed his academic career with the history department
at the University of Toronto in 1946, but had lost his zest for teaching.
Moreover, he had given up a lucrative fellowship because of his many trips
to Ottawa to deal with loose ends in the wartime intelligence world. In
early December 1948, the Minister of National Defence, and at the time
also acting secretary of state for External Affairs, wrote the president of the
University of Toronto pleading national urgency in seeking the release of
Glazebrook from his university duties.[51] Glazebrook was willing to assume
the directorship of the Canadian Joint Intelligence Bureau if he had a free
hand without interference from the Defence Research Board. To bolster a
more independent position, Glazebrook returned to the DEA but then attached himself to the DND as director of the Canadian Joint Intelligence
Bureau.[52] While he wanted to cement the relationship between the DEA
and the Canadian Joint Intelligence Bureau, and was nominally under the
authority of the CJIC, he retained doubts about the durability of the bureau
and sought the security of his old department, which offered the assurance
that he could resume conventional diplomatic work should he wish.[53]

Glazebrook assumed his new duties as director of the Canadian Joint
Intelligence Bureau in January 1949 and it was at this time the bureau
began to function.[54] Very quickly, Glazebrook divided the bureau into two
divisions, one being an economic division he headed. This unit did intelligence assessments, received and integrated material made available from

the Communications Branch of the National Research Council, and disseminated the evaluations to key clients in Ottawa.[55] The second unit was a topographic division representing much of the inter-services topographical section that had been bequeathed to the Canadian Joint Intelligence Bureau. This division was under the direction of Ivor Bowen, who had been released by the British Joint Intelligence Bureau for secondment to Canada in February 1948. A prewar assistant lecturer of geography at University College, Exeter, Bowen had spent the war in the British military intelligence service and had joined the British Joint Intelligence Bureau upon demobilization.[56]

During his tenure at the Canadian Joint Intelligence Bureau, Glazebrook acted with a great deal of autonomy and often independently of the CJIC. He had earlier been chairman of the CJIC and it was now led by his former subordinate, Bill Crean. The duties assigned by the Chiefs of Staff Committee to the Canadian Joint Intelligence Bureau in June 1948 had been general in nature. In March 1949, after Glazebrook's arrival, these were made more specific by a request from the secretary of the Cabinet Defence Committee for the Canadian Joint Intelligence Bureau to provide information for a study on the "vital points in Canada" (i.e., potential threats to critical infrastructure), a plan for economic warfare, and some early efforts on psychological warfare with particular reference to economic shortages.[57]

The Canadian Joint Intelligence Bureau recorded an increase in requests for material on foreign countries, including those countries that constituted the North Atlantic Treaty nations.[58] By the spring of 1949, the bureau's major task was providing information on the economic war potential of foreign countries; the Soviet Union and its satellites formed the first priority and the "countries of the Atlantic community or countries on the periphery of the Soviet sphere of influence ... and Argentina" formed the second tier.[59] The areas of interest focused on general information, including manpower, finance, and economic mobilization capability, food production and supply, fuels and power, mining and metallurgy, chemical industry, and armaments and engineering.[60] At about this time, Canadian missions abroad began to receive specific requests for information from the Canadian Joint Intelligence Bureau to meet its intelligence requirements.[61]

As mentioned earlier, before Glazebrook's appointment as head of the Canadian Joint Intelligence Bureau, another small foreign intelligence unit had been proposed under the authority of the CJIC to collect, research, evaluate and disseminate all foreign intelligence on foreign countries required by Canada, and to prepare strategic intelligence assessments, reports, and research papers. The Chiefs of Staff Committee granted approval in February 1947 for the CJIC to create a full-time Joint Intelligence Staff, manned by a representative from the DEA, the DND's Directorate of Scientific Intelligence, and each of the naval, military, and air intelligence directorates.[62] The idea for the Canadian Joint Intelligence Staff had first been floated in the spring of 1946 as a vehicle for preparing the Canadian contributions to Canada-US strategic intelligence appreciations for the Permanent Joint Board on Defence. Nothing had been done for the remainder of the year as Canada struggled to identify and select the appropriate leadership for the parent CJIC.

The Canadian Joint Intelligence Staff was a "virtual" organization with no physical establishment and the constituent parts coming together only irregularly. The members of the Canadian Joint Intelligence Staff remained in their home organizations but for the most part were relieved of other responsibilities so that they could direct their activities to tasks for the Canadian Joint Intelligence Staff.[63] There was no permanent chairperson, although one was appointed for each research project. A service member of the Canadian Joint Intelligence Staff served as a secretary; the position rotated annually between the army, navy, and air force.[64] The Canadian Joint Intelligence Staff prepared all intelligence assessments required by the CJIC, and recommended subjects to be considered for analysis. For the most part, the first draft of an assessment was prepared by a single member. The document was then reviewed, revised, and approved by other members.[65] The Canadian Joint Intelligence Staff issued a highly classified monthly intelligence review for limited circulation. A more widely distributed version, in a sanitized format with a lower classification, was also prepared.

The early postwar years, when the foreign intelligence units first came into being, constituted a period of dramatic reconfiguration of Canada's foreign policy. Canada's role exceeded the boundaries of its geopolitical and economic power. Canada's views were sought, and influential, in the creation of the United Nations and, later, the North Atlantic Treaty Organization. The DEA was engaged in significant expansion to meet the staffing requirements demanded of the new role Canada was called upon to play internationally. Lester B. Pearson, as the under-secretary of state for External Affairs, refused to assign DEA staff to the Canadian Joint Intelligence Staff if this prevented limited DEA resources from carrying out "studies on matters of primary importance."[66] In a long letter to the Chiefs of Staff, Pearson wrote:

> At the present time there is an acute shortage of trained officers to undertake the work in the Department, and I do not consider that the J.I.S. or the Departmental representative on it could undertake the satisfactory preparation of such a summary [the monthly intelligence review].
>
> I should like to stress that I am most anxious that such a summary should be produced, and that as soon as adequate arrangements have been made in the Department I would propose that the J.I.S. should prepare such a summary ...

I might add that papers commenting on and interpreting political developments of strategic significance will be prepared in the Department from time to time, with such assistance from the J.I.S. as may be required, and these will be available for limited distribution in Ottawa through the J.I.S.

I am arranging to provide the J.I.S. with copies of telegrams and despatches on political and economic matters so that the members may be kept up to date on current developments.[67]

In spite of refusing to be an active partner in the Canadian Joint Intelligence Staff, the DEA had no qualms about calling on them at the beginning of 1948, when Canada was elected to a seat on the UN Security Council, to prepare a long list of studies on topics expected to occupy the Canadian delegation during its tenure. Prior to January 1948, the Canadian Joint Intelligence Staff had prepared only two studies for the DEA. For the remainder of 1948, there was a steady flow of demands for reports on the capabilities, aims, and strategies of the Soviet Union, and appreciations on the Near and Middle East, Western Europe, the Far East, Palestine, Germany, Greece, Trieste, Turkey, Iran, China, and Japan.[68] The Canadian Joint Intelligence Staff succeeded in accommodating the unexpected demands.

Very few of the actual intelligence assessments prepared by the Canadian Joint Intelligence Bureau for approval by the CJIC are declassified. One of the few accessible reports is a twenty-five page analysis of Yugoslavia prepared in 1950 to assess the possibility of a Soviet or Soviet-assisted attack by 1952. A comprehensive evaluation, the report reviewed Yugoslav relations with the Soviet Union and its satellites, as well as with the West. It also assessed the country's economic resources, transportation infrastructure, and airfield and defence resources, and evaluated deficiencies that if addressed would permit Yugoslavia to successfully withstand an attack.[69]

With the outbreak of war in Korea in 1950, the Canadian Joint Intelligence Staff was charged with preparing a morning situation account based on the DEA reporting telegrams, signals available to the three service directorates of intelligence, and media coverage.[70] The reports ran two to three pages in length, and covered ground, naval, and air forces. A political segment was intermittently included, detailing events in the UN Security Council, the capture of a Russian air force lieutenant, or Canadian decisions on participation in the war. The contents were not derived from intelligence material but, rather, reflected military theatre reporting and normal diplomatic reporting. No political analysis or socio-economic information was detailed in the reports.[71]

An agreement between the CJIC and US Military Intelligence for the joint preparation of intelligence assessments for the Canada-US Basic Security Plan had been the catalyst for creating the Canadian Joint Intelligence Bureau. This original task went on to include American-British-Canadian intelligence appreciations. On 19 December 1945, the Cabinet decided that a Canadian planning team would meet with an American counterpart to form the Joint Canadian-United States Military Co-operation Committee for the purpose of revising ABC-22, the joint basic security plan.[72] From the preparation of the joint basic security plan grew the Canadian annual estimates of the Soviet threat to North America. The CJIC was tasked with "preparing an appreciation as to possible forms and scales of attack against Canada which would be amplification of the joint appreciation agreed upon by the Canadian-U.S. Committee."[73] The study concluded that the Soviet Union was the only conceivable enemy but that no large-scale attack was likely before 1950, after which point attacks of a more serious nature were possible.[74]

However, the initial Canadian effort concluded that there was a lack of intelligence about Russia, that little such intelligence was available from Canada's allies, and there was a lack of adequate intelligence staff to use available information effectively.[75] Nevertheless, the 1946 appreciation received only minor adjustment in 1947, while the 1948 appreciation was completely redone.[76] That last report was finished on 8 December 1948, having been begun already in April. Over 100 pages in length and projecting from 1949 to 1956, it was an extensive study of Soviet resources, capabilities, and intentions based on economic, political, and military factors. The major conclusion was that the Soviet Union "would not be capable of attacking Canada and the United States by conventional bombing throughout the period."[77] Nevertheless, there were obviously differences of interpretation that dogged the joint assessment exercise. A Canadian evaluation at the midpoint of the drafting states that the Americans believed that Soviet air attacks "would no longer be 'of limited strength,' whereas we [Canada] have no intelligence which indicates an increased enemy capability in this regard."[78] Canadian draft assessments drew conclusions from the available intelligence, projecting only what was supported by empirical evidence. Some American defence assessments introduced speculative material from which inferences were drawn, resulting in support for known policy direction. In a discussion of the final 1948 report by the CJIC in early 1949, there was evident Canadian concern that the Americans had proposed a marked increase in the Soviet strategic air force and attendant ability to attack North America by a factor of two and a half times the initial estimate of B-29 type aircraft (Tu-4 was the Soviet copy), and that Canada "was not prepared to accept these figures until confirmation was available."[79] No documents highlight any resolution of what may have been the beginnings of the "bomber gap."

While Canada and the United States were drafting their appreciation on the Soviet threat to North America, the British and Americans were similarly preparing an agreed intelligence evaluation of Soviet intentions and capabilities, which was concluded on 10 November 1948 and ran to about

200 pages.[80] The following year, Canada joined Britain and the United States in their preparation of a common evaluation of Soviet intentions and capabilities for 1950.[81] The decision to include Canada was probably a last-minute ruling, since the invitation was received on 1 September 1949, the Canadian Joint Intelligence Staff personnel were heading to Washington on 10 September, and the report was finished on 27 September.[82] Running over 100 pages, this assessment highlighted a divergence of analysis. The United States was of the view that if war occurred it could begin with little or no warning, while the British and Canadians estimated that armed conflict with no notice, while possible, was unlikely without necessary preparatory action by the Kremlin that would be evident to the West. Canada sought and received inclusion of "an estimate of the forms and scales of attack against North American in relation to attacks elsewhere."[83]

American interpretations often ascribed greater power to the Soviet Union than subsequent historical evidence supports. Britain and Canada seemed more dependent on hard facts in reaching their evaluations. The more pessimistic US defence assessments probably stemmed from two factors: assessments that supported demands for enhanced military resources were career supportive, and US analysts were reluctant to underestimate the potential enemy who might one day be confronted on the battlefield.

The invitation for Canada to join the British and Americans in the 1949 assessment of the Soviet threat had come shortly after finishing a Canadian-American estimate of the Soviet threat to North America, looking forward to 1957.[84] The report followed the format of earlier Canada-US reports but was significantly rewritten and probably longer (the core report was a third longer, and the appendices have not been released). While the conclusions did not significantly differ from the report of the previous year, Canada remained concerned with American perceptions of Soviet long-range bombers. The air threat had been magnified by the Americans, who claimed that Soviet bombers could use air refuelling to attack North America (and return home), although there was no specific evidence to support this possibility. In addition, the Americans envisioned a B-36 type Soviet bomber by 1957 with a range of 10,000 miles, which would threaten Newfoundland, Florida, and California. The joint assessment simply concluded that a B-36 type Soviet bomber was a possibility.[85]

The Canada-US assessment had anticipated a Soviet atomic test by mid-1950, while the later American-British-Canadian threat assessment managed to be surprised by the 1949 successful Soviet nuclear explosion. A paragraph was quickly added, stating that the Soviet Union would have no more than ten atomic bombs by the beginning of 1950.[86] Both studies were immediately outdated and a six-month study was launched in Canada (similar activities took place in Britain and the United States) to assess the new threat. The Canadian study was tasked with "a determination of targets in

Canada which the Soviet leaders may consider suitable for atomic attack and an estimation of the effect which the elimination of these targets by atomic bombs would have on the ability of Canada to wage war."[87]

During April and May 1950, Canadian and American intelligence staff met in Washington to determine the Soviet atomic threats to North America by mid-1951 and mid-1954.[88] The American side was not prepared to discuss worldwide implications of Soviet atomic power, although the Canadians attempted to include in their draft the implications for Soviet military commitments elsewhere in the world. The length of the Washington meeting was the result of excellent preparatory work by the Canadian Joint Intelligence Staff, which made "it harder for the Americans to achieve an easy acceptance of many of their points of view."[89] Acrimony also arose over a Canadian refusal to accept the US proposed draft. The Americans were invited to London for a similar Anglo-American review the following June, but declined an American-British-Canadian conference on the subject.[90]

Meanwhile, at the Canadian Joint Intelligence Bureau, George Glazebrook continued to build up the organization, and DEA officials often sought him out at a time when demands for the bureau's services were increasing with Canada's growing international stature. By November 1949, less than a year after he had assumed responsibility for the Canadian Joint Intelligence Bureau, Glazebrook felt confident enough to report to the Chiefs of Staff Committee on the bureau's progress. For the last half of the year, the incoming intelligence reaching the Canadian Joint Intelligence Bureau had doubled from the beginning of the year. Much of it was Canadian, originating primarily with the Departments of External Affairs and Trade and Commerce, though some came from defence attachés and additional material was produced by the Department of Finance, the Department of Mines and Resources, and the Bank of Canada. Some Canadian commercial firms, particularly those with developed representation abroad, agreed to pass information to the Canadian Joint Intelligence Bureau.[91] It should be underscored that the information originating from sources other than the foreign service departments was overtly collected economic and socio-political information. Intelligence material also reached the Canadian Joint Intelligence Bureau from its British counterpart, the British Joint Intelligence Bureau, with which close relations existed.

The bulk of the work of the Canadian Joint Intelligence Bureau was carried out on behalf of the DND. The Canadian Joint Intelligence Bureau responded to requests for information from the three service directorates of intelligence, but also worked for the Cabinet Secretariat, the DEA, and the Department of Mines and Resources.[92] Both Ivor Bowen and George Glazebrook had been lent to the Canadian Joint Intelligence Bureau for two years. On 1 January 1950, Glazebrook returned to the DEA, and Bowen was asked to become acting director of the Canadian Joint Intelligence Bureau; he was confirmed in the position on 1 July.[93] With a permanent appointment as director of Canadian Joint Intelligence Bureau, Bowen resigned from the British service.

From its inception, the Canadian Joint Intelligence Bureau was expected to maintain intelligence exchanges and liaison arrangements with corresponding intelligence organizations in the United States and the United Kingdom. In a practice dated back to at least the 1930s, the United Kingdom made available to Canada various intelligence reports, and it was decided in 1950 to assign an officer from the Canadian Joint Intelligence Bureau to London to act as a liaison officer to British intelligence. However, formal intelligence assessments shared by the British Joint Intelligence Committee were forwarded to the CJIC, rather than to the Canadian Joint Intelligence Bureau.[94]

A relationship with the newly created US CIA was also sought, although there were no links between the Canadian Joint Intelligence Bureau and the CIA during the first year of the bureau's existence.[95] The American National Security Act of 1947 established the CIA as an independent agency within the Executive Office of the President.[96] The earliest substantive contact between the Canadian intelligence community and the CIA dated to the first month of 1949 when Bill Crean, then chairman of the CJIC, met with CIA director Rear Admiral R.H. Hillenkoetter in Kingston to discuss placing a CIA liaison officer in Ottawa. Hillenkoetter stated, "Such a position was of benefit to both of our organizations."[97] Some contact may have preceded this meeting since already on 1 June 1948 the Chiefs of Staff Committee had authorized "the Joint Intelligence Bureau ... to establish liaison with the Central Intelligence Agency in the U.S.A. for the exchange of pertinent information within the Joint Intelligence Bureau field."[98] Exchanges of letters, some visits, and further discussions continued for more than a year, though there was little progress in the relationship. James Angleton, the CIA's counter-intelligence chief, accompanied by Colonel Schow, visited Ottawa in June 1949 at the initiative of Hillenkoetter to discuss liaison links with the CJIC.[99] Their visit was inconclusive, since the CIA wanted Canadian assistance in the counter-intelligence field, while the CJIC was interested in exchanging primarily economic and scientific intelligence.[100]

In early 1951, the relationship between the Canadian intelligence community and the CIA began to blossom, following Lieutenant General Charles Foulkes' visit to Lieutenant General Walter Bedell Smith, the director of the CIA. Foulkes met Bedell Smith at the request of the CJIC to discuss liaison arrangements and because a "close link existed between the Central Intelligence Agency and the U.K. Joint Intelligence Bureau and the Central Intelligence Agency was anxious that this link should be broadened to include Canada."[101]

The CIA invited Canadian representatives to Washington, where agency studies were made available as long as "their use [was] confined to military purposes."[102] The Canadian Joint Intelligence Bureau (and the DND's Directorate of Scientific Intelligence) began an intelligence exchange with the CIA that became particularly close following a visit to Washington in April by the director of the Canadian Joint Intelligence Bureau.[103] From this meeting emerged a Canadian decision to send to the CIA as many as possible of its CJIC papers, which were prepared by the Canadian Joint Intelligence Bureau and the Canadian Joint Intelligence Staff. Only those relating to Canadian policy toward other countries were exempted. At the same time, Canada increased the flow of Canadian intelligence assessments to the British intelligence community.[104]

The relationship between Canadian intelligence units and the CIA was not always smooth, and by 1952 the CIA was complaining that Canada was not pulling its weight, being "the poorest contributor of all those collaborating with the CIA."[105] It is difficult on the basis of incomplete archival material to draw firm conclusions about CIA allegations of insufficient Canadian effort in foreign intelligence collection. During the period from its creation in 1947 to the early 1950s, the CIA had expanded at a phenomenal rate and conducted an aggressive collection that included active measures (e.g., infiltrating large numbers of expatriates as agents into eastern Europe), many of which were often dramatic failures. Canadian intelligence collection focused on obtaining information, not necessarily covertly, that might inform policy. This approach was viewed by the CIA as cautious (it was) and not conforming to the aggressive confrontation of the Soviet foe. In reality, Canada was doing less in intelligence collection than its international role warranted, but its cautious approach met limited perceived Canadian needs and did not include the failures often associated with the more assertive CIA approach.

The CIA pushed Canada to become more aggressive in debriefing individuals in possession of information of intelligence value.[106] In June 1952, Foulkes informed the CIA of a new overt HUMINT collection initiative that was under consideration and that would exploit the knowledge and expertise of refugees and travellers with access to information of intelligence value.[107] The following year, the Canadian Joint Intelligence Bureau established the Interview Program, a non-clandestine HUMINT collection organization. Although by the late 1940s the Canadian Joint Intelligence Bureau had begun limited debriefing of travellers, it required American intervention to formalize the program.[108]

An exchange of intelligence between the Canadian Joint Intelligence Bureau and the Australian Joint Intelligence Bureau began in 1951, but it was limited for a number of years. The intelligence exchange with the New Zealand Joint Intelligence Bureau did not commence until the mid-1950s.[109]

No direct exchange of political intelligence between the DEA and any American intelligence agency existed during the late 1940s. Some discussions with the Office of Intelligence and Research of the US State Department had taken place to develop an intelligence flow, but these talks did not produce results until some time later.[110]

The rudiments of a foreign intelligence structure were defined and functioning well by the end of the decade, albeit with little entrenched political support. An internal dialogue on the country's intelligence capabilities and requirements was initiated in the summer of 1949.[111] A paper called "Canadian Intelligence Requirements," prepared by George Glazebrook, R.G. Riddell, Colonel W.A.B. Anderson, and Bill Crean,[112] initiated the process and stated: "In the widest sense, the requirements of intelligence by the Canadian Government embrace any aspect of foreign affairs in which the Government may from time to time be interested. Such requirements include both the intelligence required for the production of appreciations on strategic problems and relationships, and the intelligence required by the Services and certain of the civilian departments of government for the successful discharge of their day-to-day responsibilities."[113]

Intelligence was required for strategic political appreciations to meet four specific needs:

1 Assessment of political intentions and capabilities;
2 War potential and preparations for war;
3 Strategic plans and capabilities;
4 Vulnerability to direct attack or indirect pressure.[114]

Canada was dependent on intelligence from the United Kingdom and the United States that was "derived from various sources and of great value,"[115] but to depend entirely on foreign intelligence provided by others had consequences:

1 It would make impossible the exchange of intelligence ... Even a small quantity of intelligence supplied from original Canadian sources – provided that the quality is high – allows for a free exchange[.]
2 It would, in those matters which are of particular Canadian interest, make it difficult to provide appreciations [intelligence analysis] suited to the nature and scope of the interest.
3 [It would] reduce the possibility of creating a Canadian intelligence structure sufficiently experienced and rounded as to operate adequately under all emergencies.[116]

Canada's intelligence allies were unlikely to continue a flow of intelligence without a corresponding Canadian contribution of intelligence, and an over-dependence on the intelligence of others constricted independent choices and hampered sound policy decisions. While Canada's foreign policy making required intelligence assessments, "it does not follow that these appreciations must be based wholly on intelligence acquired from Canadian sources."[117] Information from Allied intelligence services was welcomed for augmenting and enhancing Canadian intelligence assessments.

But Canada was becoming dependent on the United States and the United Kingdom for an increasing amount of its foreign intelligence with a potential impact on independent action. At the heart of the debate were two questions: "(a) Is the Canadian intelligence organization, at home and abroad, adequate for the purposes defined above? (b) If not, what alterations or additions are necessary?"[118]

No answers to these key questions were available. The following September, Crean prepared an extensive report on the Canadian intelligence community for Arnold Heeney, who had become the under-secretary of state for External Affairs in March 1949.[119] Crean said that the DEA had two main interests in assuming a dominant role in policy relating to foreign intelligence:

a   The formation of sound foreign policy depends in large measure upon the amount and accuracy of intelligence available to the Department. Not only do we require political intelligence from our missions abroad, but also all political intelligence which can be made available from secret sources. In addition we require strategic intelligence, which can be provided by the [C.]J.I.C. While strategic considerations may often be discarded on political grounds, it is important to take them into account in forming foreign policy. Prior to the creation of the [C.]J.I.C. in its present form, a mechanism for producing collated strategic intelligence did not exist in Ottawa. Increasing use should be made of the [C.]J.I.C. for this purpose.

b   The conduct of our relations with intelligence agencies in other countries, must be kept in line with government policy toward the governments of those countries. It is thus desirable for External Affairs officers to take a leading part in negotiations and talks with such authorities. In the past four years, this has been important in working out relations with G.C.H.Q., S.I.S., the US Sigint authorities, and the US and UK Joint Intelligence Committees.[120]

Crean thought three challenges confronted the organization of foreign intelligence within the DEA. The first of these was the "S.I.S. problem," meaning that the DEA did not possess the qualified staff to evaluate the intelligence obtained from the British Secret Intelligence Service with which the department co-operated closely in overseas intelligence operations, and for which it provided protection for defectors requiring resettlement.[121] Linked with this was the need for staff to collate and disseminate the foreign intelligence that reached the DEA. The second challenge concerned counter-espionage and security intelligence. The final challenge was the inadequacy of security arrangements at Canadian missions abroad.[122]

Crean contended that the staff of the Defence Liaison Division was insufficient for the work; the department's foreign intelligence interests, intelligence liaison duties, security responsibilities, and the chairing of both the Communications Research Committee and CJIC overwhelmed the two individuals available for the tasks. An External Affairs officer was Chairman of the CJIC, Crean continued to Heeney, but

> the Chairman must be freed so far as possible from the detail of departmental duties, if he is to discharge his responsibilities to the Committee [CJIC] and to the Chiefs of Staff [at National Defence]. At the same time he must retain responsibility for his own Division in the Department in order to be fully informed of all important developments in international affairs. Under these circumstances, and with the present staffing of the Defence Liaison Division, the Head of the Division cannot possibly discharge adequately his functions as Chairman, J.I.C.[123]

The DEA's Defence Liaison Division, with responsibility for defence relations and foreign intelligence, had been established only in November 1948 as part of the administrative reforms introduced by Lester B. Pearson when he became secretary of state. Bill Crean's initiative led to the Defence Liaison Division being split into two separate divisions in 1950, one remaining responsible for bilateral and multilateral defence policy matters, and the second being exclusively tied to security and intelligence matters. The two new divisions retained the existing name but became designated 1 and 2, or DL(1), for defence matters, and DL(2) for security and intelligence affairs.[124] However, few additional resources were made available to meet the demands.

The idea of establishing a clandestine HUMINT collection service must have circulated within the Canadian intelligence community in the late 1940s, although very little related archival material has become available. The British likely urged Canada to expand its activities to include clandestine intelligence gathering, a capability the British helped the Australians develop at about this time.[125] During the spring of 1947, Canada considered drawing on the knowledge and expertise of William Stephenson, the Canadian-born head of the British Security Coordination (BSC) who had been responsible in New York for all British security and intelligence activities in the western hemisphere for most of the Second World War.

Stephenson's operation had wound up in 1945, although he continued to live much of the time in New York.[126]

No decision on creating a covert foreign intelligence unit had been made by Canada when George Glazebrook, now back at the DEA, proposed to Arnold Heeney in October 1951 that the department explore the establishment of a clandestine HUMINT service, and "examine in what way such a service is a unique provider of intelligence, how it might benefit the Government of Canada, and how such a service could be established and operated."[127] The organization would be under the authority of the DEA and the intelligence collected could provide insight into the thinking of another country that would not otherwise be available. Glazebrook feared that Canada was unlikely to have continued access to Allied HUMINT if it did not also collect and exchange this type of information. His initiative called for a modest organization with a defined geographic focus, just sufficient for Canada to be acknowledged by its intelligence partners to be engaged in HUMINT collection. However, with little tradition or involvement in and political commitment to intelligence matters, Canada followed the path of least resistance and did nothing. No action was taken on Glazebrook's proposal and Canada did not establish a clandestine HUMINT service. Glazebrook said later that the proposal was turned down for the perennial Canadian reason of a shortage of officers.[128]

By 1951, Canada had established strong intelligence links with British and American intelligence agencies extending beyond the realm of SIGINT, and the Allies sought Canadian engagement in HUMINT collection but the government would have none of it. The decision to forgo a covert HUMINT capability ultimately defined perceptions of Canada's foreign intelligence community among its intelligence allies.

There matters rested at the end of a tumultuous decade. The postwar intelligence machinery that governed the non-SIGINT side of foreign intelligence was in place. Canada had established or redefined three separate organizations (the CJIC, the Canadian Joint Intelligence Bureau, and the Canadian Joint Intelligence Staff) to perform distinct facets of the intelligence tasks, but without a clandestine HUMINT organization. While this organizational base strongly influenced the postwar structure of foreign intelligence in Canada, it was a structure built under adversity and formulated to address specific challenges with minimal resources. Nevertheless, by the end of the decade, Canada had a credible foreign intelligence infrastructure that, while organizationally cumbersome, hierarchical, and resource intensive, was functional and met the needs for which it had been constructed.

In the summer of 1945, Igor Gouzenko, the Russian cipher clerk in Ottawa, defected to Canada, although news of the event was not leaked to the media until the following year. One would assume that this event influenced the Canadian debate on the creation of postwar intelligence structures. It did not. The Gouzenko story is almost entirely absent from the debate on Canadian postwar foreign intelligence. While the Soviet Union figured prominently in Canadian foreign intelligence interests, it was not an exclusive focus. The available evidence suggests that Canada had broad foreign intelligence interests that reflected current Canadian foreign policy interests.

The postwar architecture for many of the foreign intelligence units was not ideal. The decisions made at that time have influenced the path of Canada's foreign intelligence collection until the present day. The same was not true for postwar SIGINT. In this field Canada flourished, albeit within the limiting confines of Canadian resources and capabilities. At the core of Canadian SIGINT effectiveness were the bonds forged with the wartime Allied SIGINT partners. While never a major player in the Anglo-Saxon SIGINT community, Canada was a player nevertheless.

9
The Postwar SIGINT Community

Signals intelligence was Canada's premier postwar foreign intelligence collection tool. Canada's wartime accomplishments in SIGINT were significant, given the available resources, and the value of the service was acknowledged. Nevertheless, the decision to continue SIGINT collection after the war had been in doubt in the closing months of 1945. Finally, a decision was made on 29 December 1945 to form a civilian SIGINT service that would continue to operate in peacetime.[1] An order-in-council[2] authorizing SIGINT collection was signed on 13 April[3] of the following year, and the new organization became operational on 3 September as the Communications Branch of the National Research Council (CBNRC).[4] As suggested by the name of the organization, the Canadian SIGINT service continued to be housed with the National Research Council (NRC).

The remainder of 1946 was spent making the new structure fully operational. The CBNRC was divided into four main units: communications, cryptanalysis, intelligence, and administration. The cryptanalysis unit would focus on Europe, the Far East, and South America. The prime decryption assignments were in French, Spanish, and Chinese; only the latter represented a departure from wartime interests.[5]

The newly created CBNRC had authority to staff an initial 179 positions.[6] The existing sixty-two staff members of the Communications Research Centre were transferred to the NRC to form the nucleus.[7] This figure grew to nearly 100 people by the end of 1947.[8] In spite of not yet having reached its full staff allotment, the CBNRC was authorized an additional forty-eight positions in 1947 for a total of 227 staff. However, it was not until 1949 that the CBNRC even reached the original staffing level of 179 positions.[9] From there, the CBNRC grew slowly but steadily until it reached a staff of 470 people by 1954.[10] This was not many people given the complexities and resource demands of SIGINT collection. The many hundreds of intercept collectors who were DND service personnel must be added to the number of CBNRC staff. Nevertheless, the staff resources are indicative of the limits of Canadian SIGINT capacity during this period.

By the late 1940s, the staffing levels included twenty-three people in the communications section and seventy-four people in cryptanalysis; just over half were directed at European targets (French and Spanish languages). A further seventy-eight staff members were dedicated to research, intelligence (analysis), cipher making, and various administrative duties.[11] This number of staff inexplicably adds up to only 175 positions, four short of what was authorized and supposedly on staff.

Annual salaries for staff in the new organization ranged from $5,400 for the director to $1,140 for laboratory assistants.[12] As in the past, Canada had to import some of the cryptographic expertise. Four individuals were brought from the United Kingdom to assist the new CBNRC, including Kevin O'Neill, who eventually headed the organization during the 1970s and oversaw the writing of the classified multivolume *History of CBNRC* after he retired.[13]

One of the topics that had been discussed at the Commonwealth SIGINT conference of Britain and the dominions in February-March 1946 in London was the transmission of special intelligence material between the partners. The wartime radio station Hydra, established by the British Security Coordination (BSC) in New York at Camp X near Oshawa during the war to link London, Ottawa, and Washington, still existed, although its future was in doubt. The British were ready to hand over the Oshawa facility to Canada at no cost, and Norman Robertson, the under-secretary of state for External Affairs, recommended to Prime Minister King that Canada take over Hydra "because it would seem more suitable that it should be a Canadian rather than a United Kingdom installation, and also because it would enable us to make an acceptable contribution to a field in which both London and Washington are continuing to give us valuable assistance on information."[14] Robertson went on to explain that the DND was prepared to operate Hydra.

Robertson's recommendation proved astute by establishing Canada as an important communications hub between the three principal partners, and creating for Canada a more significant role than the country's limited expertise and resources in cryptography warranted. Probably without this intent in mind, Robertson cemented Canada's intelligence partnership with its allies by assuming an important communications task. The prime minister's response was probably verbal, since no record of it has been found. A handwritten notation from a prime ministerial aide advising that the latter had returned the document without any written comment was appended to Robertson's recommendation to Mackenzie King.[15]

However, the prime minister must have assented to the recommendation because on 19 October 1946, the DEA told Sir Edward Travis of the British Government Code and Cipher School, via the Canadian High Commission in London, to proceed with the transfer of Hydra to Canadian government ownership.[16] Hume Wrong had written to warn Lester B. Pearson, in Washington but soon returning to Ottawa to assume the position of under-secretary of state for External Affairs, that the matter of Hydra was one of the issues he would face upon his return.[17] The transfer of Hydra to Canada took place in April 1947, but the station did not reach its full communications capacity until 1948 (partly due to the expansion in the number of British and Canadian users requiring encryption employing Rockex cipher equipment).[18]

Upgraded equipment had to be put in place, while the landlines continued to be cost-shared between Canada and the United States, as had been the case during the war.[19] The DEA had been eager for Canada to take over Hydra since ownership represented a substantial contribution to the postwar SIGINT effort, ensured continued Canadian access to the highly classified decrypted Ultra traffic from the Allies, and provided the department with an extremely secure communications facility for its own message traffic with London and Washington.[20] The cost of operating Hydra as a high-level secure communications link between London-Ottawa-Washington at an annual expense of $90,000 (plus $150,000 for new equipment) was not justified by the size and needs of the Canadian intelligence community. However, Hydra made Canada a communications hub for Ultra traffic between the three countries. In addition, some costs were offset by a British proposal to send 75 percent of its communications traffic with its embassy in Washington via Hydra.[21]

A triumvirate of senior staff managed the CBNRC during the early days. All had had wartime experience either with the Examination Unit or with the Joint Discrimination Unit (and its predecessors). At the helm was E.M. Drake, the former head of the military's Joint Discrimination Unit, by now a civilian, who as director of the CBNRC concentrated on administration and security. A second individual, whose name has never been made public, headed operations and plans as the assistant technical director. The third member of the triumvirate was Mary Oliver, who was officially the administrative assistant and, incidentally, was the sister of Norman Robertson, the under-secretary of state for External Affairs. She was principally occupied with personnel matters, assisted by a number of young women she trained and directed. She had had much the same responsibilities with the Examination Unit during the war.[22] It was to her that many of the tasks of identifying and selecting staff fell, although final decisions were normally made by Drake. These three were the architects of the CBNRC. C.J. Mackenzie, who had played such an important role in the creation of the Examination Unit in 1941, remained as president of the NRC until early 1952. After overseeing the conversion of Canada's wartime SIGINT units into the CBNRC, Mackenzie tended to treat the organization "with an attitude of benevolent neglect."[23]

The NRC had already been home to the Examination Unit and was familiar with the purpose and goals of a SIGINT collection organization. The budget for the CBNRC was easily concealed within the larger budget of the NRC. A greater, immediate challenge was camouflaging money for the initial cost of the intercept stations and the 100 intercept positions (i.e., work stations, not staff). The capital costs (the physical plant and equipment) would run to just over $1 million, although that figure quickly grew to $3 million, a substantial amount when converted to current values. Lester B. Pearson sought C.J. Mackenzie's assistance in hiding the funding for the intercept stations within the NRC.[24] Mackenzie was cool toward the proposal, suggesting that the NRC was a civilian agency and that the intercept stations, staffed by military personnel, were unlikely to be perceived as conventional research facilities. Mackenzie proposed that the money for the intercept stations (not for the CBNRC, per se) be placed with the Defence Research Board, which would be a more credible and defensible location for the funds, and was also an organization that was expected to have funding for secret research. Indeed, the funding was eventually placed with the Defence Research Board.[25]

A cover story for the CBNRC was developed in February 1947, and obscured the clandestine nature of SIGINT operation by focusing on the defensive nature of some of its activities. After some initial debate, a public line was agreed upon, which read, "It will be realized that most of the Government and Service authorities in Canada have security means whereby they could exchange confidential messages internally or with external authorities. To preserve the security aspects of such communications some form of ciphering or encoding devices are used. It is the duty of this Branch [CBNRC] to analyze such devices from a security point of view and recommend improvements where need be to ensure that the devices are safe to use."[26]

Overseeing the operations of the CBNRC was the Communications Research Committee, which, under a chairman from the DEA, held its first meeting on 20 June 1946.[27] Its mandate was to guide the SIGINT effort. A technical steering committee was also formed in April 1947.[28] A more senior policy-directing body was created in November 1948, under the undersecretary of state for External Affairs, and included participants of corresponding rank from other departments. Initially called the Senior Committee, it was later renamed the Communications Security Board.[29] George Glazebrook disdainfully dismissed this board, stating that "it hardly ever met [and] we didn't want it to meet."[30] When queried about his strong stance, Glazebrook added that, "Because they didn't know enough about it [SIGINT collection] and were liable to be a nusicence [sic] they were called only occasionally and they had this committee because the British had a similar one."[31] Glazebrook's recollections ignore the imposed checks and balances, represented by the Communications Security Board, that were built into the oversight of the CBNRC through different levels of increasingly senior managing committees that framed policy and may have provided advice on operational objectives.

In 1947, the CBNRC assumed control of cryptographic keying material, the means of coding of communications. Prior to that time, both the DEA and the DND services had made use of cost-free ciphering material supplied by the United Kingdom. Of course, this did not ensure confidentiality for Canadian enciphered communications.[32] At the Commonwealth SIGINT conference in London in February-March 1946, the British had asked Canada, Australia, and New Zealand to develop their own cipher requirements.[33] When the CBNRC was established, it had been specifically stipulated that one of its functions was to assume responsibility for Canada's code and cipher requirements.[34] Nevertheless, as late as October 1946, no agreement had been reached as to what Canadian government authority would have responsibility for cipher security policy,[35] and it was two years later, in June 1948, before the Communications Security Board was established as a subcommittee of the Communications Research Committee to set communications security policy. Some initial conflicts arose with the DND, which sought an autonomous committee that "would not have to include intelligence representatives" for formulating policy regarding the production and security of ciphers.[36] The conflict appears to have been resolved by the end of the decade. The first Canadian-made One Time Key Tape (i.e., the encryption coding tape for the Rockex secure communications equipment) became available in September 1948.[37]

The CBNRC was initially located at the LaSalle Academy on Guigues Street in downtown Ottawa. However, space was at a premium and the steady growth of the CBNRC required that new facilities be found. A move followed in late 1949 to the former psychiatric ward of the Rideau Military Hospital on Alta Vista Drive in Ottawa.[38] The CBNRC remained at this last location until November 1956.[39]

With the establishment of the CBNRC, the armed forces were called upon to man the collection sites. The army provided forty intercept positions staffed by some 100 personnel. The station in Vancouver had twenty-five of the positions, while the rest were located in Ottawa. Because of the shortage of qualified staff to meet all of the personnel requirements, former Department of Transport operators and others were taken on as civilians as an interim measure. At this time, the army was still operating stations in Grande Prairie and Victoria. However, it is unclear whether these were meant to close shortly after CBNRC was established.[40]

The navy was also accorded forty positions to be located at Coverdale, New Brunswick (twenty), Churchill, Manitoba (thirteen), and Prince Rupert, British Columbia (seven). Coverdale already existed but had only four positions operating, while authority to build the Churchill station had not yet been granted. The existing wartime facility at Churchill was only an iono-spheric station. Only Prince Rupert was operating at full capacity.[41] The RCAF was asked to man twenty positions, all to be located at a station near Whitehorse, Yukon. At the point the request was made, there was no authority to establish the Whitehorse station and no operators were available for deployment.[42]

By the end of the decade, and notwithstanding a slow Canadian start in establishing and manning intercept stations, intercept facilities had been built up in Churchill (1950); Aklavik, Northwest Territories (1949); Coverdale (since 1941); Fort Chimo, Quebec (1949); Vancouver-Victoria, British Columbia (1942); and Whitehorse, Yukon (1948).[43] By the 1950s, extending beyond the period covered by this study, there were additional stations at Frobisher Bay on Baffin Island; Gander, Newfoundland; Masset, British Columbia; Alert, Northwest Territories; and Ladner, British Columbia.[44] Later intercept sites were also established at Inuvik, Northwest Territories; Bermuda; Flin Flon, Manitoba; and likely others. Some stations were also closed over the years. The focus on stations in the north of Canada reflected Canada's intercept responsibility for Soviet air force and air defence communications.

The resources initially authorized for the CBNRC were only slightly dif-ferent from what had been projected for a postwar SIGINT collection estab-lishment while the Second World War still raged. In August 1944, the armed forces had assumed that three army and three navy intercept stations would be required to operate a SIGINT collection program after the end of hostili-ties.[45] When expanding upon the 1944 document two years later, and in preparation for making the CBNRC operational, Drake stated that a sound appreciation of the resource requirements for peacetime SIGINT monitor-ing was entirely dependant on what the Canadian collection requirements would be. Drake suggested that the Canadian priorities ought to be:

1 Interception of commercial transmitters for P/L and code traffic – auto-matic high speed.
2 Interception of Service traffic (foreign Navy, Military and Air Force traf-fic) – high and hand speeds.
3 Interception of clandestine traffic – hand speeds.[46]

In peacetime, Drake envisaged the greatest collection resource would be foreign high-speed commercial transmitters; the diplomatic traffic on com-mercial lines would be the most critical.

Following his attendance at the Commonwealth SIGINT conference in London from 22 February to 8 March 1946, Drake modified some of his pro-posals to accord with the co-operative agreement reached between British, Canadian, Australian, New Zealand, and Indian SIGINT authorities.[47] The 1946 conference recommended "that Canada should supply 100 intercept positions 35 of which should be located on the East Coast and 65 on the West Coast."[48] The focus of the Canadian effort was to be on Russian, Western European, Chinese and Asiatic, search and development, and illicit international targets, as well as some minor South American targets. Apart from acting as intercept stations, the Commonwealth partners would maintain a direction-finding network with worldwide, interconnected stations operating in the United Kingdom, Gibraltar, Malta, Cyprus, India, Ceylon, the Cocos Islands, Hong Kong, Fiji, Canada, Bermuda, and Sierra Leone.[49]

Canada's participation in a SIGINT alliance with the United States, the United Kingdom, Australia, and New Zealand provided Canada with significant access to SIGINT. The alliance, many of the details of which are still murky after more than fifty years, bound the partners together through a series of bilateral and multilateral agreements to provide communications intercept coverage of much of the world. Each partner had access to all, or at least most, of the collected material while making a contribution commensurate with its individual abilities and resources.

Neither the Government of Canada nor those of the other members of the alliance have provided details of the agreements that govern the postwar SIGINT collection activities, nor have they released or avowed the applicable treaties. Nevertheless, it is possible to reconstruct some of what occurred during the late 1940s relating to forging the intelligence alliance. However, the formal beginning of the alliance admittedly remains very much in the shadows.

Prior to launching formal talks for postwar SIGINT co-operation between Britain and the United States, Sir Edward Travis had paid a visit to Ottawa in October 1945. He urged that a British-Canadian cryptanalytic agreement be reached to allow Britain to speak for Canada in talks with the United States. The Americans, learning shortly thereafter about the British-Canadian agreement, objected to the idea. Because of "Canada's strategic position with respect to the United States and Russia, [the Americans] believed that all consideration of U.S. intelligence relations with that nation should be made independently."[50] At a Commonwealth ministers' conference in London during April and May 1946, both Canada and Australia argued successfully for greater latitude in managing their respective national intelligence efforts, including negotiating their own bilateral cryptologic agreements with the Americans.[51] There is no record of any Canadian perceptions of lacking a voice in discussions that must have been recognized even at the time as being very important. Whatever the Canadian position and argument may have been behind the scene, the outcome was that Britain spoke for Canada and the other senior Commonwealth states during the British-American talks that followed in 1946, but the Americans did not delay in initiating talks with Canada, the result of which was the CANUSA Agreement.

The creation of the alliance benefited from fortuitous circumstances that built confidence among the partners and underscored the value of continued co-operation. The wartime alliance of the United States and the United Kingdom was the foundation. Forged by the needs of the moment and bound by a common heritage, it was natural that Britain and the United States began an exceptional intelligence relationship in the Second World War. The old Commonwealth nations, particularly Canada, were easily subsumed within the alliance.[52] While the wartime alliance provided the foundation and confidence on which the postwar relationship was built, it was this conference between the British and the Americans that provided the catalyst for much of what followed.

The unifying theme of mutual dependence brought the wartime Anglo-Saxon partners together to forge a strong intelligence alliance. Fiscal austerity and the unprecedented perceived enormity of the threat from the Soviet Union made it clear that no single member of the future Anglo-Saxon alliance was capable by itself of allotting the resources necessary to provide intelligence coverage of the Soviet Union and its allies so as to fully meet the potential threat and requirements of national needs.[53]

The 1946 conference in London grew from talks that had begun in the spring of 1945. The initiative came from the British who, in spite of their "undoubted brilliance in cryptanalysis, realised that it would be they who would need partners and not the other way around."[54] The head of the British Government Code and Cipher School, Sir Edward Travis, was the moving force for a postwar relationship with the Americans. He initially saw the co-operative agreements as being limited to SIGINT, although with time the relationships came to encompass sharing a broad range of intelligence products.

The environment in which these events occurred should be recalled. Britain had already somewhat scaled back its postwar intelligence community, and Canada had only just concluded that it would indeed continue with SIGINT. The US Army Signal Security Agency and the navy's Op-20-G had had 36,500 personnel at the end of the war and were down to 7,000 by mid-1946.[55] The Americans had also dismantled the Office of Strategic Services and only just created the Central Intelligence Group on 22 January 1946, as an interim intelligence-gathering entity while internal politics coalesced around an intelligence vision for the future. The CIA was not established until June 1947. There was a general feeling in the United States, Britain, and Canada that the conclusion of hostilities would return the victors to traditional parochial interests and mark an end to SIGINT co-operation.[56] It was the emerging perceived threat from the Soviet Union that provided the motivation for continuing wartime intelligence co-operation into the postwar era.

At the time of the Travis' visit to discuss postwar SIGINT co-operation, the United States was already taking steps toward returning to a prewar position of withdrawal from global affairs; it took a presidential directive and an allusion to "possible hostile intentions of foreign nations ... [to] authorize continuation of collaboration between the United States and the United Kingdom in the field of communications intelligence."[57] What emerged from the British-American talks was the 1946 British-United States Communications Intelligence Agreement (BRUSA), which was successfully concluded during the last week of January 1946. However, the twenty-five-page agreement wasn't signed until 5 March 1946, in London.[58]

The UKUSA Agreement, also known as the UKUSA Security Agreement or UKUSA COMINT Agreement, is said to have followed in June 1948.[59] There is still some confusion over this. Some sources cite 1947 as the year in which it came into force, while more current sources list 1948 as the year in which the UKUSA Agreement entered into being.[60] The June 1948 UKUSA Agreement is said to have formally added Canada, Australia, and New Zealand to the 1946 BRUSA Agreement, but retained Britain as the dominant partner among the Commonwealth members.[61] Britain is supposed to have again signed on behalf of the Commonwealth members.

No reference to the existence of a UKUSA Agreement has actually been found in the documentation released to archives by the US National Security Agency. Matthew Aid, an American historian who has researched this period in considerable detail, is of the view that there may not be any formal UKUSA Agreement. The negotiations over cryptologic co-operation between Britain and the United States, which followed the signing of the 1946 BRUSA Agreement, continued in London throughout 1946, including the June UKUSA Technical Conference to finalize some technical details. This was followed by the negotiation of supplementary agreements governing the security and collection of communications intelligence (COMINT, which encompasses all facets of electronic intelligence collection) and other aspects of British-American co-operation. These technical clarifications were added as appendices to the core BRUSA Agreement. Nearly two years of negotiations, updates, revisions, and clarifications were required to articulate the detailed cryptologic co-operation between Britain and the United States. In Aid's view, these extensive negotiations have mistakenly been identified as a UKUSA Agreement.[62] In his book *For the President's Eyes Only*, Christopher Andrew acknowledges that the BRUSA Agreement was followed by two years of negotiations, which clarified the agreement, but concludes that the culmination was a separate UKUSA Agreement in 1948.[63]

The expansion of the agreement, whether as a more detailed BRUSA Agreement or as a separate UKUSA Agreement, provided for a division of responsibilities among the Allies. An early postwar British Joint Intelligence

Committee paper called "Sigint Intelligence Requirements – 1948" lists fifty-two collection priorities, forty-five of which relate to the Soviet Union.[64] Each of the partners was given primary responsibility for SIGINT collection in a specific part of the world commensurate with its location and capability; Canada looked after the Russian polar regions.[65] In addition to the northernmost regions of the Soviet Union, Canada was also given responsibility for SIGINT collection on parts of northern Europe and the Far East.[66]

As early as 1948, the SIGINT co-operation between the Anglo-Saxon nations had evolved to such an extent that a senior US intelligence official could write, "At the present time, there is complete interchange of communications intelligence between the cognisant United States and British [i.e., Commonwealth] agencies. It is not believed that the present arrangement on the interchange of this information could be improved."[67]

While little information has become available on the details of Canada's SIGINT mission, the limited accessible resources and the demands of transforming the wartime organizations into the new CBNRC served to confine what could be achieved. To this must be added the communications security role of the CBNRC – that is, the protection and securing of Canada's own official communications. Nevertheless, one of the CBNRC histories records that in August 1946 "the workload was not high."[68]

Following the 1946 London conference, talks continued between the principal intelligence partners. In 1947, the Commonwealth Sigint Organization Agreement, at British instigation, was concluded among the Commonwealth partners.[69] Somewhere between 1946 and 1948, Canada seems to have found an independent voice with which to represent its national intelligence interests. While no details of the CANUSA Agreement have been made public, it has been suggested that it is modelled on the BRUSA Agreement, although the terms of the relationship are more confined and the exchanges are limited to a "need to know" basis. An American official related at the time that "the Canadians have no information to exchange."[70] CANUSA governed all Canadian-American co-operation on COMINT, which was defined as comprising "all processes involved in the collection, production and dissemination of information derived from the communications of countries other than the U.S.A., the British Empire, and the British Commonwealth of Nations."[71] Negotiations between the United States and Canada began in early 1948 to establish a comparable agreement to the 1946 BRUSA Agreement between Britain and the United States. The resulting agreement between Canada and the United States has sometimes been said to have concluded on 15 September 1950 through an exchange of letters giving formal acknowledgment of the "Security Agreement Between Canada and the United States of America"[72]; an Arrangement for Exchange of Information between the United States, the United Kingdom, and Canada followed two months later.[73] The 1950 date for the agreement is not supported in accessible Canadian archival documents.

Agreements already existed among Britain, Canada, and Australia through the Commonwealth SIGINT Organization Agreement of 1947 when Canada and the United States commenced bilateral discussion. By May 1948, a draft of the CANUSA Agreement had been concluded between the US Communications Intelligence Board and the Canadian Communications Research Committee; it governed the exchange of COMINT translations and traffic between the two countries, taking into account the much more limited resources of Canada.[74]

The Canada-US negotiations continued throughout the summer of 1948, then recessed for half a year while the extended detailed appendices to the BRUSA Agreement were concluded. Negotiations resumed in December 1948 with the Americans stating that they were in a much better position to pursue definite discussions. Talks continued for most of 1949, culminating in a conference in November-December 1949 that ended with the signing of the CANUSA COMINT Agreement.[75]

Following closely on the CANUSA Agreement was another Canadian-US SIGINT agreement, concluded in 1950, which established a Canadian-American naval high-frequency direction-finding net.[76] There likely were similar additional specialized agreements signed during this period, traces of which have not yet emerged in publicly accessible archives.

Notwithstanding a less than fully sovereign stance on some postwar intelligence negotiations, Canada took an early initiative that cemented its role as a key member of the alliance. We have already seen that Canada decided early in the postwar period to assume responsibility from the British for Hydra, the wartime communications station at Camp X near Oshawa that linked London–Ottawa–New York–Washington. The British, who had managed the station but did not have the funds to ensure its postwar continuance, welcomed the Canadian initiative. Lester B. Pearson summed up the significance of Hydra in a letter to C.J. Mackenzie at the NRC:

> The chief purpose of the link is for trans-Atlantic communication, which will link the London Signal Intelligence authorities with the United States Communications Authorities and ourselves. Its chief purpose is to carry traffic from the intercept stations in its raw form and to make for ease of handling and speed at the various centres. In addition, it will carry Foreign Office traffic to Washington and External Affairs traffic to the U.K. The Oshawa station is, therefore, an important link in the general signals intelligence network and is of vital importance to the United Kingdom and the United States, as for political reasons they do not want to pass the traffic direct.[77]

This decision seems to signal that Canada was aware of its subservient role in some aspects of intelligence negotiations and sought avenues for articulating a national position.

Canada's SIGINT collection activity, both during the war and in the decades that followed, remained a closely held secret. British and American SIGINT activities, and other facets of their foreign intelligence collection programs, became known in the postwar world partly as the successes of the Second World War emerged and as some of the more egregious intelligence failures of the postwar world reached the media. However, little attention was paid to anything Canada might be doing in collaboration with the significant international intelligence players.

While Canada's involvement in postwar SIGINT activity was a natural outgrowth of all that had gone before, it came as a surprise to the Canadian public when the existence of the CBNRC and its close relationship to the Allied services were revealed on the CBC's *The Fifth Estate* television magazine, which aired on 9 January 1974. Questions followed in the House of Commons, but there was no government admission that Canada carried out SIGINT activities in co-operation with other countries.[78]

Details of the secret relationships slowly emerged. A 1995 government statement before a House of Commons committee provided the first public acknowledgment that Canada was engaged in "the collection of foreign signals intelligence," an activity that was carried out in co-operation with the SIGINT agencies of the United States, the United Kingdom, Australia, and New Zealand, and was founded in "international agreements, which ... date back to the Second World War."[79]

The postwar SIGINT alliance emerged from fortuitous circumstances. Wartime collaboration, which had proven highly beneficial to all the partners, was the foundation of the co-operative agreements. The perceived postwar threat from the Soviet Union to all the partners in the alliance, and the recognition that none of the countries could fulfill the information requirements by themselves, was the catalyst to co-operation. During the period of this study, the alliance proved mutually beneficial in spite of unequal contributions. The resources that were eventually harnessed for the task proved gargantuan, as were the collection resources. In the decades that followed, well beyond the scope of this study, the Anglo-Saxon countries established at least 420 intercept stations worldwide operated by the member states, plus an additional twenty-seven stations manned by third-party members (Denmark, Norway, and Germany) to the alliance.[80] The SIGINT alliance, in which Canada was a small but significant cog, proved to be a boon for Canadian sovereign intelligence needs by providing a steady flow of independently produced foreign intelligence vital to the country's foreign-policy-making process.

Outside of the postwar intelligence alliance, with limited resources and facing gargantuan technological challenges that could only be overcome by the senior alliance partners, Canada could not have established a credible SIGINT organization capable of addressing the national needs. Details of Canada's contribution to the alliance during these early years have never been made public, but one can presume that it was limited and represented only a fraction of the SIGINT material to which reciprocal access was gained. SIGINT, as well as other intelligence products, provided Canada with significant benefits in the form of information with which to inform the foreign-policy-making process. Intelligence could provide insights not normally attainable through the conventional diplomatic process. Similarly, intelligence could confirm or validate information that did become available through diplomatic channels. By making available separate sources of information on issues of vital importance to Canada's foreign policy interests, intelligence served to articulate a more secure international role for Canada by allowing confident decision making.

Conclusion

Canada's foreign intelligence community, which was established during the Second World War and in the immediate years thereafter, is a testimony to the vision, determination, and hard work of a relatively small number of individuals centred primarily in the Departments of External Affairs and National Defence. These individuals recognized the need for Canada to have access to foreign intelligence to complement information more overtly collected by the country's small diplomatic service.

As the world approached war in the late 1930s, Canadian civil servants, mostly military officers or diplomats, sought to draw attention to the need for access to foreign intelligence collected by Canada to meet national requirements and provide a sovereign source of information with a uniquely Canadian perspective. This was to augment intelligence traditionally provided by the British services to the dominions. The determination of those engaged in building the nation's foreign intelligence tools, during the war and in the years thereafter, never wavered, although they did not always agree or share a single vision of what the country needed, what it could afford, and where limited resources should be focused.

While they might have differed and bickered over the details surrounding the creation of Canada's foreign intelligence community, there was little argument over the broad framework chosen for the nation's foreign intelligence structure. The mandarins at the DEA, such as Robertson, Pearson, Heeney, Glazebrook, Stone, and Crean, constituted a common thread of experience and vision that, with others at the DND, such as Foulkes, Murray, Drake, and de Marbois, surmounted any "fragmentation" that arose from the understaffed units that constituted the Canadian intelligence community. While debate existed and could be dramatic, the broad perspective of Canada's foreign intelligence requirements remained a unifying theme transcending divergent views.

Canada's political leadership did not intimately participate in building the country's foreign intelligence tools. The political leadership was not ignorant of what was happening but willingly delegated to civil servants a broad mandate for managing things relating to foreign intelligence. During the war years, the involvement of political leaders in intelligence matters surfaced intermittently in the archival records as testimony to their awareness and broad support for action taken in their name. Both the prime minister (who was also his own secretary of state for External Affairs) and the Minister of National Defence provided guidance or sanctioned intelligence-related activities at critical junctures. For example, Mackenzie King clearly knew and approved of the Examination Unit, located at one point next door to his own residence, and regularly read Canadian and Allied SIGINT material. As stated earlier, many examples have found their way into the Mackenzie King files at Library and Archives Canada. Similarly, the Minister of National Defence made a critical intervention when the British sought authority to establish Camp X in Canada.

While Canada's politicians may have been kept apprised of the establishment of the nation's intelligence resources during the war period, they remained distant from the details of the effort. Canada's political leadership demonstrated no discernible interest in the manner in which intelligence policy was being formulated. Nor did the nation's political leaders articulate a clear vision of what sort of intelligence architecture was required and to what extent a foreign intelligence collection capacity should be developed. These were regrettable omissions. The political leadership seemingly followed the advice of senior civil servants and rarely questioned the ad hoc evolution of Canada's foreign intelligence activities. Foreign intelligence collection may at its simplest be merely a tool contributing to the foreign-policy-making process. However, intelligence activities are fraught with potential political danger, and it was an abrogation of their responsibilities for Canada's political leadership to divorce themselves from the daily involvement of an undertaking with a risk for abuse and adverse political and public attention arising from mistakes. That such things did not occur does not diminish the responsibilities of the politicians but does speak well of the civil servants, largely in the DEA and DND, who assumed daily responsibility for establishing Canada's modest intelligence effort.

The outcome of a minimalist approach to building a Canadian foreign intelligence capability may have been the same whether the process had significantly engaged the attention of political leaders during the critical war years or, as was the case, it remained in the hands of civil servants. Funding was ultimately the key to the scope of any intelligence effort and defined what was done. Nevertheless, the remoteness of much of the political leadership from foreign intelligence matters during the wartime years contributed to the absence of a foreign intelligence culture in Canada and public disinterest in the subject matter until recently.

Foreign intelligence units evolved incrementally and in a manner responsive to changing circumstance in Canada from about 1940 to 1951, and probably continued in much the same way for some years thereafter. The results were testimony to the work of a very small number of individuals, many of whom were engaged in intelligence activities only as a minor peripheral element to their normal duties. Most of the individuals charged with overseeing Canada's foreign intelligence activities often carried out these duties as secondary tasks to broader responsibilities. The officers at the DEA often had a host of other responsibilities unrelated to intelligence. The same is true of the intelligence staff at the DND, whose primary duties were to support the Chiefs of Staff.

To understand the absence of Canadian political leaders from issues pertaining to intelligence matters, one must recognize Canada's very limited engagement in foreign intelligence. Little was done before the Second World War with respect to foreign intelligence, and some of what was done was conducted on behalf of the United Kingdom. With a very small DEA and limited foreign policy objectives, the need for foreign intelligence before the Second World War was not significant.

During the Second World War, intelligence was but one minor element in the broader conduct of a war in which Canada played a moderate role. Canada's intelligence activities were complementary to the more significant intelligence tasks of its allies. Furthermore, there was no culture of intelligence in Canada, meaning that intelligence was largely unknown in the country before the war, something that did not significantly change during the rest of the 1940s. In Britain, and even in the United States, political leaders were more aware of the potential use and benefit of foreign intelligence. The media had provided some coverage of the subject in those countries, and intelligence had often been a factor in Britain's imperial policy. In the United States, Herbert Yardley, who went on to play a role in Canada's own intelligence history, publicly disclosed the existence of the American "Black Chamber," the country's SIGINT organization, drawing the ire of the American intelligence establishment with important repercussions when he was employed by Canada. In Canada, little coverage of or attention to intelligence matters existed beyond the subject of security intelligence, the purview of the RCMP at the time, and often this was viewed simply as a police matter.

By 1945, the attitude in Canada toward intelligence had evolved. The world was no longer at war. There was uncertainty about whether Canada should continue to collect foreign intelligence. A dramatic shift in attitude toward foreign intelligence occurred at the DEA. Long a champion of foreign intelligence collection, as were individuals at the DND, the constituency within the department for such activities suddenly and temporarily evaporated. This merely underscores the absence of a clear interdepartmental vision of what foreign intelligence collection should be. An ardent supporter of foreign intelligence and a key participant in its collection, the DND was for some time the lone but determined voice calling for the continuance of a Canadian foreign intelligence program.

By the end of 1945 and after a dark period of uncertainty, the DEA again favoured a foreign intelligence capability for Canada. In the structures that were debated during the closing period of the Second World War and put in place in the years that followed, the DEA played a pivotal role by often assuming the chairmanship of the institutions that were created.

Mackenzie King's government did not spend money idly, and Canada's foreign intelligence activities were ruled by the credo of doing just enough to ensure engagement with Canada's partners. One can argue that such an approach was short-sighted. Conversely, one can view the approach as the responsible actions of a small nation that has been provided a singularly unique opportunity and must scrounge sufficient resources to harvest the rewards. Those engaged in building a Canadian intelligence community in the early postwar period must have known that they were constructing something that had to be durable and had to remain in place for a long time, if not forever. However, a minimalist approach that made use of several small, inadequately staffed units did not easily accommodate an expansion of responsibilities. This approach was followed because it was British. Although General Foulkes had articulated a different vision, one that was analogous to the model the United States ultimately followed, Canada followed British guidance during this period. The ties to the United Kingdom were still very firm and, frankly, the British were the only ally with substantial intelligence collection experience. Any Canadian shortcomings with the British model arose from the scale with which British institutions were replicated in Canada.

Canada committed just enough resources to gain broad access to collective Allied intelligence. The Canadian contribution to the Allied pool of information was important, but Canada did not independently collect enough intelligence consistently to ensure a unique Canadian perspective on important international questions. Notwithstanding the shortfall in Canadian-produced intelligence, Canada's choice of acquiring access to some Canadian-collected intelligence, and a great deal of Allied intelligence, was a preferable option to an alternative of little or no intelligence. Canadian intelligence analysis might be skewered by insufficient sovereign intelligence, although the risk was similar in conventional diplomatic relations. The prime defence against being unduly influenced by others was always access to sufficient knowledge to gain an understanding of an issue.

In the space of a decade, Canada created a foreign intelligence capability that laid the foundation for its postwar involvement in intelligence matters.

There was much that was not right with the intelligence structures put in place in the postwar period. Foreign intelligence was inadequately funded and seemed hampered by too many small functional units and an abundance of managing committees. However, the continued engagement in foreign intelligence collection in the postwar period reflected a maturing nation.

The achievements of the Canadian intelligence community during the 1940s pale in comparison with those of its senior allies. Canada did not conduct any intelligence activity that altered or significantly influenced the outcome of the war. Nor was the Canadian intelligence contribution ever more than that of a junior partner provided with specific tasks that fed into broader objectives. However, that should not detract from the real accomplishments. During the war, Canada carried out extensive, although not very technically complex, decryption of French (Vichy and Free French) diplomatic traffic, as well as German, Japanese, and Spanish language decryption. The archival documents do not identify which among the decrypted documents were the results of Canada having broken a foreign code and what reflected entry into a foreign code as a result of code breaking initially achieved by an Allied SIGINT organization. During the early years of the Examination Unit, there was certainly considerable overlap in what was carried out by the partners. However, it is very evident that Canada did not possess the ability to decrypt machine-enciphered communications. On the other hand, the French material appears to have been based largely on Canadian decryption, and Canada played a significant role in this area.

Canada also made an important contribution to the intelligence war in the North Atlantic through its direction-finding skills and the beginnings of scientific intercepts that interpreted ionospheric conditions to pinpoint locations of signals. Canada's involvement in the Mousetrap operation in the United States was entirely a support role carried out on behalf of Britain for its broader objectives. More important were the activities of the No. 1 Special Wireless Group, which made a contribution in its own right against the Japanese from its location in Australia. Debriefing Canadian repatriates and analysis of POW correspondence provided a large quantity of important but probably not unique information.

Canada's strength was evident in its analysis of information, even when much of that information was not derived from Canadian sources. The few available wartime evaluations prepared by Herbert Norman's special intelligence section indicate that these were detailed assessments of their subjects, seemingly merging SIGINT material and other material and placing the information in context. The postwar Canadian contributions to the Canada-US assessments of the Soviet threat to North America show dependable analysis of information that avoided the trap of ascribing to the Russians more power and abilities than they possessed. The Canadians consistently questioned American conclusions, though not always successfully, about Soviet resources, particularly the number of bombers that, at the time, posed the greatest potential threat.

While Canadian interpretations of events were influenced by the intelligence provided by its allies, this was probably not more so than the case of any of the partners, including Britain and the United States. Raw intelligence does not contain a national "interpretation." Any interpretive or policy bias is introduced during the analytical phase – and all the partners probably displayed some bias at one time or another. Canadian assessments of events, based on intelligence material available to all the alliance partners, were valued for the perspective they presented. In an industry in which interpretations are determined from sometimes insufficient data, perspectives drawn from different insights, different intuitions, and different past experiences are valued as contributions to understanding of issues. In this respect Canada was not particularly unique, but did make a valuable contribution. More significant perhaps is the question of whether Canada was unduly influenced by its allies by virtue of its high reliance on foreign intelligence that was not Canadian in origin. To some extent this possibly was the case in the sense that analysts within the alliance probably often drew similar conclusions since they had access to virtually the same material – that is, the raw intelligence. Differing conclusions likely arose whenever outside factors like policy determinants influenced intelligence assessments. This certainly seems to have been the case when difference arose during joint Canada-US evaluations of the Soviet threat to North America in the immediate postwar period. Given that many information elements contribute to intelligence assessments, including open-source knowledge of the subject or area, the conclusions drawn by Canadian intelligence analysts were probably as correct as such assessments can be.

Canada's achievement in foreign intelligence matters during the war and in the years that followed was significantly less for the immediate results than for the foundation it laid in providing a resource that could task, collect, collate, evaluate, and disseminate foreign intelligence in sufficient quantity and quality to meet the national requirements. Much of the raw intelligence may not have been Canadian in origin, but the interpretation placed upon it was entirely Canadian and provided an autonomous source of information vital to the foreign-policy-making process.

Notwithstanding that Canada had travelled a long journey in developing a foreign intelligence community, at a time when it was also developing a stronger foreign policy capability, the reality of what Canada had the capacity to produce on its own was very limited. Canada was not and would never be in the same intelligence league as its two senior partners. Canada did succeed in gaining access to many, if not all, the secrets of its allies when its contribution was very limited and, at times, verged on being practically nil. This is evident from the intelligence agreements concluded shortly after the war. One factor in easing Canadian access to the intelligence of its allies was certainly the wartime alliance, when a need for a Canadian contribution was recognized. Another was the British interest in speaking to its American partner as the representative of the senior Commonwealth members. At the same time, the United States had an interest in drawing Canada into its sphere of interest to ensure its own defence. American action at the beginning of the war and earlier, as reflected in the Ogdensburg Agreement, attests to US concerns with having a "safe" northern border. Lastly, since the postwar Anglo-Saxon alliance has lasted for more than half a century, one must conclude that the contributions of the junior partners, Canada, Australia, and New Zealand, have proven their worth. All three countries added value to the alliance by virtue of their geographic placement and political opportunities for collection purposes, and possibly for their individual collation and evaluation of raw intelligence into finished intelligence assessments that informed policy making without being policy proscriptive, something that dogged the two senior alliance members at varying times.

By the early 1950s, the achievements of Canada's foreign intelligence community were significant in providing the country its own voice in this area, and were attributable to the vision and conceptualization of a handful of exceptional individuals. What they accomplished was done quietly, with little public attribution or recognition.

Glossary

Arlington Hall Headquarters of US Army's signals intelligence (SIGINT) service. It was formerly a girls' private school.

Army Security Agency US Army SIGINT organization. Succeeded the Signal Security Agency on 15 September 1945.

British Security Coordination (BSC) Amalgamated British security and intelligence agencies headquartered in New York under William Stephenson ("Intrepid") during the Second World War.

BRUSA Agreement SIGINT agreement between Great Britain and the United States, signed 5 March 1946.

Camp X British special operations training school near Oshawa, Ontario. Camp X was the name used by David Stafford in his study of the camp. The actual name was Special Training School 103 (STS103), the British designation, but it was also known by the Department of External Affairs (DEA) as "The Country House," and by the Department of National Defence (DND) as "S25-1-1," the name of the relevant file.

Canadian Joint Intelligence Committee (CJIC) Created in 1942 by the DND to conduct intelligence studies; in the postwar period, its membership expanded and it became the coordinating body for Canadian foreign intelligence activities.

CANUSA Canadian-United States Intelligence Agreement on SIGINT, concluded in May 1948 but not signed until 1949.

COMINT Communication intelligence. Sometimes used to denote the broad range of technical intelligence gathering. Term came into use during the postwar period.

Combined Intelligence Objectives Subcommittee British and American-led initiative, with Canadian participation, tasked to collect scientific and technical intelligence from the enemy. Initiated in September 1944; lasted till the end of the war.

Commonwealth SIGINT Organization SIGINT agreement between Great Britain, Canada, Australia, and New Zealand, concluded in 1947.

Communications Branch of the National Research Council (CBNRC) Postwar name for Canada's SIGINT collection agency. The name was disclosed by the media in 1974 and the CBNRC became the Communications Security Establishment, the name still in use today.

Communications Research Centre Name given to Canada's postwar SIGINT organization in April 1946. The successor to the Joint Discrimination Unit, the Communications Research Centre eventually became the CBNRC.

Communications Security Board Postwar name of senior committee overseeing SIGINT matters.

Coordinator of Information US intelligence predecessor to the Office of Strategic Services. Existed briefly during the time leading up to American involvement in the war. Headed by William "Wild Bill" Donovan.

Defence Liaison 2 (DL2) Postwar unit within the DEA charged with responsibility for foreign intelligence matters.

Department of External Affairs (DEA) The name of Canada's foreign ministry during the period covered in this study. Today named the Department of Foreign Affairs and International Trade.

Department of National Defence (DND) The Department of National Defence is charged with defending Canadian territory and providing assistance to civil authorities, as required and mandated.

Direction Finding SIGINT activity involving several intercept stations that identify the location of a radio signal by triangulation of intercepts.

Directorate of Military Operations and Intelligence The DND military intelligence unit in the prewar period.

Discrimination Unit Radio signals intercept unit operated by the DND. Created on 12 June 1942, in addition to collecting signals for decryption, it was also involved in direction-finding work and inventory of foreign radio transmitters.

Enigma German encryption machine that became operational before the Second World War. A series of rotors electronically scrambled letters that were typed on the machine, to create an encrypted document.

Examination Unit Canada's SIGINT organization during the Second World War. Established in 1941 under the policy direction of the DEA and housed with the National Research Council (NRC).

Foreign Intelligence Section Canadian naval intelligence unit established in 1939 as a direction-finding signals collector.

Government Code and Cipher School Wartime name of Britain's SIGINT service.

Government Communications Headquarters   Postwar name of Britain's SIGINT service. Succeeded Government Code and Cipher School in June 1946.

HUMINT   Human intelligence; relates to intelligence derived from a human source.

Hydra   A secret Canadian communications installation located at Camp X during and after the Second World War.

Joint Discrimination Unit   Merger of Examination Unit and Discrimination Unit under DND control. Came into being in August 1945.

Joint Intelligence Bureau   Postwar Canadian intelligence unit created in 1947 and tasked with collecting and collating information for defence purposes. Housed with the DND.

Joint Intelligence Committee   See CJIC. British and American JICs also existed; the British JIC continues to this day.

Joint Intelligence Staff   Postwar Canadian intelligence unit created in 1947 and tasked with providing intelligence assessments.

Magic   Code word given to American decryption of Japanese ciphered communications.

Mousetrap   British-Canadian diplomatic and economic intelligence collection program, which operated in Canada and the United States from 1942 to 1943.

National Research Council (NRC)   The National Research Council has been active since 1916 as Canada's national research and development organization.

Office of Strategic Services (OSS)   US wartime intelligence organization headed by William "Wild Bill" Donovan.

Op-20-G   US Navy SIGINT organization.

Privy Council Office   Canadian government department that acts as the administrative arm of the prime minister; often acts as a centralized coordinator of policy. Established during the war.

Purple   Name of Japanese code broken by the United States in 1940. See also **Magic**.

Radio Fingerprinting   See "Z" work.

Secret Intelligence Service   Britain's covert foreign intelligence HUMINT collector. Sometimes known popularly as MI6.

Security Intelligence   Relates to counter-intelligence (catching spies) or, otherwise, protecting the nation (counter-terrorism, counter-insurgency, etc.).

SIGINT   Signals intelligence; information obtained from technical monitoring and interception of signals or communications that travel through the air waves or on telegraphic wires (during the period of study). At its core, SIGINT is the listening to, recording of, and interpretation of electromagnetic signals captured from the air or from taken from wires used to transmit information.

Signal Security Agency US Army SIGINT organization.

Signals Intelligence Service US Army Signals Corps wartime SIGINT agency.

Special Intelligence Section Established within the DEA in September 1942 as the analytical unit that interpreted decrypted SIGINT material and circulated it to a select readership.

Special Operations Executive (SOE) British clandestine service during the Second World War charged with coordination of all action, including subversion and sabotage, in enemy-controlled areas.

Telekrypton Enciphered communication, using hand-punched tapes, which was used by BSC to provide secure communications between Ottawa, New York, and Washington. The first phase was introduced in January 1942. Canada came "on line" in May 1942.

UKUSA Agreement Postwar SIGINT agreement between the United Kingdom and the United States, concluded in 1948. Canada, Australia, and New Zealand became parties to the agreement later.

Ultra Code word given to British decrypted SIGINT derived from breaking German Enigma codes. In the postwar period, it came to be the code word for all SIGINT material among the UKUSA partners.

"Y" Committee Created on 2 June 1942. Lt. Col. W.W. Murray of Army Intelligence was the chairman. Committee oversaw SIGINT (W/T, or Wireless Telegraphy) collection by the three armed services. It was not responsible for cryptographic analysis.

"Y" Discrimination System for collecting data and plotting the locations of enemy radio signals. Direction-finding triangulation, employed to locate other radio transmitters, was called "Y" work, a holdover from the First World War, when it was discovered that three stations homing in on the strongest signal from a radio transmitter acted much like the spokes of the "Y" to pinpoint the location of a signal where the three spokes intersected.

"Z" Work The identification of wireless transmitters by the characteristics of the signals emitted and of the radio operators by the rhythm of their Morse transmissions.

Notes

Introduction

1 James Eayrs, *In Defence of Canada,* vol. 2, *Appeasement and Rearmament* (Toronto: University of Toronto Press, 1967), ix.

2 The Department of External Affairs was established in 1909. The name was changed to Department of Foreign Affairs and International Trade in 1981.

3 See, for example, Donald Creighton, *The Forked Road: Canada 1939-1957* (Toronto: McClelland and Stewart, 1989).

4 *Canada's Balance of International Payments: Historical Statistics, 1926 to 1992* (Ottawa: Statistics Canada, 1993).

5 Graham D. Taylor and Peter A. Baskerville, *A Concise History of Business in Canada* (Toronto: Oxford University Press, 1994), 397; and J.L. Finlay and D.N. Sprague, *The Structure of Canadian History* (Scarborough, ON: Prentice-Hall of Canada, 1979), 291.

6 Memorandum, 1 July 1946, Library and Archives Canada [LAC], RG25, vol. 5805, file 300-B(s).

7 John Hilliker, *Canada's Department of External Affairs,* vol. 1, *The Early Years, 1909-1946* (Montreal: McGill-Queen's University Press, 1990), 195-96 and 321.

8 The original name was the Department of External Affairs, followed by the Department of Foreign Affairs and International Trade and (briefly) Foreign Affairs Canada.

9 See John Bryden, *Best Kept Secret: Canadian Secret Intelligence in the Second World War* (Toronto: Lester Publishing, 1993); Wesley K. Wark, "Cryptographic Innocence: The Origins of Signals Intelligence in Canada in the Second World War," *Journal of Contemporary History* 22, 4 (1987): 639-66; and Peter St. John, "Canada's Accession to the Allied Intelligence Community 1940-45," *Conflict Quarterly* 4, 4 (1984): 5-21.

10 Wesley K. Wark, "Creating a Cold War Intelligence Community: The Canadian Dilemma," in *Intelligence in the Cold War,* eds. Lars Christian Jenssen and Olav Riste, 103-14 (Oslo: Norwegian Institute for Defence Studies, 2001), 21n. Dr. Wark, one of the most respected Canadian academics on intelligence, acknowledges, "The conclusions I then drew are, in the light of the full archives, wrong-headed." The archives are still limited but continue to become available, albeit slowly.

11 See, for example, Richard Cleroux, *Official Secrets* (Toronto: McGraw-Hill Ryerson, 1990); Larry Hannant, *The Infernal Machine: Investigating the Loyalty of Canada's Citizens* (Toronto: University of Toronto Press, 1995); Steve Hewitt, *Spying 101: The RCMP's Secret Activities at Canadian Universities, 1917-1997* (Toronto: University of Toronto Press, 2002); and Andrew Mitrovica, *Covert Entry: Spies, Lies and Crimes inside Canada's Secret Service* (Toronto: Random House, 2002).

12 I am indebted to James Gannon for this excellent example. *Stealing Secrets, Telling Lies: How Spies and Codebreakers Helped Shape the Twentieth Century* (Washington, DC: Brassey's, 2001), 55-58.

13 Bryden, see note 9 above.

14 Maj. S.R. Elliot, *Scarlet to Green: A History of Intelligence in the Canadian Army, 1903-1963* (Toronto: Canadian Intelligence and Security Association, 1981); and David Stafford, *Camp X: Canada's School for Secret Agents 1941-45* (Toronto: Lester and Orpen Dennys, 1986).

15 J.L. Granatstein and David Stafford, *Spy Wars: Espionage and Canada from Gouzenko to Glasnost* (Toronto: McClelland and Stewart, 1992).

16 Nigel West, ed., *British Security Coordination: The Secret History of British Intelligence in the Americas, 1940-45* (New York: Fromm International, 1999).

17 Intrepid was the cable address for the BSC in New York; Stephenson's designation was 48000.

18 The documents were taken to Camp X where they were burnt.

19 West, see note 16 above. The format is difficult to comprehend given that the book had a high security classification and a circulation restricted to the British intelligence community. A copy was also provided to Canada and one perhaps to the United States.

20 Kurt F. Jensen, review of *British Security Coordination: The Secret History of British Intelligence in the Americas, 1940-45*, ed. Nigel West, *Intelligence and National Security* 15, 3 (2000): 163-65.

21 St. John, see note 9 above; Scott Anderson, "The Evolution of the Canadian Intelligence Establishment, 1945-1950," *Intelligence and National Security* 9, 3 (1994): 448-71; Wark, "Cryptographic Innocence," see note 9 above; Wesley K. Wark, "The Evolution of Military Intelligence in Canada," *Armed Forces and Society* 16, 1 (1989): 77-98; and Wark, "Creating," see note 10 above.

22 Jeffrey T. Richelson and Desmond Ball, *The Ties That Bind: Intelligence Cooperation Between the UKUSA Countries*, 2nd ed. (Boston: Unwin Hyman, 1990).

23 Jeffrey T. Richelson, *The U.S. Intelligence Community*, 5th ed. (Boulder, CO: Westview Press, 2008).

24 Richard J. Aldrich, *The Hidden Hand: Britain, America and Cold War Secret Intelligence* (Woodstock, NY: Overlook Press, 2002); and Richard J. Aldrich, "British Intelligence and the Anglo-American 'Special Relationship' during the Cold War," *Review of International Studies* 24, 3 (1998): 331-51.

25 Christopher Andrew, "The Making of the Anglo-American SIGINT Alliance," in *In the Name of Intelligence*, eds. Hayden B. Peake and Samuel Halpern, 95-109 (Washington, DC: NIBC Press, 1994).

26 See, for example, G. de B. Robinson, ed., *A History of the Examination Unit 1941-45* (Ottawa, 1945); Communications Security Establishment [CSE], *History of the CBNRC* (Ottawa: CSE, 1987); Communications Security Establishment, *25 Years of Signals Intelligence and Communications Security* (Ottawa: CSE, 1971). The CSE is the successor to the wartime Examination Unit and the postwar Communications Branch of the National Research Council, and is Canada's SIGINT organization.

27 Private information to the author.

28 See, for example, LAC, RG25, series A-3-b, vol. 5805, file 303-E(s), pt. 1, and -F, -G, -H, -K; and LAC, RG25, series A-3-b, vol. 5809, file 338-E(s), pt. 1, and -M-1, -N, and -N-1. The file covers became accessible only through Access to Information Program requests.

Chapter 1: Foreign Intelligence at the Beginning of the War

1 O.D. Skelton, Memorandum, 25 August 1939, Library and Archives Canada [LAC], MG26 J4, reel C-4288, vol. 228, file C155079.

2 Lester B. Pearson to O.D. Skelton, 8 September 1938, LAC, MG26 N1, vol. 14, Skelton, O.D. 1935-38.

3 King Diaries, 1 September 1939, LAC, MG26 J13; C.P. Stacey, *Canada and the Age of Conflict: A History of Canadian External Policies*, vol. 2, *1921-1948* (Toronto: University of Toronto Press, 1981), 260.

4 James Eayrs, *The Art of the Possible: Government and Foreign Policy in Canada* (Toronto: University of Toronto Press, 1961), 131-32.

5 Letter from Lester B. Pearson, 23 February 1939, LAC, MG26 N1, vol. 14, Skelton, O.D. 1939-40.

6 Maj. S.R. Elliot, *Scarlet to Green: A History of Intelligence in the Canadian Army, 1903-1963* (Toronto: Canadian Intelligence and Security Association, 1981), 63.

7   Directorate of Military Operations and Intelligence to Rand McNally, 29 January 1932, LAC, RG24, reel C-5068, file 4720; and Elliot, see note 6 above at 66-67.
8   Memorandum, Allotment of Funds for Intelligence Services, Fiscal Year 1933-34, 19 June 1933, LAC, RG24, reel C-5068, file 4720.
9   Various memoranda dated 1938, LAC, RG24, reel C-5070, file 4720.
10 Much of the work was done under the direction of Col. J Sutherland-Brown, whose historical reputation has suffered as a result.
11 Elliot, see note 6 above at 74.
12 Norman Hillmer and J.L. Granatstein, *Empire to Umpire: Canada and the World to the 1990s* (Toronto: Copp Clark Longman, 1994), 127.
13 G.J. Desbarats to the British Admiralty, 28 October 1910, LAC, RG24, vol. 3856, file 1023-4-1.
14 British Admiralty to G.J. Desbarats, 14 December 1910, see note 13 above.
15 Ibid.
16 Department of National Defence, Directorate of History and Heritage [DND], *Notes on the History of Operational Intelligence Centre in Canada* (Ottawa: n.d.), chap. "First Phase 1910-1939," 3, file S1440-18 (1940).
17 Ibid., 5.
18 G.J. Desbarats to the USSEA, External Affairs, 16 April 1920, LAC, RG24, vol. 3856, file 1023-4-3.
19 Director, Naval Service, Ottawa, Memorandum, to Director, Naval Intelligence, Admiralty, 11 February 1921, LAC, RG24, vol. 3816, file 1012-11-1, pt. 1. Locations "covered" at the time included Savannah, GA; Newport News, VA; Baltimore, MD; New York, NY; Philadelphia, PA; Portland, ME; Portland, OR; Boston, MA; Los Angeles, CA; San Diego, CA; San Francisco, CA; Seattle, WA; Charleston, SC; Honolulu, HI; St. John's, NL; Managua and Corinto, Nicaragua; San Salvador, Guatemala; Salina Cruz and Colima in Mexico; Colon and Panama City in Panama.
20 Director, Naval Service, Ottawa, to Director, Naval Intelligence, Admiralty, 23 September 1921, LAC, RG24, vol. 3817, file 1012-11-1.
21 Various memoranda from 1939 and early 1940 suggest information being provided to Canadian officers by friendly Americans. LAC, RG24, vol. 3816, file 1012-11-1, pt. 1.
22 DND, *Notes,* chap. "Operational Intelligence," 1; and John Bryden, *Best Kept Secret: Canadian Secret Intelligence in the Second World War* (Toronto: Lester Publishing, 1993), 8.
23 Memorandum, 9 June 1930, LAC, RG24, reel C-5061, file 3493.
24 Elliot, see note 6 above at 460.
25 Appendix A to unavailable report, undated but written after the start of the war, LAC, RG24, vol. 29164, file WWII-9, pt. 1, XU.
26 Ibid.
27 Attachment, 5 April 1938, to Canadian Joint Intelligence Committee memorandum, 27 August 1945, LAC, RG24, vol. 8088, file 1274-10, vol. 1.
28 Ibid.
29 Ibid.
30 Attachment, 20 April 1938, see note 27 above. Earnshaw's first name is not recorded.
31 Ibid.
32 Attachments, 23 April 1938 and 27 April 1938, see note 27 above.
33 Memorandum, 27 August 1945, see note 27 above.
34 Elliot, see note 6 above at 81-82.
35 Memoranda, 23 April 1938 and n.d. May 1938, LAC, RG24, vol. 4052, file 1078-11-30.
36 Memorandum, 31 May 1938, see note 35 above.
37 Memorandum, n.d., May 1938, see note 35 above.
38 Attachment to memorandum, 3 May 1938, see note 27 above.
39 S.A. Gray, *Getting to the Roots of a 291er* (Ottawa: DND, 1993), 3.
40 Ibid.
41 Memorandum, 27 August 1945, see note 27 above. The document lists the first army station as commencing operations in December 1939. This is incorrect, since the Rockcliffe station began operating in October 1939.

42 DND, *Notes,* introduction, 1.
43 Ibid.; and E.S. Brand, "Not All the Work Was Done at Sea," in *Salty Dips Project,* vol. 3, edited by Mack Lynch (Ottawa: NOAC, 1988), 75-88.
44 Bryden, see note 22 above at 11.
45 At this time, direction-finding triangulation, employed to locate other radio transmitters, was called "Y" work, a holdover from the First World War when it was discovered that three stations homing in on the strongest signal from a radio transmitter acted much like the spokes of the "Y" to pinpoint the location of a signal where the three spokes intersected.
46 Lt. Cdr. John (Jock) de Marbois, Memorandum, 17 May 1943, LAC, RG24, vol. 3806, file 1008-75-19, vol. 1.
47 Ibid.
48 DND, *Notes,* chap. "1939," 3.
49 C.H. Little, "Early Days in Naval Intelligence, 1939-41," in *Salty Dips Project,* vol. 2, edited by Mack Lynch (Ottawa: NOAC, 1985), 111-18.
50 Brand, see note 43 at 85.
51 DND, *Notes,* chap. "1939," 1-2.
52 Ibid.; and Gray, see note 39 at 7-8.
53 Gray, see note 39 at 7.
54 Memoranda, 13 February 1941 and 7 March 1941, LAC, RG24, vol. 3805, file NSS 1008-75-10, vol. 1.
55 Ibid., 13 February 1941 at 5.
56 Capt. E.M. Drake, Memorandum, to Col. W.W. Murray, n.d. November 1940, White Files, Examination Unit folder; and Memorandum, 20 November 1940, National Archives and Records Administration, United States [NARA], box 798, nr. 2282, CBLL35, 11622A, 19401120. The White Files are released by the Communications Security Establishment to LAC, and copies were provided to the author to overcome lengthy processing times at LAC. They are archival records pertaining to Canadian wartime SIGINT activities that were forwarded to LAC in 2001 but had not all been processed at the time this study was being prepared. This material is expected to be fully integrated into the LAC public records.
57 Lt. Col. H.E. Taber, Memorandum, to Col. Letson, Canadian military attaché in Washington, 11 November 1940, White Files, Examination Unit folder.
58 Details of Drake's visit to Washington can be found in G. de B. Robinson, ed., *A History of the Examination Unit 1941-45* (Ottawa, 1945), 3-10; Memoranda, 20 November 1940 and 26 November 1940, White Files, Examination Unit folder; and Memorandum, 20 November 1940, NARA, RG457, box 798, nr. 2282, CBLL35, 11622A, 19401120.
59 If these talks took place and dealt with foreign intelligence matters, they were likely of a very preliminary nature since no substantive agreements emerged, and there is no trace of such talks evident in Canadian or American archival records. Possibly, Mauborgne could have been referring to a British proposal in the talks with the Americans to use Canada as an intelligence platform.
60 See note 58.
61 Ibid.
62 Ibid.
63 Robinson, see note 58 at 9.
64 J.L. Granatstein, *A Man of Influence: Norman A. Robertson and Canadian Statecraft, 1929-68* (Ottawa: Deneau, 1981), 184.
65 Eayrs, see note 4 at 137.
66 C.P. Stacey, *Arms, Men and Governments: The War Policies of Canada 1939-1945* (Ottawa: Queen's Printer, 1970), 534 and 599.
67 Memorandum, 13 February 1941, LAC, RG24, vol. 3805, file NSS 1008-75-10.
68 Memorandum, 3 April 1941, see note 67.

Chapter 2: The Birth of the Examination Unit
1 Capt. E.S. Brand to Dr. H.L. Keenleyside, 21 January 1941, White Files, Examination Unit folder.

2   H.L. Keenleyside to Capt. E.S. Brand, 27 January 1941, White Files, Examination Unit folder.
3   Capt. E.S. Brand to Dr. H.L. Keenleyside, 29 January 1941, see note 2.
4   Robertson succeeded O.D. Skelton, who died as a result of a massive heart attack while driving home for lunch on 28 January 1941. Skelton had led the DEA for much of its history until then, and had been one of Mackenzie King's key advisors and confidants. See Norman Hillmer and J.L. Granatstein, *Empire to Umpire: Canada and the World to the 1990s* (Toronto: Copp Clark Longman, 1994), 164-66.
5   Communications Security Establishment [CSE], *History of the CBNRC* (Ottawa: CSE, 1987), 5.
6   L.B. Pearson to Norman Robertson, 1 February 1941, White Files, Examination Unit folder.
7   G. de B. Robinson, ed., *A History of the Examination Unit 1941-45* (Ottawa, 1945), Addendum, chap. 5, "Entry of DEA and NRC," 1-2.
8   H.L. Keenleyside to C.J. Mackenzie, 13 February 1941, White Files, Examination Unit folder.
9   Robinson, see note 7 at 11.
10 Ibid., 11-12; and C.J. Mackenzie to Norman Robertson; and communication signed WMH to the Canadian Legation in Washington, both 24 April 1941, White Files, Examination Unit folder.
11 H.S.M. Coxeter and G. de B. Robinson, Report, to C.J. Mackenzie, 3 May 1941, White Files, Examination Unit folder and Yardley folder.
12 Following his employment with the US cryptography bureau, Herbert O. Yardley wrote *The American Black Chamber* (Indianapolis, IN: Bobbs-Merrill, 1931), an exposé of American SIGINT successes during the First World War. Yardley also wrote *The Chinese Black Chamber* (published years after his death [Boston: Houghton Mifflin, 1983]) on his SIGINT experience in China before coming to Canada, as well as several novels (one was made into a film) and a book about poker.
13 H.S.M. Coxeter and G. de B. Robinson, Report to the National Research Council of Canada re Cryptographic Project, 3 May 1941, White Files, Examination Unit folder.
14 H.M. Wrong to the Secretary of State for External Affairs, 3 May 1941, White Files, Examination Unit folder and Yardley folder.
15 Ibid.
16 C.J. Mackenzie to H.L. Keenleyside, 6 May 1941, White Files, Examination Unit folder.
17 H.L. Keenleyside to C.J. Mackenzie, 7 May 1941, White Files, Examination Unit folder.
18 D. Geary, Report of Conference of the Interdepartmental Committee on Cryptography, 12 May 1941, White Files, Examination Unit folder and Yardley folder; and NARA, RG457, box 1358, nr. 4166, ZEMA 168, 44121A, 19410201.
19 Geary, see note 18.
20 Herbert O. Yardley, *The Chinese Black Chamber* (Boston: Houghton Mifflin, 1983), xv. Yardley and Ramsaier were married in 1944.
21 Report on Further Conference of the Interdepartmental Committee on Cryptography, 13 May 1941, White Files, Examination Unit folder and Yardley folder; and letter, 16 May 1941, NARA, see note 18.
22 Cabinet War Committee Minutes, item on Report on Financial Assistance to the National Research Council, 5 March 1941, Library and Archives Canada [LAC], RG2, reel C-11789.
23 Cabinet War Committee Minutes, item on Report on Further Conference of the Interdepartmental Committee on Cryptography, 13 May 1941, White Files, Examination Unit folder and Yardely folder.
24 T.A. Stone to C.J. Mackenzie, 3 June 1941, White Files, Examination Unit folder and Yardley folder. "Herbert Osborn" were, in fact, Yardley's first and middle names.
25 Yardley, see note 20 at 3.
26 T.A. Stone to Commissioner S.T. Wood, 23 May 1941, White Files, Examination Unit folder and Yardley folder.
27 Robinson, see note 7 at 16.
28 It is difficult to follow the constant name changes of committees overseeing Canada's intelligence activities. Since the titles were often largely descriptive, it is conceivable that some of the names reflected individual descriptive whimsy at the moment of writing a memorandum.
29 Robinson, see note 7 at 5.

30 R.M. Macdonnell to T.A. Stone, 17 June 1941; and T.A. Stone to R.M. Macdonnell, 23 June 1941, White Files, Examination Unit folder.
31 T.A. Stone to Herbert Osborn (Yardley), 25 July 1941; and Herbert Osborn (Yardley) to T.A. Stone, 26 July 1941, White Files, Examination Unit folder.
32 More information about this part of Stone's intelligence role will be found in Chapter 4.
33 Mr. George Glazebrook, interview, 8 February 1977, 21, Department of Foreign Affairs and International Trade [DFAIT] Special Registry; and David Stafford, *Camp X: Canada's School for Secret Agents 1941-45* (Toronto: Lester and Orpen Dennys, 1986), 41.
34 T.A. Stone to DND, 26 September 1941, LAC, RG25, vol. 1967, file 867-B.
35 Secretary of State for External Affairs, Telegram, to the High Commissioner, London, 5 June 1941, White Files, Examination Unit folder and Yardley folder.
36 Financial Statement, Examination Unit, 31 July 1941; memoranda from Herbert Osborn (Yardley) to Chairman, Supervisory Committee, Examination Unit, 5 August 1941, and 15 August 1941, White Files, Examination Unit folder and Yardley folder; also found in NARA, RG457, box 1358, nr. 4166, ZEMA 168, 44121A, 19410201.
37 Robinson, see note 7 at 7.
38 N.A. Robertson to Vincent Massey, 7 July 1941, White Files, Examination Unit folder and Yardley folder.
39 Robinson, see note 7 at 8; and Herbert Yardley to Vincent Massey, 22 August 1941, NARA, RG457, box 1358, nr. 4166, ZEMA 168, 44121A, 19410201.
40 John Bryden, *Best Kept Secret: Canadian Secret Intelligence in the Second World War* (Toronto: Lester Publishing, 1993), 79; and Bradley F. Smith, *The Ultra-Magic Deals and the Most Secret Special Relationship, 1940-1946* (Shrewsbury, UK: Airlife Publishing, 1993), 89.
41 T.A. Stone or L.B. Pearson (names are penned in, accompanied by a question mark) to Vincent Massey, 23 September 1941; and H.H. Wrong to T.A. Stone, 8 October 1941, White Files, Examination Unit folder and Yardley folder; letter of 23 September 1941 is also in NARA, RG457, box 1358, nr. 4166, ZEMA 168, 44121A, 19410201.
42 T.A. Stone to Hume Wrong, 22 November 1941, White Files, Examination Unit folder and Yardley folder.
43 Memorandum on Visit to Washington to Enquire into the Situation Regarding H.O. Osborn [Yardley], 28 November 1941 (first page records 26 November, which is incorrect), White Files, Examination Unit folder and Yardley folder.
44 Bryden, see note 40 at 84. See pages 80-85 for the full account.
45 David Kahn, "Nuggets from the Archives: Yardley Tries Again," *Cryptologia* 2, 2 (1978): 139-43.
46 L.B. Pearson to Vincent Massey, 9 December 1941, White Files, Examination Unit folder.
47 N.A. Robertson to Major H.O. Yardley, 6 January 1942; N.A. Robertson to C.J. Mackenzie, 9 January 1942; and unsigned draft letter to C.J. Mackenzie, 12 January 1942, White Files, Examination Unit folder.
48 Malcolm MacDonald to N.A. Robertson, 24 December 1941, LAC, RG24, vol. 5264, file 24-14-3. The laudatory terms coming so shortly after British efforts to oust Yardley may be more reflective of British fears than genuine acceptance of Canadian capabilities.
49 N.A. Robertson to Malcolm MacDonald, 27 December 1941, LAC, RG24, vol. 5264, file 24-14-3.
50 Chief of Naval Personnel, Memorandum, to Director of Naval Intelligence, 24 February 1942; and Report of Work Undertaken by Far Eastern Intelligence, 13 February 1942, LAC, RG24, reel C-5849, file 1023-4-15.
51 Memorandum for the War Committee of the Cabinet, 26 January 1942, White Files, Examination Unit folder and Yardley folder. One of the copies of the memorandum has added by hand, "Approved by War Committee. 28.1.42." A copy of the annotated document is available in NARA, RG457, box 1358, nr. 4166, ZEMA 168, 44121A, 19410201.
52 J.L. Granatstein and David Stafford, *Spy Wars: Espionage and Canada from Gouzenko to Glasnost* (Toronto: McClelland and Stewart, 1992), 34.
53 T.A. Stone to Commissioner, RCMP, 19 January 1942, White Files, Examination Unit folder. Variations of the committee name cited in other documents suggest that members had trouble recalling the cumbersome title.

54 C.J. Mackenzie, Memorandum, to Mr. Eagleson, 4 February 1942, White Files, Examination Unit folder.
55 Robinson, see note 7 at 24.
56 CSE, see note 5 at 8-9.
57 Mackenzie King's files in the LAC contain many examples of SIGINT that were provided to the prime minister during the war, and that were made available to the public by LAC staff at a time when Canada had yet to acknowledge that this type of SIGINT had been collected. The SIGINT pieces are not distinguishable but represent reports about progress of the war from an enemy perspective, often Japanese or Italian, which could only have been obtained from decrypted enemy diplomatic reporting.
58 Bryden, see note 40 at 135.
59 Robinson, see note 7 at 21.
60 John Hilliker, *Canada's Department of External Affairs,* vol. 1, *The Early Years, 1909-1946* (Montreal: McGill-Queen's University Press, 1990), 269.
61 T.A. Stone to C.J. Mackenzie, 24 September 1942, LAC, RG24, vol. 29165, file WWII-15, pt. 4.
62 Arthur Menzies, interview by Harjit Virdeeh, 8 December 2003. Provided by Mr. Virdeeh.
63 N.A. Robertson, Memorandum for Messrs. Beaudry, Wrong, Read, and Keenleyside, 25 September 1942, LAC, RG24, vol. 29165, file WWII-15, pt. 4.
64 Special Intelligence Section of the Department of External Affairs, 19 March 1945, LAC, RG24, vol. 29164, file WWII-8 XU.
65 Ibid.
66 See note 62.
67 See note 64.
68 Ibid.
69 Ibid.
70 Ibid.
71 Ibid.; N.A. Robertson to C.J. Mackenzie, 11 January 1945, LAC, RG24, vol. 29167, file WWII-33; and Memorandum to N.A. Robertson, 25 August 1944, LAC, RG24, vol. 29164, file WWII-8 XU.
72 Memorandum to N.A. Robertson, 25 August 1944, LAC, RG24, vol. 29164, file WWII-8 XU.
73 See note 62.
74 The Spanish language intercepts have not been traced but may exist in the LAC backlog of material awaiting processing. An evaluation of the French decrypts, both Vichy and Free French, is provided in Chapter 6.
75 The Japanese in the Dutch East Indies, 16 October 1943, LAC, RG24, vol. 29163, file WWII-5, pt. 3.
76 Harold A. Skaarup, *Out of Darkness – Light: A History of Canadian Military Intelligence,* vol. 1 (New York: iUniverse, 2005), 42; and Jeffrey T. Richelson, *Foreign Intelligence Organizations* (Cambridge, MA: Ballinger Publishing, 1988), 69.
77 Although controversy continues to haunt Norman's memory, and two books (taking opposing views) have been written about his alleged Communism, there has never been a shred of concrete evidence presented to show that he betrayed his country. More telling, in the almost half-century since his death, no defector from the then USSR or its East European satellites has ever suggested that Norman was a traitor.
78 Skaarup, see note 76 at 109.
79 Ibid., 41.
80 Capt. H.R. Sandwith R.N., Report on Canadian Military "Y" Organization, 23 May 1942, LAC, RG24, vol. 3806, file 1008-75-20.
81 A figure of nineteen sites is cited in S.A. Gray, *Getting to the Roots of a 291er* (Ottawa: DND, 1993), 15; and Capt. H.R. Sandwith R.N., Report on Royal Canadian Naval "Y" Organization, 19 May 1942, LAC, RG24, vol. 3806, file 1008-75-20, lists fifteen stations with an additional four proposed sites: Harbour Grace, NL; Botwood, NL; Hartlen Point, NS; Cap D'Espoir, QC; Pennfield, NB; St. Hubert, QC; Ottawa, ON; Strathburn, ON; Winnipeg, MB; Portage la Prairie, MB; Rivers, MB; Point Grey, BC; Gordon Head, BC; Coal Harbour, BC; and Ucluelet, BC; additional stations were proposed for Masset, BC; Grande Prairie, AB; Red Deer, AB; and Lethbridge, AB. Some of the stations were operated by the Department of Transport.

Chapter 3: Building Alliances

1 Bradley F. Smith, *The Ultra-Magic Deals and the Most Secret Special Relationship, 1940-1946* (Shrewsbury, UK: Airlife Publishing, 1993).

2 Ibid., 36.

3 Nigel West, introduction in *British Security Coordination: The Secret History of British Intelligence in the Americas, 1940-45* (New York: Fromm International, 1999), ix-x. Stephenson had also made an earlier brief visit to Washington in April 1940.

4 Smith, see note 1 at 37.

5 Memorandum, "Traffic Exchange," n.d., Department of National Defence, Directorate of History and Heritage [DND], 97/3, file 4566. It was probably written in late 1944 or 1945; see also Smith, see note 1 at 88-89.

6 Canadian Legation, Washington, to Department of External Affairs [DEA], 26 November 1941, Library and Archives Canada [LAC], RG24, vol. 5264, file 24-14-3.

7 Thomas F. Troy, *Donovan and the CIA: A History of the Establishment of the Central Intelligence Agency* (Washington, DC: CIA, Center for the Study of Intelligence, 1981), 423.

8 See note 6.

9 Ibid.

10 Canadian Legation, Washington, to DEA, 21 January 1942, LAC, RG24, vol. 5264, file 24-14-3.

11 FBI Minutes of Working Committee of Hemispheric Intelligence Conference held in office of FBI, 29 January 1942, LAC, RG24, vol. 5264, file 24-14-3.

12 Troy, see note 7 at 36. Stephenson, through his contact with Bill Donovan, had very close access to the White House. He was able to inform London of the favourable decision on the bases-for-destroyers deal before the official announcement was made.

13 See note 11.

14 Minutes of the Western Hemisphere Intelligence Conference held (blacked out) on Monday, 16 March 1942, Canadian Security Intelligence Service, Access to Information Program [ATIP] 117-91-71. Much of the ATIP-released information has been blacked out, including the location, but the RCMP participant "left" Ottawa and, presumably, travelled to Washington.

15 Minutes of the Western Hemisphere Intelligence Conference held at Ottawa, on Monday, 3 August 1942, Canadian Security Intelligence Service, ATIP.

16 Letter, addressee blacked out (presumably Hoover), "Re: Co-ordination of Intelligence Activities in the Western Hemisphere"; and letter to N.A. Robertson, both dated 20 October 1942, Canadian Security Intelligence Service, ATIP.

17 Letter to Commissioner S.T. Wood, 21 October 1942, Canadian Security Intelligence Service, ATIP.

18 Letter to N.A. Robertson, 24 October 1942, Canadian Security Intelligence Service, ATIP.

19 Memorandum to the DCI, 25 November 1943, Canadian Security Intelligence Service, ATIP.

20 Final Report, British-Canadian-American Radio Intelligence Discussions, Washington, DC, 6-17 April 1942, DND, 97/3, file 3848; and US National Archives and Records Management [NARA], RG457, box 1292, nr. 3848, ZEMA 108, 32863A, 19420417. The DND copy is a photocopy obtained from NARA; Canada has not released the report. The report is eleven page long, but its appendices total hundreds of pages of dense, highly technical electronic intelligence information. Several copies are in US Archives.

21 DND, *Notes on the History of Operational Intelligence Centre in Canada* (Ottawa: n.d.), chap. "1942," 1, file S1440-18 (1940).

22 W.A.B. Douglas and Jürgen Rohwer, "'The Most Thankless Task' Revisited: Convoys, Escorts, and Radio Intelligence in the Western Atlantic, 1941-43," in *The RCN in Retrospect, 1910-1968*, ed. James A. Boutilier, 187-234 (Vancouver: UBC Press, 1982), 192.

23 Peter St. John, "Canada's Accession to the Allied Intelligence Community, 1940-45," *Conflict Quarterly* 4, 4 (1984): 7.

24 DND, *Notes*, chap. "Between the Wars," 4a.

25 Notes on the "Y" Committee Conference in Washington, DC, 17 April 1942, White Files, Y Material folder.

26 See note 20.

27 Ibid. The Final Report lists five Canadian delegates, although records of the subcommittees indicate that there was at least one other Canadian in attendance.
28 Ibid.
29 Report of the Sub-Committee Appointed to Study "Y" Intelligence; and Memorandum on the Canadian "Y" Committee, 15 November 1942. White Files, Y Material folder.
30 Memorandum to N.A. Robertson, 3 June 1942, White Files, Y Material folder.
31 See note 25.
32 Traffic Exchange, n.d. (probably late 1944 or early 1945), DND, 97/3, file 4566. The copy in the DND files is obtained from NARA.
33 Report of Conference with British and Canadian Representatives on Traffic Exchange, 12 April 1943, DND, 97/3, file 4566; and NARA, RG457, box 800, nr. 2305, CBLL37, 16433A, 19420330.
34 Report of Conference with British and Canadian Representatives, 7 September 1943, DND, 97/3, file 4566; and NARA, RG457, box 800, nr. 2305, CBLL37, 16433A, 19420330.
35 Minutes, 18 June 1943, LAC, RG24, vol. 29163, file History of No. 1 Discrimination Unit.
36 Ibid.
37 Smith, see note 1 at 151. It was only after signing the BRUSA Agreement that the Americans were informed of the Government Code and Cipher School's early "computer" (the "bombe") used for breaking the Enigma ciphers.
38 Jeffrey T. Richelson, *The U.S. Intelligence Community,* 3rd ed. (Boulder, CO: Westview Press, 1995), 277.
39 C.H. Little, "Now It Can All Be Told," in *Salty Dips Project,* vol. 3, edited by Mack Lynch · (Ottawa: NOAC, 1988), 217-37.
40 Harold A. Skaarup, *Out of Darkness – Light: A History of Canadian Military Intelligence,* vol. 1 (New York: iUniverse, 2005), 119.
41 Ibid., 50.
42 F.H. Hinsley, *British Intelligence in the Second World War,* abrid. ed. (New York: Cambridge University Press, 1993), 308n.
43 West, see note 3 at xxvi; and Troy, see note 7 at 34.
44 Maj. S.R. Elliot, *Scarlet to Green: A History of Intelligence in the Canadian Army, 1903-1963* (Toronto: Canadian Intelligence and Security Association, 1981), 386-87.
45 F.H. Hinsley and C.A.G. Simkins, *British Intelligence in the Second World War,* vol. 4 (London: HMSO, 1990), 146.
46 West, see note 3 at xxvii.
47 George Glazebrook, interview, 8 February 1977, 15, Department of Foreign Affairs and International Trade [DFAIT] Special Registry. The UK Public Record Office [PRO] is attempting to recreate the BSC archives by collecting copies of BSC correspondence and documents from other files.
48 George Glazebrook, interview, 29 January 1980, 2, DFAIT Special Registry.
49 Ibid.
50 L.B. Pearson to W.S. Stephenson, 31 July 1942 and 6 August 1942, NARA, RG457, box 1358, nr. 4166, ZEMA 168, 44121A, 19410201. An overview of the special intelligence section can be found in G. de B. Robinson, ed., *A History of the Examination Unit 1941-45,* chap. 3, "Special Intelligence Section of the Department of External Affairs," E.H. Norman, 50-59 (Ottawa, 1945). The same chapter can also be found in NARA, RG457, box 1358, nr. 4166, ZEMA 168, 44121A, 19410201.
51 Letter, 26 February 1942, LAC, RG24, vol. 29163, file WWII-5, pt. 2. Pearson writes that an earlier letter was supposed to have contained a special report but he found only a blank piece of paper enclosed and he claimed, alas, not to be an expert on secret ink.
52 Meeting of the Advisory Committee on the Examination Unit, 19 March 1942, 18 June 1942, and 16 October 1942, NARA, RG457, box 1358, nr. 4166; ZEMA 168, 44121A, 19410201.
53 No document found at LAC or at the DND's Directorate of History and Heritage contains the name "Camp X."
54 Memorandum to the Minister, 21 October 1941, DND 112.3S2009 (D190).
55 T.G. Drew-Brook, interview, 12 January 1977, 3-5, DFAIT Special Registry.

56 Glazebrook, see note 47 at 19-20.
57 Memorandum to the Minister, 25 October 1943, DND 112.3S2009 (D190).
58 Glazebrook, see note 47 at 16; and Drew-Brook, see note 55 at 4-5.
59 David Stafford, *Camp X: Canada's School for Secret Agents 1941-45* (Toronto: Lester and Orpen Dennys, 1986).
60 W.S. Stephenson to Maj. Gen. J.C. Murchie, 30 August 1944, LAC, MG26 N1, vol. 72, "World War II – Special Training School"; and West, see note 3 at 424.
61 DND Headquarters to Maj. Gen. Pearkes, 24 March 1944; and Memorandum to the Minister, 25 August 1944, DND 112.3S2009 (D190).
62 Memorandum to the Minister, 29 August 1944, DND 112.3S2009 (D190); and Stafford, see note 59 at 249-50.
63 Minutes of the Meeting of the Advisory Committee on the Examination Unit, 23 September 1942; and T.A. Stone to W.S. Stephenson, 21 October 1942, both NARA, RG457, box 1358, nr. 4166, ZEMA 168, 44121A, 19410201.
64 Memorandum, 22 June 1943, LAC, RG24, vol. 29163, file WWII-5, pt. 2.
65 N.A. Robertson to L.B. Pearson, 12 October 1944, LAC, RG24, vol. 29166, file WWII-30, pt. 1 XU.
66 Ibid.
67 Ibid.

Chapter 4: Canadian HUMINT Collection

1 Joint Intelligence Committee, Memorandum on Foreign Intelligence in Peacetime, to the Chiefs of Staff Committee, 29 September 1945, Library and Archives Canada [LAC], RG24, vol. 6178, file 22-1-43, pt. 1.
2 Maurice A. Pope, *Soldiers and Politicians: The Memoirs of Lt.-Gen. Maurice A. Pope* (Toronto: University of Toronto Press, 1962), 135 and 137. Pope makes only passing reference to his involvement in intelligence matters early in the war.
3 Ibid.; and Memorandum, "Censorship," n.d., LAC, RG25, vol. 5805, file 300-B(s).
4 Report on Censorship. A Narrative on the Organization, Activities and Demobilization of Censorship during the War of 1939-1945, Department of National Defence [DND], 72/295. The document is undated but 22 October 1953 is stamped on the cover.
5 A good account of the use of censorship for propaganda or psychological warfare can be found in Don Page, "Tommy Stone and Psychological Warfare in World War Two: Transforming a POW Liability into an Asset," *Journal of Canadian Studies* 16, 3-4 (1981): 110-20.
6 Report SA-171524, 25 June 1943, LAC, RG24, vol. 2846, file 1520-40, pt. 2.
7 Canadian Postal Censorship, Report on Conditions in Germany, 12 March 1945, LAC, RG24, vol. 8034, file 1182-4, pt. 3.
8 Maj. S.R. Elliot, *Scarlet to Green: A History of Intelligence in the Canadian Army, 1903-1963* (Toronto: Canadian Intelligence and Security Association, 1981), 502 and 505.
9 John Joseph Kelly, "Intelligence and Counter-Intelligence in German Prisoners of War Camps in Canada during World War II," *Dalhousie Review* 58, 2 (1978): 285-94.
10 Staff Officer (Intelligence), Ottawa, Report, to Naval Intelligence Halifax, St. John's and Vancouver, 30 December 1942; and subsequent reports to March 1943, LAC, RG24, vol. 11942, file 1960-1.
11 George Glazebrook, interview, 11 January 1977, 2-5, Department of Foreign Affairs and International Trade [DFAIT] Special Registry. Glazebrook recollects that L.B. Pearson and Norman Robertson decided that censorship intelligence gathering should be completely reorganized, since it was not working properly.
12 Memorandum, see note 3. The text of the document suggests that it was a postwar assessment of the role of the Department of External Affairs [DEA] in censorship activities.
13 John Hilliker, *Canada's Department of External Affairs*, vol. 1, *The Early Years, 1909-1946* (Montreal: McGill-Queen's University Press, 1990), 268.
14 Directorate of Prisoners of War Intelligence Report, 24 June 1944, LAC, RG24, series C-1, reel C-8250, file 31-15-3.
15 Information Summary for June 1944, 30 June 1944, LAC, RG24, series C-1, reel C-8250, file 31-15-3.

16 Report on Conditions in Germany, 22 February 1945, LAC, RG24, vol. 8034, file 1182-4, pt. 3.
17 LAC, RG24, vol. 11250, file 81; and Report on Conditions in Germany, 18 July 1944, LAC, RG24, reel C-5417.
18 Report on Conditions in France, 1 June 1945, LAC, RG25, vol. 2846, file 1520-C-40, pt. 2.
19 Ibid.
20 Memorandum for the Chief Postal Censor, "Postal Censorship and Intelligence Liaison Officers," 15 January 1942, LAC, RG2, vol. 5987, file DC15.
21 Memorandum to the Prime Minister on Censorship Organization, 5 March 1942, LAC, RG25, vol. 5805, file 300-B(s).
22 Report on Censorship, Order-in-Council, P.C. 4012, DND, 72/295. The OIC was put in place on 13 May 1942.
23 Minutes of the Advisory Committee on Service Intelligence, 21 May 1942, LAC, RG25, vol. 1933, file 724-BW.
24 Ibid.
25 Hilliker, see note 13 at 289-90.
26 N.A. Robertson to L.B. Pearson, 11 February 1943; and unsigned letter (likely from N.A. Robertson) to Vincent Massey, 23 February 1943, with appended memorandum for the Under-Secretary on Organization for Political Warfare, 15 February 1943, LAC, RG25, vol. 3207, file 5353-40C, pt. 1.
27 Memorandum to the Prime Minister, 17 June 1943, LAC, RG25, vol. 3207, file 5353-40C, pt. 1; and unsigned memorandum to Mr. Robertson, Mr. Grierson, Mr. Wrong, 11 June 1943, LAC, RG25, vol. 3207, file 5353-40C, pt. 1; and DND 119.009 (D22). As with so many elements of Canadian wartime intelligence, the names of committees were often fluid and changed from one memorandum to the next. The Psychological Warfare Committee, the Political Intelligence Committee, and the Political Warfare Planning Committee were not the same but often shared a purpose that flowed from one into the other. Membership in the committees often overlapped in Canada's small intelligence community.
28 T.A. Stone to the Chief of the General Staff, 22 July 1943, DND 119.009 (D22); DND 193.009 (D29); and LAC, RG25, vol. 3211, file 5353-Q-40C. The file copies were not typed at the same time but the text is identical.
29 T.A. Stone to Maj. Gen. H.F.G. Letson, 23 July 1943, DND 119.009 (D22); DND 193.009 (D29); and LAC, RG25, vol. 3211, file 5353-Q-40C.
30 George Glazebrook, Memorandum, to the Chief of the General Staff, 16 September 1943, DND 119.009 (D22); DND 193.009 (D29); and LAC, RG25, vol. 3211, file 5353-Q-40C.
31 Memorandum, "Psychological Warfare," 3 July 1946, LAC, RG25, vol. 3207, file 5353-40C, pt. 2.
32 Draft memorandum on Psychological Warfare, 3 July 1946, LAC, RG25, vol. 3207, file 5353-40C, pt. 2.
33 Memorandum, "Political Warfare Organization," 14 December 1942, LAC, RG25, vol. 3180, file 4858-C-40, pt. 1.
34 Prisoner of War Mail Extracts, 15 November 1944 and 5 December 1944, LAC, RG25, vol. 3226, file 5454-C-40C, pt. 8.
35 Col. W.W. Murray, Director of Military Intelligence, Memorandum, to the Chief of the General Staff, "Political Warfare, Prisoners of War Intelligence Section," 15 November 1943, DND 193.009 (D29); and LAC, RG25, vol. 3211, file 5353-Q-40C. The two copies were typed at different times but the text is identical except for a half line missing from the RG25 copy (probably the result of folded carbon paper).
36 Ibid.
37 Memorandum on the Special Prisoners of War Intelligence Unit, 8 November 1943, LAC, RG25, vol. 3211, file 5353-Q-40C.
38 W.W. Murray returned to military service in 1939 as a lieutenant colonel and was promoted to colonel in the fall of 1940. For the sake of simplicity, Murray will be referred to as colonel for the remainder of this book. Harold A. Skaarup, *Out of Darkness – Light: A History of Canadian Military Intelligence*, vol. 1 (New York: iUniverse, 2005), 37 and 40.
39 See note 35.

40 Minutes of Chiefs of Staff Committee, section on Political Warfare – Prisoners of War Intelligence Section, 4 January 1944 and 14 January 1944, DND 193.009 (D29); and LAC, RG25, vol. 3211, file 5353-Q-40C.
41 See note 35.
42 N.A. Robertson to the Secretary, Chiefs of Staff Committee, 8 March 1944, LAC, RG25, vol. 3211, file 5353-Q-40C.
43 Memorandum to the Prime Minister, 10 March 1944, LAC, RG25, vol. 3211, file 5353-Q-40C.
44 Memorandum to the Ministers, "Political Warfare – Directorate of Prisoners of War Intelligence," 28 March 1944, DND 193.009 (D29) and LAC, RG25, vol. 3211, file 5353-Q-40C.
45 Chronology Relating to Establishment of P[risoners]/W[ar] Intelligence Sections Within Directorate of Military Int[elligence], LAC, RG25, vol. 3211, file 5353-Q-40C; undated but likely prepared in 1944 or 1945.
46 Elliot, see note 8 at 507.
47 See note 31.
48 George Glazebrook, Memorandum, to Hume Wrong, with an appended memorandum, "Psychological Warfare," 13 September 1944, LAC, RG25, vol. 3707, file 5353-40C, pt. 2.
49 Ibid.
50 Partial List of the Staff of the Marine Kriegsschule, FLENSBURG-MUERWIK, 3 March 1945, LAC, RG24, vol. 8034, file 1182-4, pt. 3.
51 Michael L. Hadley, *U-Boats against Canada: German Submarines in Canadian Waters* (Kingston: McGill-Queen's University Press, 1985), 168-92.
52 T.A. Stone, Teletype, to Mahoney, Canadian Legation, Washington, DC, 3 April 1943; USSEA to Colonel H.N. Steight, Commissioner, Internment Operations, 5 April 1943; T.A. Stone to George Glazebrook and Saul Rae, 6 April 1943; T.A. Stone to Robert C. Tryon, OSS, 15 April 1943; Robert C. Tryon to T.A. Stone, 30 April 1943, LAC, RG25, vol. 3180, file 4858-B-40, pt. 1.
53 T.A. Stone to L.B. Pearson, 18 May 1943, LAC, RG25, vol. 3180, file 4858-B-40, pt. 1.
54 Ibid.
55 See note 11 at 45.
56 Ibid.
57 Thomas F. Troy, *Donovan and the CIA: A History of the Establishment of the Central Intelligence Agency* (Washington, DC: CIA, Center for the Study of Intelligence, 1981), 155.
58 Ibid., 45.
59 Memorandum to file on OSS and Canadian Postal Censorship, 31 May 1943; Robert C. Tryon, OSS, to George Glazebrook, 1 November 1943; and F.E. Jollitte, Chief Postal Censor, to George Glazebrook, 2 December 1943, LAC, RG25, vol. 3180, file 4858-B-40, pt. 1.
60 Hume Wrong to L.B. Pearson, 4 March 1942, NARA, RG457, box 1358, nr. 4166, ZEMA 168, 44121A, 19410201.
61 Document, "Exchange of P[risoners]/W[ar] Information Between Canadian and United States Censorship, 21 July 1943, LAC, RG2, vol. 5987, file DC 15.
62 The POWs went to great lengths to communicate clandestinely with Germany. Canada issued special sensitized paper, which would more easily reveal invisible inks, to enemy POWs for their correspondence. Insight into the challenges of intercepting secret writings can be found in an undated memorandum (likely prepared in 1945) titled "Censorship Security," DND, 72/295, Report on Censorship.
63 Digest of Proceedings, Miami Conference, LAC, RG25, vol. 1939, file 724-WD. Interestingly, the higher quality of Canadian writing paper available to POWs in Canada initially made it more difficult to identify secret writing than was the case for both British and American paper.
64 Report on Censorship, Censorship Security, DND, 72/295. Undated document prepared sometime after August 1945.
65 Memorandum, "General Observations on Censorship Operations," n.d., LAC, RG25, vol. 1923, file 724-M.
66 Canadian Legation, Washington, DC, Telegram, to USSEA, no. WA-1569, 1 July 1942, LAC, RG24, vol. 5372, file 45-19-3, pt 1.
67 Ibid.

68 Pearson makes no mention in his memoirs of this incident or his other intelligence-related experiences, except for one humorous incident when he acted as an ad hoc diplomatic courier carrying an envelope from London to the BSC offices in New York. Lester B. Pearson, *Mike: The Memoirs of the Right Honourable Lester B. Pearson,* vol. 1 (Toronto: University of Toronto Press, 1972), 194.

69 Memorandum, Interrogation of Repatriates from the Orient on board the GRIPSHOLM, 26 August 1942, LAC, RG24, vol. 11923, file PC.

70 LAC, RG24, reel C-5061, file 3448. The file in its entirety comprises documents pertaining to the repatriation and debriefing of Canadians returning from Japanese captivity.

71 Memorandum, Interrogation of Canadian Repatriates from the Orient Aboard the GRIPSHOLM, 26 August 1942, LAC, RG24, vol. 11923, vol. 09-6. The individual debriefing reports total probably 100 pages of socio-political and military intelligence.

72 Memorandum, Results of Intelligence Interrogation of Repatriates from HONG KING [sic] on "GRIPSHOLM," 26 August 1942, LAC, RG24, vol. 11923, file PC.

73 Intelligence Report: Tokyo and Vicinity, 25 August 1942, 26 August 1942, LAC, RG24, vol. 11923, file PC.

74 James Barros, *No Sense of Evil. Espionage: The Case of Herbert Norman* (Toronto: Deneau, 1986), 27; and William L. Langer to Colonel William J. Donovan, 12 October 1942, LAC, RG24, vol. 29165, file WWII-15, pt 4x4. The letter from Langer, a noted American historian, refers to Norman being repatriated on the SS *Gripsholm.* Norman's name is not cited among those for whom Tokyo interview reports have been located. See note 73.

75 Document, "Edgerton Herbert Norman" with 1950 handwritten in upper right corner. Canadian Security Intelligence Service, Access to Information Program [ATIP], 117-89-109, Item 72.

76 Information Secured from Repatriates Returning from Orient, Interviewed on Sealed Train en route from New York to Montreal, 26 August 1942, LAC, RG24, vol. 11923, file PC.

77 See note 70.

78 Minutes of the Canadian Joint Intelligence Committee, 27 October 1943, LAC, RG24, vol. 2468, file 715-10-161-3, pt. 2.

79 Minutes of the Canadian Joint Intelligence Committee, 26 April 1944, LAC RG24, vol. 8088, file 1274-10-1, pt. 1.

80 Minutes of the Joint Intelligence Committee, 23 November 1943, and 8 December 1943, LAC, RG24, vol. 2469, file 715-10-16-1-3, vol. 3.

81 Minutes of the Ad Hoc Joint Intelligence Committee Meeting with the DEA, 16 December 1943, LAC, RG24, vol. 2469, file 715-10-16-1-3, vol. 3.

82 E.H. Norman to David Bowes-Lyon, 29 January 1944, LAC, RG24, vol. 29166, file WWII-30, pt. 2 XU.

83 T.A. Stone, Memorandum, to Mr. Norman, 7 February 1944, LAC, RG24, vol. 29166, file WWII-30, pt. 2 XU.

Chapter 5: The Mousetrap Operation, 1942-43

1 G. de B. Robinson, ed., *A History of the Examination Unit 1941-45* (Ottawa, 1945), chap. 5, "Entry of DEA and NRC," 16-18. Portions of the chapter clearly relate to Mousetrap. The code word has been removed as have some of the details and names of participants. Although released under the Access to Information Act [ATIP], most of the excisions appear to relate to technical means of collecting and decrypting communications. These do not prevent the reader from gaining a good insight into the Examination Unit.

2 Ibid., 17-18.

3 Ibid., 17.

4 Memorandum re contacts in Washington, 13 October 1944, Library and Archives Canada [LAC], RG24, vol. 29164, file WWII-8 XU.

5 John Bryden, *Best Kept Secret: Canadian Secret Intelligence in the Second World War* (Toronto: Lester Publishing, 1993), 140.

6 David Kahn, *Seizing the Enigma: The Race to Break the German U-Boat Codes, 1939-1943* (New York: Barnes and Noble, 2001), 188.

7 F.H. Hinsley, *British Intelligence in the Second World War,* vol. 1 (London: HMSO, 1979), 223-25.

8 The few details that have emerged do not explain the meaning of "Mousetrap." Some documents imply that the term was the "address" of Denniston's organization. One document speaks of "transmission [of telegraphic messages] to Mousetrap." See C. des Graz to Colonel O.M. Biggar, 10 September 1943, LAC, RG24, vol. 5989, file DC9/3. Also, "sent ... to Mousetrap (MEW)," cited in Minutes of "Y" Committee, 15 November 1942, LAC, RG24, vol. 8125, file NSS1282-85, vol. 1. Most references, however, use the code word as a verb, as in "Mousetrapping," suggesting that it refers to a type of collection program.

9 Henry LeRoy Lewis to W. Hill-Wood, 7 August 1942, LAC, RG24, vol. 29165v, file WWII-15, pt. 4x4.

10 Unsigned letter from the Information and Records Branch to Cmdr. A.G. Denniston, 7 August 1942, LAC, RG24, vol. 29165, file WWII-15, pt. 4x4.

11 See note 9.

12 L.B. Pearson to H.H. Wrong, 25 February 1942; and H.H. Wrong to L.B. Pearson, 4 March 1942, US National Archives and Records Administration [NARA], RG457, box 1358, nr. 4166, ZEMA 168, 44121A, 19410201. Mousetrap is not mentioned in either letter that NARA obtained under the ATIP from Canada. Some words have been excised from both, including the specifics of the "highly confidential matter." The context of both letters leaves no doubt that the correspondence relates to Mousetrap-type telegraphic collection efforts. LAC has no copy of the letters accessible to the public.

13 L.B. Pearson to H.H. Wrong, 25 February 1942, NARA, RG457, box 1358, nr. 4166, ZEMA 168, 44121A, 19410201.

14 Ibid.

15 Ibid.; H.H. Wrong to L.B. Pearson, 4 March 1942, NARA, RG457, box 1358, nr. 4166, ZEMA 168, 44121A, 19410201.

16 Harold A. Skaarup, *Out of Darkness – Light: A History of Canadian Military Intelligence*, vol. 1 (New York: iUniverse, 2005), 119-20.

17 T.A. Stone, Teletype message, to [William] Stephenson and [C.] des Graz, 28 August 1942, LAC, RG2, vol. 5987, file DC9/3.

18 Handwritten notes from a meeting between Stephenson, des Graz, Hill-Wood, Maidment, and Stone, 26 August [presumably] 1942, Department of Foreign Affairs and International Trade [DFAIT], file 5-2-1, vol. 1.

19 Memorandum on the Disposition of Certain Cable and Wireless Telegraph Intercepts, signed TAS [T.A. Stone], 27 October 1942, LAC, RG24, vol. 29165, file WWII-15, pt. 4x4.

20 Note to file, "Procedure in United States Censorship Offices New York in Respect of Government Messages," 27 August 1942, DFAIT, file 5-2-1, vol. 1.

21 See note 19.

22 Originals of the schematic document are available in White Files, "Y" Material; and Minutes of the "Y" Committee, relating to Mousetrap, 15 November 1942, LAC, RG24, vol. 8125, file NSS1282-85, vol. 1.

23 See note 17. The message is cited as coming from the director of censorship, a position Stone did not hold.

24 T.A. Stone to Colonel O.M. Biggar, 1 September 1942; and E.A. Martin to W. Eggleston, 1 September 1942, LAC, RG2, vol. 5987, file DC9/3.

25 T.A. Stone, Telekrypton message, to B. de F. Bayly, 23 December 1942, LAC, RG2, vol. 5987, file DC9/3. Telekrypton denotes a highly secure communications system.

26 Signature indecipherable, Memorandum, 23 December 1942, LAC, RG2, vol. 5987, file DC9/3.

27 T.A. Stone to the Director of Censorship, 4 January 1943, LAC, RG2, vol. 5987, file DC9/3.

28 Minutes of the "Y" Committee, relating to Mousetrap, 25 September 1942, LAC, RG2, vol. 8125, file NSS1282-85, vol. 1.

29 Minutes of the "Y" Committee, relating to Mousetrap, 15 November 1942, LAC, RG24, vol. 8125, file NSS1282-85, vol. 1; and Public Record Office, UK [PRO], WO208, box 5036, file 29603.

30 See note 19.

31 Director of Censorship, Memorandum, 27 October 1942, LAC, RG24, vol. 29165, file WWII-15, pt. 4x4.

32 Ibid.
33 See note 19.
34 [Benjamin deForest] Bayly, Teletype message, to [T.A.] Stone, 30 August 1943, DFAIT, file 5-2-1, vol. 1.
35 Ibid.
36 Ibid.
37 O.M. Biggar, Memorandum re New York Cable Traffic, 1 September 1943, DFAIT, file 5-2-1, vol. 1.
38 T.A. Stone, Teletype message, to [L.B.] Pearson, 8 September 1943, DFAIT, file 5-2-1, vol. 1.
39 See note 17.
40 Ibid.
41 C. des Graz to Colonel O.M. Biggar, 17 September 1943, LAC, RG2, vol. 5987, file DC9/3. The letter has a signature that appears to be that of C. des Graz and clearly came from British Security Coordination.
42 Ibid.
43 C. des Graz to Colonel O.M. Biggar, 10 September 1943, LAC, RG2, vol. 5987, file DC9/3.
44 [Probably from] Colonel O.M. Biggar to C. des Graz, 15 September 1943, LAC, RG2, vol. 5987, file DC9/3. The signature is indecipherable but the contextual link with the letter from des Graz to Biggar cited in note 41 clearly establishes the writers of the letters.
45 Ibid.
46 See note 41; and B. deF. Bayly, Teletype message, to T.A. Stone, 30 August 1943, DFAIT, file 5-2-1, vol. 1.
47 See note 38.
48 [T.A.] Stone, Teletype message, to [Capt. K.J.] Maidment, 8 September 1943, DFAIT, file 5-2-1, vol. 1. The message is annotated, "Not sent, wired Mike [Pearson] instead."
49 See note 37.
50 Ibid.
51 E.A. Martin, Memorandum, to Director of Censorship, Report of visit to Washington on 24 September to 4 October 1943, LAC, RG2, vol. 5987, file DC9/3.
52 Ibid.
53 Ibid.

Chapter 6: Canadian Intelligence at War

1 Christopher Andrew, "The Making of the Anglo-American SIGINT Alliance," in *In the Name of Intelligence,* eds. Hayden B. Peake and Samuel Halpern, 95-109 (Washington, DC: NIBC Press, 1994), 101.
2 Patrick Beesly, *Very Special Intelligence: The Story of the Admiralty's Operational Intelligence Centre 1939-1945* (London: Greenhill Books, 2000), 95.
3 Michael L. Hadley, *U-Boats against Canada: German Submarines in Canadian Waters* (Kingston: McGill-Queen's University Press, 1985), 55.
4 Beesly, see note 2 at 147.
5 Hadley, see note 3 at 30-31.
6 Marc Milner, "Royal Canadian Navy Participation in the Battle of the Atlantic Crisis of 1943," in *RCN in Retrospect, 1910-1968,* ed. James A. Boutilier, 158-74 (Vancouver: UBC Press, 1982), 159.
7 Patrick Beesly, "Operational Intelligence and the Battle of the Atlantic: The Role of the Royal Navy's Submarine Tracking Room," in *RCN in Retrospect, 1910-1968,* ed. James A. Boutilier, 175-86 (Vancouver: UBC Press, 1982), 184.
8 S.A. Gray, *Getting to the Roots of a 291er* (Ottawa: Department of National Defence [DND], 1993), 15.
9 Lt. Col. W.W. Murray, Report of the Sub/Committee Appointed to Study "Y" Intelligence etc., 19 May 1942, White Files, "Y" Material folder.
10 "The History of O.I.C.5 (U/B Tracking Room) 1942," undated but probably prepared in 1945, Library and Archives Canada [LAC], RG24, vol. 29163, file OIC5: U-Boat Tracking.
11 Ibid.

12 "History of 'Z' in Canada," undated but probably 1945, LAC, RG24, vol. 29163, file OIC7: W/T Intel "Z." "Z" work was more than "familiarity" with a radio. Cathode ray oscillographs were used to identify individual transmitters, and Morse characteristics were recorded and analyzed from undulator tape or even photographic film. Although the document appears to have been prepared as part of the DND's *Notes on the History of Operational Intelligence Centre in Canada*, it is not available at the Directorate of History and Heritage at the DND.

13 Gray, see note 8 at 11.

14 See note 12.

15 Ibid.

16 DND, *Notes on the History of Operational Intelligence Centre in Canada* (Ottawa: n.d.), chap. "1942," 8, file S1440-18 (1940).

17 Jürgen Rohwer and W.A.B. Douglas, "Canada and the Wolf Packs, September, 1943," in *The RCN in Transition 1910-1985*, ed. W.A.B. Douglas, 159-86 (Vancouver: UBC Press, 1988), 159; and Michael Smith, *The Emperor's Codes: Bletchley Park and the Breaking of Japan's Secret Ciphers* (London: Bantam Press, 2000), 219.

18 David Syrett, "The Infrastructure of Communications Intelligence: The Allied D/F Network and the Battle of the Atlantic," *Intelligence and National Security* 17, 3 (2002): 163-72 at 165.

19 Lt. Cdr. John (Jock) de Marbois, Memorandum, 17 May 1943, LAC, RG24, vol. 3806, file 1008-75-19, vol. 1.

20 DND, *Notes*, chap. "1943," 2.

21 Ibid.

22 Ibid.

23 DND, *Notes*, chap. "Naval Intelligence in Canada," 4a-5.

24 Ibid.

25 Ibid., 5.

26 Ibid.

27 DND, *Notes*, chap. "1944 W/T 'Y' – German," 2.

28 White Files, "Y" Material folder; and DND, *Notes*, chap. "1943."

29 See note 10, pt. 1.

30 Ibid.

31 DND, *Notes*, chap. "1944," 1.

32 The prime minister and other members of the Canadian decision-making establishment already had access to Enigma decrypts, but these intercepts had not always been shared with Canadian officials at the operational level. In Cabinet War Committee writings, King stated, "All are entitled to have equal knowledge except on some ultra secret matters." Ultra was the code word for decrypted enemy communications, although King may have used the term only to suggest especially secret matters. The Mackenzie King diaries contain references to decrypted SIGINT material. Copies of decrypt, or memoranda referring to such, can be found in the files. Mackenzie King Diaries, entry for 25 March 1943, LAC, MG26 J13, fiche 184.

33 DND, *Notes*, chap. "1944," 1.

34 Ibid.

35 DND, *Notes*, chap. "1943," 2.

36 DND, *Notes*, chap. "Outline of Trans-Pacific Coverage Plan Op-20G, 17 March 1944," 1.

37 DND, *Notes*, chap. "1943," 7, and chap. "'Y' Liaison Officer, Bainbridge," 1.

38 Smith, see note 17 at 194.

39 Telecommunication from London for [T.A.] Stone, 6 November 1943, White Files, Meteorological Unit folder. Two copies exist; one appears to be the original decoded message and the second is a retyped version on National Research Council stationery. See also DND, *Notes*, chap. "1943," 6.

40 Minutes of the Ad Hoc Committee of the Wireless Intelligence Board, 14 December 1943, White Files, Meteorological Unit folder.

41 T.A. Stone, Memorandum, to the Hon. Mr. Ralston, 6 January 1944, White Files, Meteorological Unit folder.

42 Ibid.
43 D.S.C. [BSC], Telegram, to T.A. Stone, 19 February 1944, White Files, Meteorological Unit folder.
44 [T.A.] Stone, Telegram, to [Charles] Ritchie, 18 January 1944; unsigned note to F.A. Kendrick, 19 January 1944; T.A. Stone, Memorandum, to Lt. Col. Hugh O'Connor, 28 January 1944; and two separate memoranda for the MET Unit file, both 28 January 1944, White Files, Meteorological Unit folder. There is no evidence that US cryptographic staff were ever offered to Canada, although naval liaison exchanges did take place.
45 Acting President of the National Research Council [NRC], Memorandum, to the Deputy Minister of National Defence, 29 February 1944, White Files, Meteorological Unit folder.
46 N.A. Robertson to the Deputy Minister of National Defence (Army), 1 March 1944, White Files, Meteorological Unit folder.
47 Acting President of the NRC to the Secretary of the Naval Board, 2 March 1944, White Files, Meteorological Unit folder.
48 A. Heeney to W.C. Ronson, 11 March 1944, White Files, Meteorological Unit folder.
49 Unsigned memorandum to the prime minister, 4 March 1944, White Files, Meteorological Unit folder; and LAC, MG24 J4, reel H-1529, frames C240627-31.
50 Unsigned memorandum to the prime minister, 28 March 1944, White Files, Meteorological Unit folder.
51 See note 36.
52 John Bryden, *Best Kept Secret: Canadian Secret Intelligence in the Second World War* (Toronto: Lester Publishing, 1993), 226-27.
53 DND, *Notes,* chap. "Canadian Army Japanese Language School, Subsection 1944," 1.
54 BRUSA was also the name allotted to all or some of the postwar intelligence treaties between the United States, Britain, Canada, Australia, and New Zealand. There is no evidence that the use of BRUSA by Op 20-G was linked to the postwar agreements.
55 DND, *Notes,* see note 36 at 1-3.
56 DND, *Notes,* chap. "Outline of Trans-Pacific Coverage Plan, Subsection 1943," 1-2.
57 G. de B. Robinson, ed., *A History of the Examination Unit 1941-45* (Ottawa, 1945), 32-33.
58 Memorandum reporting on visit of Samuel Snyder and Capt. R.J. McCartney to the Examination Unit, 8 September 1944, NARA, RG457, box 766, nr. 1991, CBLJ48, 4874A, 19440908.
59 Ibid.
60 Ibid.
61 Lt. C.H. Little, Memorandum, to DNI and FIS on Interception of French Naval W/T Traffic, 11 June 1942, LAC, RG24, vol. 3806, file 1008-75-19, vol. 1.
62 Message No. 343, 12 September 1941, LAC, RG24, series C-22, reel T-17429 and reel T-17427.
63 Memorandum on French Traffic, 22 November 1943, LAC, RG24, vol. 29163, file WWII-5, pt. 3.
64 Memorandum to F.A. Kendrick, 27 November 1943, LAC, RG24, vol. 29163, file WWII-5, pt. 3.
65 LAC, RG24, series C-22, reel T-17429.
66 Message Nos. 130-36, 28 March 1943, LAC, RG24, series C-22, reel T-17427.
67 Message Nos. 375, 377-79, 16 April 1943, LAC, RG24, series C-22, reel T-17427.
68 Robinson, see note 57, chap. "French Intelligence," at 61.
69 Memorandum on French Diplomatic and Colonial Wireless Traffic, n.d., with June 1942 added in pencil; and T.A. Stone, Memorandum, to F.A. Kendrick, 29 September 1942, NARA, RG457, box 1358, nr. 4166, ZEMA 168, 44121A, 19410201.
70 F.A.K. [Kendrick] to George [Glazebrook], 3 March 1945, LAC, RG24, vol. 29164, file WWII-9 XU.
71 F.A.K. [Kendrick], Memorandum, to George Glazebrook, 20 June 1944, White File, Examination Unit folder.
72 Message Nos. 400-7, 19 February 1943, LAC, RG24, series C-22, reel T-17427.
73 LAC, RG24, series C-22, reel T-17425.
74 Antoine de St. Exupéry, author of *The Little Prince,* sent a message to his wife in New York announcing that he was embarking with his comrades in arms. Message No. 658, 9 May 1943, LAC, RG24, series C-22, reel T-17427.

75 Message Nos. 4959-71, 7 August 1944, LAC, RG24, series C-22, reel T-17426.
76 Message Nos. 37-92, 16 January 1945, LAC, RG24, series C-22, reel T-17425.
77 Examination Unit note, 20 April 1944, LAC, RG24, reel C-8306, vol. 2, file 6074-3.
78 Memorandum to Deputy Chief of the General Staff, 25 April 1944, LAC, RG24, reel C-8306, vol. 2, file 6074-3.
79 Memorandum to War Committee of Cabinet, 30 May 1944, LAC, RG24, reel C-8306, vol. 2, file 6074-3.
80 Maj. S.R. Elliot, *Scarlet to Green: A History of Intelligence in the Canadian Army, 1903-1963* (Toronto: Canadian Intelligence and Security Association, 1981), 384-85.
81 Ben. A. Yolleck, Canadian Walkabout, DND 73/1557; Vehicles – No. 1 Special Wireless Group, 29 April 1944, LAC RG24, reel C-8336, file 7428-12; and Appendix "B" Designation, 9 December 1944, LAC, RG24, vol. 29166, file WWII-26, pt. 1, No.1 SWG.
82 Yolleck, see note 82; and 1 SWG Souvenir Booklet, 1944-45, LAC, RG24, vol. 29166, file WWII-26, pt. 2.
83 Canadian Special Wireless Group, 28 July 1945, LAC, RG24, vol. 29166, file WWII-26, pt. 1, No. 1 SWG.
84 Gil Murray, *The Invisible War: The Untold Secret Story of Number One Canadian Special Wireless Group, Royal Canadian Signal Corps, 1944-46* (Toronto: Dundurn Group, 2001), 186.
85 Letter marked SECRET-THUMP, 22 August 1945, LAC, RG24, vol. 29166, file WWII-26, pt. 1, No. 1 SWG.
86 Murray, see note 85 at 188-89.
87 Ibid., 227, 266, and 287.
88 Ibid., 290.
89 C.P. Stacey, *The Canadian Army 1939-1945: An Official Historical Summary* (Ottawa: King's Printer, 1948), 292.
90 C.P. Stacey, *Six Years of War: The Army in Canada, Britain and the Pacific* (Ottawa: Queen's Printer, 1955), 510.
91 Private information.
92 Examination Unit 1943 [a staff list], unsigned, 21 February 1943, White Files, Examination Unit folder.
93 F.A. Kendrick, Memorandum, to George Glazebrook, 20 June 1944, White Files, Examination Unit folder.
94 N.A. Robertson, "Examination Unit" Authority for expansion of activities, 12 January 1944, White Files, Examination Unit folder.
95 G. de B. Robinson, Statement of Financial Position of Examination Unit, 1 May 1943; F.A. Kendrick, Examination Unit Expenses for 1944, 27 November 1943, White Files, Examination Unit folder.

Chapter 7: Planning for Postwar SIGINT

1 Lester B. Pearson, *Mike: The Memoirs of the Right Honourable Lester B. Pearson,* vol. 3 (Toronto: University of Toronto Press, 1975), 167.
2 F.A. Kendrick to T.A. Stone, 30 November 1943, White Files, Main File folder.
3 George Glazebrook, Memorandum, to T.A. Stone, 8 December 1943; and T.A. Stone, Memorandum, to F.A. Kendrick, 9 December 1943, White Files, Main File folder, and Library and Archives Canada [LAC], RG24, vol. 29163, file WWII-5, pt. 3.
4 G. de B. Robinson, ed., *A History of the Examination Unit 1941-45* (Ottawa, 1945), Addendum, chap. 5, "Entry of DEA and NRC," 20-21n; and F.A. Kendrick to A.G. Denniston, 18 December 1943, LAC, RG24, vol. 29163, file WWII-5, pt. 3.
5 Unsigned draft memorandum on the organization of secret intelligence work in Canada, 1 May 1944, White Files, General File folder. A different typed copy but with the same text is available in LAC, RG24, vol. 8125, file NSS 1282-85, vol. 2.
6 Ibid.; and Minutes of the Advisory Committee on the Examination Unit, 4 May 1944, LAC, RG24, vol. 29164, file WWII-14, pt. 1 XU.
7 Hume Wrong, Memorandum for the Under-Secretary, 9 June 1944, White Files, Main File folder and Joint Discrimination Unit [JDU] and Examination Unit folder, and LAC, RG24, vol. 29164, file WWII-8 XU.

8 Ibid.
9 Ibid.
10 George Glazebrook, interview, 12 January 1977, 58, Department of Foreign Affairs and International Trade [DFAIT] Special Registry.
11 George Glazebrook, Memorandum, to N.A. Robertson, 8 September 1944, White Files, Main File folder and JDU and Examination Unit folder, and LAC, RG24, vol. 29164, file WWII-8 XU, Post-war Org.
12 See note 10 at 58-59. Robertson did not want the Examination Unit in External Affairs so as to avoid it being subject to Civil Service Commission oversight.
13 Minutes of the Advisory Committee on the Examination Unit, 20 September 1944, LAC, RG24, vol. 29164, file WWII-14, pt. 1 XU.
14 George Glazebrook, Memorandum for the Under-Secretary, 20 September 1944, White Files, Main File folder and JDU and Examination Unit folder, and LAC, RG24, vol. 29164, file WWII-8 XU.
15 Ibid.
16 Minutes of the Advisory Committee on the Examination Unit, 4 May 1944, LAC, RG24, vol. 29164, file WWII-14, pt. 1 XU.
17 See notes 13 and 14.
18 George Glazebrook, Memorandum, to N.A. Robertson, 5 October 1944, LAC, RG24, vol. 29164, file WWII-8 XU, Post-war Org.; and see note 16.
19 See note 13.
20 Hume Wrong, Memorandum, to N.A. Robertson, 11 October 1943, LAC, RG24, vol. 29164, file WWII-14, pt. 1 XU.
21 George Glazebrook, Memorandum for the Under-Secretary, 1 November 1944, White Files, Main File folder and JDU and Examination Unit folder, and LAC, RG24, vol. 29164, file WWII-8 XU, Post-war Org.
22 G. de B. Robinson to N.A. Robertson, 2 November 1944, White Files, Main File folder and JDU and Examination Unit folder. An extract of the letter is also available in Robinson, see note 4 at 21, and LAC, RG24, vol. 29164, file WWII-8 XU, Post-war Org.
23 T.A. Stone to George Glazebrook, 21 November 1943, White Files, JDU and Examination Unit folder, and LAC, RG24, vol. 29164, file WWII-8 XU, Post-war Org.
24 T.A. Stone to George Glazebrook, 27 November 1943, White Files, Main File folder, and LAC, RG24, vol. 29164, file WWII-8 XU, Post-war Org.
25 John Bryden, *Best Kept Secret: Canadian Secret Intelligence in the Second World War* (Toronto: Lester Publishing, 1993), 245.
26 F.A. Kendrick, Memorandum, to the Under-Secretary for External Affairs, "Plans for the Future of the Examination Unit," 8 December 1944, White Files, Main File folder, and LAC, RG24, vol. 29164, file WWII-8 XU, Post-war Org.
27 Minutes of the Advisory Committee on the Examination Unit, 14 December 1944, LAC, RG24, vol. 29164, file WWII-14, pt. 1 XU.
28 George Glazebrook, Memorandum, to the Under-Secretary, 19 January 1945, White Files, JDU and Examination Unit folder, and LAC, RG24, vol. 29164, file WWII-8 XU, Post-war Org.
29 George Glazebrook, Memorandum, to Major-General Pope, 22 February 1945, White Files, JDU and Examination Unit folder, and LAC, RG24, vol. 29164, file WWII-8 XU, Post-war Org.
30 N.A. Robertson, Memorandum, to the Chief of the General Staff, 9 April 1945; and Lt. General J.C. Murchie, Memorandum, to N.A. Robertson, 26 April 1945, LAC, RG24, vol. 29164, file WWII-8 XU, Post-war Org.
31 George Glazebrook, Memorandum, to Mr. Robertson, 28 February 1945, LAC, RG24, vol. 29164, file WWII-8 XU, Post-war Org.
32 N.A. Robertson, Telegram, to Sir Edward Travis (Government Code and Cipher School), 27 February 1945, LAC, RG24, vol. 29164, file WWII-8 XU, Post-war Org. For an inexplicable reason, the closure date was now August, while a month earlier the target date had been July. Later correspondence again refers to July.

33 N.A. Robertson to Lester B. Pearson, 19 March 1945, LAC, RG24, vol. 29164, file WWII-8 XU, Post-war Org.
34 This is the claim of Bryden, see note 25 at 253-54. See also Robinson, see note 4 at 24-25.
35 Bryden, see note 25 at 253-54.
36 G. de B. Robinson to George Glazebrook, 25 May 1945, LAC, RG24, vol. 29164, file WWII-8 XU, Post-war Org.
37 George Glazebrook to N.A. Robertson, 27 April 1945, White Files, JDU and Examination Unit folder.
38 Ibid.
39 Ibid.
40 Memorandum, "Notes on Discussions Held During Dr. Robinson's Visit to Signal Security Agency," 17-20 May 1945, LAC, RG24, vol. 29163, file History of No. 1 Discrimination Unit, and LAC, RG24, vol. 29164, file WWII-8 XU, Post-war Org.
41 Washington, DC, Telegram, to George Glazebrook and T.A. Stone, 31 May 1945, LAC, RG24, vol. 29164, file WWII-8 XU, Post-war Org.
42 Minutes of the "Y" Committee, 30 May 1945, LAC, RG24, vol. 8125, file NSS1282-85, vol. 1.
43 Minutes of the "Y" Committee, 5 May 1945, LAC, RG24, vol. 8125, file NSS1282-85, vol. 2.
44 Minutes of the Canadian Joint Intelligence Committee [CJIC], 24 November 1942, LAC, RG24, vol. 2468, file HQ 715-16-1-3, vol. 1. Good summaries of the responsibilities of the wartime CJIC can be found in Memorandum on Canadian Joint Intelligence Committee, 13 April 1943 and 19 May 1944, LAC, RG24, vol. 5190, file C-15-9-73.
45 See note 42.
46 Lt. Col. E.W.T. Gill to N.A. Robertson, 30 June 1945, DFAIT, file 29-1-1-Cda, vol. 1; and George Glazebrook, Teletype message, to the Canadian Ambassador in Washington (for attention of T.A. Stone), 9 July 1945, White Files, JDU and Examination Unit folder.
47 N.A. Robertson to the Secretary, Chiefs of Staff Committee, 13 July 1945, White Files, JDU and Examination Unit folder, and LAC, RG24, vol. 29164, file WWII-8 XU, Post-war Org.
48 See note 40.
49 T.A. Stone to George Glazebrook, 9 June 1945, DFAIT, file 29-1-1-Cda, vol. 1.
50 George Glazebrook to T.A. Stone, 14 June 1945, White Files, JDU and Examination Unit folder, and LAC, RG24, vol. 29164, file WWII-8 XU, Post-war Org.
51 Ibid.
52 Memorandum to Mr. Courtice: Estimate of Examination Unit Expenses for 1945, 9 August 1945, White Files, Main File folder. The document is ambiguous about whether this amount represents the cost for the remainder of the year or for the whole year.
53 Col. W.W. Murray, Chairman, Joint Intelligence Committee, Memorandum, "The Canadian Joint Intelligence Committee: 1. Statement of the Problem," 27 August 1945, LAC, RG24, vol. 8088, file 1274-10, vol. 1.
54 Unsigned but cites GG [George Glazebrook] as drafter, to T.A. Stone, 16 August 1945, White Files, JDU and Examination Unit folder, and LAC, RG24, vol. 29164, file WWII-8 XU, Post-war Org.
55 Unsigned and untitled, drafted by George Glazebrook, Memorandum, 23 August 1945, White Files, JDU and Examination Unit folder, and LAC, RG24, vol. 2469, file 15-10-16-1-3, vol. 4.
56 Minutes of the CJIC, 24 August 1945, LAC, RG24, vol. 2469, file 15-10-16-1-3, vol. 4.
57 See note 53.
58 Ibid.
59 Ibid.
60 G. de B. Robinson, Memorandum, "Blue-Print for a Permanent DU [Discrimination Unit] by 18 September 1945," White Files, JDU and Examination Unit folder, and LAC, RG24, vol. 29164, file WWII-8 XU, Post-war Org.
61 Memorandum for the Under-Secretary, 27 September 1945, Department of External Affairs [DEA], 29-1-1-Cda, vol. 1.

62 Minutes of the CJIC, 22 October 1945, LAC, RG24, vol. 2469, file 15-10-16-1-3, vol. 5, and LAC, RG24, vol. 8088, file 1274-10 pt. 1.
63 N.A. Robertson, Telegram, to Hume Wrong, 18 October 1945, White Files, JDU and Examination Unit folder.
64 See note 62.
65 Memorandum on Post-War Plans for Intelligence and Counter-Intelligence, 3 November 1945, White Files, JDU and Examination Unit folder, and LAC, RG2, vol. 81, file I-40, 1945-47, and LAC RG24, vol. 29164, file WWII-8 XU, Post-war Org.
66 See note 10 at 76.
67 J.L. Granatstein, *A Man of Influence; Norman A. Robertson and Canadian Statecraft, 1929-68* (Ottawa: Deneau, 1981), 181. Granatstein states that it is obvious that Robertson had received the prime minister's permission to proceed.
68 Communications Security Establishment [CSE], *History of the CBNRC* (Ottawa: CSE, 1987), 2.
69 Lt. Col. E.M. Drake, Memorandum, to Chairman, CJIC, "Canadian Post-War Intercept Facilities," 16 January 1946, LAC, RG24, vol. 8088, file 1274-10, pt. 1. The six stations would be located at Coverdale, NB; Vancouver-Victoria (Navy), BC; Ottawa, ON; Grande Prairie, AB; Vancouver-Victoria (Army), BC; and Whitehorse, YT (RCAF). The navy and army had separate stations in Vancouver-Victoria.
70 Minutes of the CJIC, 6 February 1946, LAC, RG24, vol. 8088, file 1274-10, pt. 1.
71 Minutes of the CJIC, 2 February 1946, LAC, RG24, vol. 2469, file 15-10-16-1-3, vol. 5.
72 Matthew M. Aid, "All Glory Is Fleeting: The U.S. Communications Intelligence Effort: 1945-1950," paper presented at the Annual Conference of Society for Military History, Calgary, Alberta, 25-27 May 2001, 8-10. Made available by the author.
73 Stephen Dorril has suggested that a UKUSA SIGINT conference took place concurrently in London during February and March. There is no independent corroboration of this suggestion, and it seems illogical since the senior US SIGINT community representatives were in Washington for the signing of the BRUSA Agreement on 5 March 1946. A technical conference to implement BRUSA did follow in London in late March. See Stephen Dorril, *MI6: Inside the Covert World of Her Majesty's Secret Intelligence Service* (New York: Free Press, 2000), 54. BRUSA details were provided by Matthew Aid.
74 Lt. Col. E.M. Drake, Memorandum, "Canadian Post-War Intercept Facilities," 2 May 1946, LAC, RG24, vol. 8088, file 1274-10, pt. 1.
75 G.G. Crean, Memorandum, "Canadian Intelligence Policy," 10 October 1946, DFAIT, file 29-1-1-Cda, vol. 1.
76 Ibid.
77 Minutes of Chief of Staff Committee, extract, 28 March 1946, White Files, JDU and Examination Unit folder; and Robinson, see note 4, Addendum, chap. 5, "Entry of DEA and NRC," 26.
78 Minutes of the CJIC, 2 April 1946, LAC, RG24, vol. 2469, file 15-10-16-1-3, vol. 5.
79 C.D. Howe, Memorandum, to His Excellency, the Governor General in Council, 13 April 1946, White Files, Communications Branch of the National Research Council [CBNRC] folder; and Robinson, see note 4, Addendum, chap. 5, "Entry of DEA and NRC," 27. The White File contains a copy with the signatures of the three ministers and a separate copy signed by Mackenzie King.
80 Robinson, see note 4, Addendum, chap. 1, "Wartime SIGINT (1939-45)," 001176 of the Access to Information Program [ATIP] version; and A. Heeney to W.C. Ronson, Treasury Board, 18 May 1946, White Files, CBNRC folder. A copy of the 13 April 1946 order-in-council is attached.
81 Memorandum, "Communications Research Centre," 29 March 1946, White Files, Communications Research Centre folder.
82 Robinson, see note 4, Addendum, chap. 1, "Wartime SIGINT (1939-45)," 001177 of the ATIP version, and see note 68 at 3.
83 Ibid.
84 CBNRC would remain the name of Canada's SIGINT service until Canada's involvement in foreign intelligence gathering was disclosed by the media in 1974.

Chapter 8: Postwar Intelligence Structures

1 Memorandum to the Prime Minister, 4 March 1944, White Files, Meteorological Unit folder; and Library and Archives Canada [LAC], MG24 J4, reel H-1529, frames C240627-31.

2 Col. W.W. Murray, Chairman, Canadian Joint Intelligence Committee [CJIC], Memorandum, to the Chiefs of Staff Committee, "Foreign Intelligence in Peace-Time," 26 September 1945, LAC, MG24 J4, reel H-1529, frames C240627-31. The memorandum is also found in LAC, RG24, vol. 6178, file 22-1-43.

3 G.G. Glazebrook, Memorandum, to the Under-Secretary, "Discrimination, Cryptography, Intelligence and Security," 27 September 1945, White Files, JDU and Examination Unit folder.

4 D. Jenness to George Glazebrook, 15 June 1945 and 20 June 1945, Department of Foreign Affairs and International Trade [DFAIT], file 29-1-1-Cda, vol. 1. The two letters are almost identical, although the 20 June version has been shortened. A separate cover letter from Jenness to Glazebrook, dated 20 June 1945, explains that two versions of letters on the inter-service topographical section are enclosed.

5 Maj. S.R. Elliot, *Scarlet to Green: A History of Intelligence in the Canadian Army, 1903-1963* (Toronto: Canadian Intelligence and Security Association, 1981), 521.

6 D. Jenness to George Glazebrook, 15 June 1945, DFAIT, file 29-1-1-Cda, vol. 1.

7 Hume Wrong, Memorandum, to A. Heeney, 7 November 1945, LAC, RG2, vol. 81, file I-40, 1945-47.

8 Lt. Gen. Charles Foulkes, A Proposal for the Establishment of a National Intelligence Organization, 22 December 1945, LAC, RG2, vol. 248, file I-40 (1945-47).

9 Ibid.

10 Walter, Secretary, Joint Staff Mission, London, Telegram, to Lt. Col. Gill, Secretary, Chiefs of Staff Committee, 16 November 1945, LAC, RG24, vol. 6178, file 22-1-43, vol. 1. The telegram is recorded as an appendix to Minutes of the CJIC, 20 November 1945.

11 N.A. Robertson to the Secretary, Chiefs of Staff Committee, 2 May 1946, with an attachment, "Co-Ordination of Intelligence," 3 May 1946, LAC, RG24, vol. 6178, file 22-1-43, pt. 1.

12 L.M.C., Memorandum, to Chief of General Staff, 13 May 1946, Department of National Defence [DND] 112.21009 (D152).

13 F.F. Lambert, Memorandum, to Maj. J.F. Lays, 30 May 1946, LAC, RG24, vol. 6178, file 22-1-43, pt. 1.

14 Minutes of Meeting of the Chiefs of Staff Committee, extract, 14 May 1946, DND 112.3M2 (D116); and L.M.C., Memorandum, to Chief of General Staff, 20 May 1946, DND 112.21009 (D152).

15 The reader should be cautioned about the confusing names that will follow: the Canadian Joint Intelligence Committee (CJIC), the Canadian Joint Intelligence Bureau, and the Canadian Joint Intelligence Staff. Each is a distinct organization existing in proximity to each other and with some overlapping membership.

16 Minutes of Meeting of the Chiefs of Staff Committee, 11 July 1946, LAC, RG24, vol. 6178, file 22-1-43, pt. 1.

17 G.G. Crean, Memorandum, to A. Heeney, 2 September 1949, DFAIT, file 11-4-1 DL2.

18 Joint Planning Committee, Memorandum, to the Chiefs of Staff Committee, 10 May 1946, LAC, RG24, vol. 8088, file 1274-10, pt. 1.

19 Ibid.

20 Ibid.

21 Memorandum, "Co-Ordination of Intelligence," 29 March 1946, LAC, RG2, vol. 81, file I-40 (1945-47).

22 The early archival material is vague about what departments were being discussed. DND officials even considered what the departments might be, although it seems likely that the departments were External Affairs and Trade and Commerce. See note 12.

23 George Glazebrook, interview, 12 January 1977, 66, DFAIT Special Registry.

24 Minutes of the CJIC, 30 July 1946, LAC, RG24, vol. 8088, file 11274-10, vol. 2.

25 Minutes of Cabinet Defence Committee, 24 July 1946 and 18 September 1946, LAC, RG2, vol. 2748, v. I; Minutes of Cabinet Defence Committee, 31 January 1946, LAC, RG2, vol. 2748, v. II; and R.H. Macdonald, Defence Research Board, Memorandum, to Secretary, CJIC,

"Organization of Joint Intelligence Bureau, Ottawa," 12 July 1948, with attachment "Memorandum for the Cabinet Defence Committee on Joint Intelligence Bureau," 16 July 1946, LAC, RG25, vol. 5805, file 303-J(s). The date of establishing the Canadian Joint Intelligence Bureau is cited as 31 January 1947 in an appendix to G.G. Crean's memorandum to A. Heeney, see note 17.

26 Memorandum for the Cabinet Defence Committee, 30 January 1947, LAC, RG24, vol. 6178, file 22-1-43, pt. 1; and D.M. Johnson, note to file "Following is a brief history of the J.I.B.," 5 May 1947, LAC, RG25, vol. 5805, file 303-J(s).

27. As soon as the inter-service topographical section was identified as forming the core of the new Canadian Joint Intelligence Bureau, D. Jenness, the head of the inter-service topographical section who had fought so strenuously to protect the organization, asked to return to his home department of Mines and Resources, or be permitted to retire. This left the inter-service topographical section with few officers, nearly all of whom were scheduled to leave during the summer, and a handful of clerks. Memorandum, 14 May 1947, LAC, RG2, vol. 81, file I-40 (1945-47).

28 Draft CJIC paper on Joint Intelligence Bureau Topographic Section, 7 May 1947, LAC, RG25, vol. 5805, file 303-J(s).

29 Lt. Col. J.A.K. Rutherford, Secretary, Memorandum, CJIC on Joint Intelligence Bureau – Expansion, 20 May 1948, LAC, RG25, vol. 5805, file 303-J(s).

30 CJIC, Memorandum, to Secretary, Chiefs of Staff Committee, 13 July 1946, LAC, RG24, vol. 8164, file 1700-51; and Minutes of the CJIC, 5 July 1946, LAC, RG24, vol. 8088, file 11274-10, vol. 2.

31 Col. W.A.B. Anderson, Memorandum, to Deputy General Chief of Staff – Army, "Intelligence Aspects Permanent Joint Defence," 30 April 1946; and memorandum to L.M.C. to Vice Chief of General Staff, 11 May 1946, DND 112.21009 (D153).

32 Appreciation of Russian Ability to Engage in a War with the Object of Obtaining Supremacy of the Western Hemisphere, 12 March 1946, LAC, RG24, vol. 8088, file 1274-10-5.

33 Hume Wrong, Memorandum, to Lester B. Pearson, "Intelligence Questions," 5 October 1946, DFAIT, file 29-1-1-Cda, vol. 1.

34 Ibid.

35 Minutes of the CJIC, 5 February 1947 and 9 May 1947, LAC, RG24, vol. 8088, file 11274-10, vol. 2; and Minutes of the CJIC, 16 May 1947, LAC, RG24, vol. 6178, file 22-1-43, pt. 2.

36 G.G. Crean, Memorandum, "Canadian Intelligence Policy," 10 October 1946, LAC, RG24, vol. 6178, file 22-1-43, pt. 2.

37 Minutes of Meeting of Chiefs of Staff Committee, 21 January 1947, LAC, RG24, vol. 6178, file 22-1-43, pt. 1.

38 Minutes of the CJIC, 16 May 1947, LAC, RG24, vol. 6178, file 22-1-43, pt. 2; and Minutes of the CJIC, 9 May 1947, LAC, RG24, vol. 8088, file 11274-10, vol. 2.

39 Minutes of the CJIC, 19 May 1947 and 20 June 1947, LAC, RG24, vol. 8088, file 11274-10, vol. 2.

40 Joint Intelligence Bureau reports dated October and November 1948. The North Atlantic Treaty was not signed till 4 April 1949, but exploratory talks had begun the previous spring. LAC, RG2, vol. 81, file I-40 (1948-49).

41 Memorandum, Joint Intelligence Bureau, Personnel and Financial Requirements, "25 July 1947" added in pencil, LAC, RG2, vol. 81, file I-40 (1945-47).

42 D.A. Camfield, Canadian Joint Intelligence Bureau, to J.J. McCardle of DL(2) at the Department of External Affairs [DEA], 13 August 1965, DFAIT, file 1-3-14-1, vol. 1.

43 Memorandum for the CJIC, Distribution of CJIC Papers, 30 April 1951, LAC, RG24, vol. 8088, file 12740-10-6.

44 R.H. Macdonald to Secretary, CJIC, 12 July 1947, LAC, RG25, vol. 5805, file 303-J(s), and LAC, RG24, vol. 6178, file 22-1-43, vol. 3.

45 Col. W.A.B. Anderson to Secretary, CJIC, 16 August 1948, LAC, RG25, vol. 5805, file 303-J(s).

46 Ibid.

47 D.A. Camfield, Canadian Joint Intelligence Bureau, to J.J. McCardle of DL(2) at the DEA, 13 August 1965, DFAIT, file 1-3-14-1, vol. 1. The tasks and organization of the Joint Intelli-

gence Bureau are also quoted in a memorandum from Cdr. F.W.T. Lucas, CJIC, to the Secretary, Chiefs of Staff Committee, 18 March 1949, LAC, RG2, vol. 248, file I-40 (1948-49).

48 Memorandum to Secretary, Chiefs of Staff Committee, 4 June 1948, LAC, RG24, vol. 6178, file 22-1-43, vol. 2. The resignation became effective on either 1 July 1948 or 1 August 1948. Both dates are cited in documents in the file.

49 DMI, Memorandum, to the CJIC, 16 August 1948, LAC, RG24, vol. 6178, file 22-1-43, vol. 3.

50 Minutes of the Personnel Members Committee, 28 October 1948, LAC, RG24, vol. 6178, file 22-1-43, vol. 3.

51 T.W.L. MacDermot to Dr. S.E. Smith, University of Toronto, 7 December 1948, LAC, RG2, vol. 81, file I-40 (1948-49).

52 T.W.L. MacDermot, note to file, 6 November 1948, LAC, RG25, vol. 5805, file 303-J(s).

53 George Glazebrook to G.G. Crean, 20 November 1947, LAC, RG25, vol. 5805, file 303-J(s). Glazebrook did eventually return to conventional diplomatic work (and some intelligence activities) with the DEA after his tour with the Canadian Joint Intelligence Bureau.

54 D.A. Camfield, Canadian Joint Intelligence Bureau, to J.J. McCardle of DL(2) at the DEA, 13 August 1965, DFAIT, file 1-3-14-1, vol. 1.

55 See note 23 at 67.

56 Minutes of the CJIC, 25 February 1948, LAC, RG24, vol. 6178, file 22-1-43, vol. 2; and CJIC, Memorandum, to the Secretary, Chiefs of Staff Committee, 31 October 1949, LAC, RG24, vol. 6178, file 22-1-43, vol 3.

57 Cdr. F.W.T. Lucas, CJIC, Memorandum, to the Secretary, Chiefs of Staff Committee, 18 March 1949, LAC, RG2, vol. 248, file I-40 (1948-49).

58 Ibid.

59 G.G. Crean, Circular Document No. A. 38, to Heads of Canadian Missions Abroad, 31 May 1949, LAC, RG2, vol. 248, file I-40 (1948-49).

60 Ibid.

61 Ibid.

62 Lt. Col. J.A.K. Rutherford, Memorandum, to the Secretary, Chiefs of Staff Committee, 17 February 1947, LAC, RG2, vol. 81, file I-40 (1945-47).

63 See note 17.

64 Chiefs of Staff Committee, Memorandum on Joint Intelligence Staff, 15 March 1947; and Lt. Cdr. F.W.T. Lucas, CJIC, to the Secretary, Chiefs of Staff Committee, 21 July 1947, LAC, RG2, vol. 81, file I-40 (1945-47); and Minutes of the CJIC, 20 June 1947 and 25 June 1947, LAC, RG24, vol. 6178, file 22-1-44. Although almost certainly an error, the date of establishing the Canadian Joint Intelligence Staff is cited as August 1947 in an appendix to G.G. Crean's memorandum to A. Heeney. See note 17.

65 See note 17.

66 Lester B. Pearson to Secretary, Chiefs of Staff Committee, 2 September 1947, LAC, RG24, vol. 6178, file 22-1-44.

67 Ibid.

68 DEA, Memorandum, to the CJIC, 29 January 1948, LAC, RG24, vol. 6178, file 24-14-5; and G.G. Crean, CJIC Memorandum, to Secretary, Chiefs of Staff Committee, 13 December 1948, LAC, RG24, vol. 6178, file 22-1-44.

69 CJIC, Paper No. 5(51): Yugoslavia, 18 May 1950, LAC, RG24, series C-1, reel C-11665, file 9042-34/352.

70 Memorandum to the CJIC, 29 June 1950, LAC, RG24, series C-1, reel C-11665, file 9042-34/178-3.

71 Korea: Joint Intelligence Committee Sitrep, July to September 1950, LAC, RG24, series C-1, reel C-11665, file 9042-34/178-3.

72 Joint Canadian-United States Basic Security Plan, 18 June 1946, DND 112.3M2(D116).

73 CJIC Appreciation on Forms and Scales of Attack, 29 May 1946, LAC, RG24, vol. 8088, file 1274-10, vol. 1.

74 Outline of CJIC Appreciation Leading to Canadian-U.S. Basic Security Plan, 28 May 1946, LAC, RG24, vol. 8088, file 1274-10, vol. 1.

75 Intelligence – Russia, 10 May 1946, DND 112.3M2(D116).

76 Long-Term Strategic Appreciation, 2 September 1948, LAC, RG24, reel C-11665, file 9042-32/21-3.

77 Soviet Capabilities and Probable Courses of Action Against Canada, the United States, and the Areas Adjacent Thereto, 1949-1956, 8 December 1948, DND Access to Information Program [ATIP] No. (A) 1999-01289.

78 Report on the Acceptability of the American Revisions to the Appreciation of the Requirements of Canada-United States Security, 12 June 1948, LAC, RG24, reel C-11665, file 9042-32/21-3.

79 CJIC Minutes, 9 March 1949, LAC, RG24, reel C-11665, file 9042-32/21-3.

80 American-British-Canadian Agreed Intelligence: Soviet Intentions and Capabilities, 10 November 1948, LAC, ATIP No. AH-2000-00257.

81 American-British Agreed Intelligence 15: Soviet Intentions and Capabilities – 1950, 27 September 1949, DND ATIP No. (A) 1999-01290.

82 [US] Joint Intelligence Group to G.G. Crean, 1 September 1949; and Directive to Joint Intelligence Staff, 8[?] September 1949, LAC, RG24, series C-1, reel C-11665, file 9042-3072-2, pt. 1.

83 CJIC, Memorandum to the Secretary, Chiefs of Staff Committee, 19 October 1949, LAC, RG24, series C-1, reel C-11665, file 9042-3072-2, pt. 1.

84 Probable Soviet Courses of Action Against Canada, the United States, and the Areas Adjacent Thereto, 1 January 1957, DND ATIP No. (A) 1999-01288, and LAC RG24, vol. 20887, file 14-8-11-3.

85 Brief for Chiefs of Staff Committee, 22 August 1949, DND ATIP No. (A) 1999-01288.

86 See note 84 and note 81.

87 Revision of ABC Intelligence, 10 November 1949; and Revision of ABC Intelligence, 15 November 1949, DND ATIP No. (A) 1999-01290.

88 Report on Joint U.S.-Canadian Intelligence Conference, 24 April to 11 May 1950, 15 May 1950; and Preliminary and Tentative Study of Soviet Unconventional Use of Weapons (Mid-1951) and (Mid-1954), LAC, ATIP No. AH-2000-00257 and LAC, RG24, vol. 20888, file 14-8-11-4, pt. 1.

89 Ibid.

90 Ibid. Canadian-US assessment of Soviet threat to North America continued until at least the 1970s.

91 CJIC, Report on the Joint Intelligence Bureau, to the Secretary, Chiefs of Staff Committee, 30 November 1949, LAC, RG2, vol. 248, file I-40 (1948-49).

92 Ibid.

93 See note 54.

94 Ibid.

95 See note 91.

96 Thomas F. Troy, *Donovan and the CIA: A History of the Establishment of the Central Intelligence Agency* (Washington, DC: CIA, Center for the Study of Intelligence, 1981), 351-79.

97 Rear Adm. R.H. Hillenkoetter to G.G. Crean, 24 February 1949, LAC, RG24, vol. 6178, file 24-14-5.

98 Minutes of the Meeting of the Chiefs of Staff Committee, 18 March 1949, LAC, RG24, vol. 6178, file 24-14-5.

99 Rear Adm. R.H. Hillenkoetter to G.G. Crean, 23 May 1949, LAC, RG24, vol. 6178, file 24-14-5. The idea of establishing a liaison function between the Canadian Joint Intelligence Bureau and the CIA had been under consideration since March 1949. See Rear Adm. R.H. Hillenkoetter to G.G. Crean, 15 April 1949, LAC, RG24, vol. 6178, file 24-14-5.

100 See note 17.

101 Minutes of the Meeting of the Chiefs of Staff Committee, 28 February 1951, DFAIT, file 11-4-1 DL2.

102 Ibid.

103 General Charles Foulkes to Bedell Smith, Director, CIA, 7 March 1951; Bedell Smith to General Charles Foulkes, 3 April 1951; General Charles Foulkes to Air Vice Marshall H.L. Campbell, 13 April 1951; and General Charles Foulkes to Bedell Smith, 13 April 1951, DND 73/1223, series 9, file 3170 Intelligence.

104 Ibid.; see also Minutes of the Meeting of the Chiefs of Staff Committee, 24 April 1951, LAC, RG24, vol. 6178, file 24-14-5; and Lt. Col. R.L. Raymont, Memorandum, to Chairman, CJIC, "Intelligence Relationship with CIA," 24 April 1951, LAC, RG24, vol. 6178, file 24-14-5.

105 Lt. Gen. Charles Foulkes to George Glazebrook, 3 June 1952, DND 73/1223, series 9, file 3170 Intelligence.

106 Ibid.

107 Ibid.

108 Kurt F. Jensen, "Canada's Foreign Intelligence Interview Program, 1953-90," paper presented at the annual meeting of the Canadian Association of Security and Intelligence Studies, Ottawa, Ontario, 26-28 September 2002; also see Jensen's article of the same title in *Intelligence and National Security* 19, 1 (2004): 95-104. The Interview Program, now located at DFAIT, is the only element of the Canadian Joint Intelligence Bureau still in existence.

109 See note 105. The exchange of intelligence between the Canadian Joint Intelligence Bureau and the New Zealand Joint Intelligence Bureau began in 1956.

110 See note 105.

111 G.G. Crean to Mr. Gill, Secretary, Chiefs of Staff Committee, 14 July 1949, LAC, RG2, vol. 248, file I-40 (1948-49).

112 G.G. Crean, Memorandum, to Mr. Gill, 14 July 1949, LAC, RG2, vol. 248, file I-40 (1948-49). Although first circulated on 14 July, the paper had been drafted about a month earlier.

113 F.W.T. Lucas, Memorandum, to Mr. Gill, 18 July 1949, LAC, RG2, vol. 248, file I-40 (1948-49).

114 See note 112.

115 Ibid.

116 Ibid.

117 Ibid.

118 Ibid.

119 See note 17.

120 Ibid.

121 Ibid.

122 Ibid.

123 Ibid.

124 John Hilliker and Donald Barry, *Canada's Department of External Affairs*, vol. 2, *Coming of Age, 1946-68* (Montreal: McGill-Queen's University Press, 1995), 50.

125 Jonathan Bloch and Patrick Fitzgerald, *British Intelligence and Covert Action* (Kerry, Ireland: Brandon Book Publishers, 1984), 65.

126 David Stafford, *Camp X: Canada's School for Secret Agents 1941-45* (Toronto: Lester and Orpen Dennys, 1986), 252. Stafford attributes the information to the scrapbook of Charles Arthur McLaren Vining (a Canadian who was the British security coordination representative in Canada) and may have some of the details incorrect (private information). No Canadian documents supporting the statement have been released.

127 George Glazebrook, Memorandum, to A. Heeney, "Memorandum on a Canadian Secret Intelligence Service," 26 October 1951, DFAIT, 29-1-1-Cda, vol. 2.

128 See note 23 at 49.

Chapter 9: The Postwar SIGINT Community

1 J.L. Granatstein, *A Man of Influence: Norman A. Robertson and Canadian Statecraft, 1929-68* (Ottawa: Deneau Publishers, 1981), 181.

2 Communications Security Establishment [CSE], *History of the CBNRC*, Vol. 1, chap. 1, 1 (Ottawa: CSE, 1987). The OIC was P.C. 54/3535.

3 C.D. Howe, Memorandum, to His Excellency, the Governor General in Council, 13 April 1946, White Files, CBNRC folder; and G. de B. Robinson, ed., *A History of the Examination Unit 1941-45*, Addendum, chap. 5, "Entry of DEA and NRC," 27 (Ottawa, 1945).

4 See note 2. The date authorized for the start of the Communications Branch of the National Research Council [CBNRC] was 1 September. However, this was a Sunday and was followed by Labour Day.

5 Survey of the Organization of the Communications Research Centre, 18 July 1946, White Files, General File folder.

6 Robinson, see note 3. The addendum was added some time after the original *History* was completed. The date when this occurred is unclear but was at least after May 1946. Other addenda to the *History* refer to events as late as 1975.

7 The address for classified correspondence was Director, Communications Branch of the National Research Council, c/o Dept of External Affairs, Room 117, East Block, Ottawa; E.M. Drake, Telegram to Government Communications Headquarters (UK), 28 August 1946, White Files, CBNRC folder.

8 See note 2. Vol. 1, chap. 3, 1-2.

9 Robinson, see note 3, chap. "SIGINT in Canada," 001206-001207 of the Access to Information Program [ATIP] version. This section consists of material that appears to have been appended to the original history but was clearly written many years later. The chapter and pagination is disrupted from many excisions. The ATIP page number is consistent on all copies.

10 Communications Security Establishment, *25 Years of Signals Intelligence and Communications Security* (Ottawa: CSE, 1971), 2.

11 See note 5.

12 Treasury Board, Supplementary List of Temporary Positions Authorized by Treasury Board on 23 May 1946, attached to letter to S. Preston Eagleson, 29 May 1946, White Files, Communications Research Centre folder.

13 S.P. Eagleson to A.L. Jolliffe, Director of Immigration, 1 August 1946, White Files, Communications Research Centre folder. The letter concerned the admission of the four British nationals to Canada.

14 N.A. Robertson, Memorandum to the Prime Minister, 12 July 1946, White Files, Communications Research Centre folder.

15 Ibid.

16 High Commissioner, London, Telegram, to the Secretary of State for External Affairs, 19 October 1946, White Files, Communications Research Centre folder.

17 Hume Wrong, Memorandum, to Lester B. Pearson, "Intelligence Questions," 5 October 1946, Department of Foreign Affairs and International Trade [DFAIT], file 29-1-1-Cda, vol. 1.

18 G.G. Crean to T.A. Stone, 18 November 1947, DFAIT, file 5-1-2, vol. 1.

19 British Government Code and Cipher School, Telegram, to MI2, Ottawa, 5 March 1946, DFAIT, file 5-1-2, vol. 1. The text indicates the message is to N.A. Robertson from George Glazebrook.

20 G.G. Crean, Memorandum, to N.A. Robertson, 4 April 1946, DFAIT, file 5-1-2, vol. 1.

21 See note 19. The costs were soon revised upward to $120,000 annual operating costs and $200,000 for equipment. See note 20.

22 See note 2, vol. 6, chap. 27, 1-2 and 4.

23 Ibid., 7.

24 John Bryden, *Best Kept Secret: Canadian Secret Intelligence in the Second World War* (Toronto: Lester Publishing, 1993), 291 and 295.

25 Ibid., 296.

26 See note 2, vol. 3, chap. 17, 5.

27 See note 10.

28 See note 2, vol. 4, chap. 14, 6.

29 See note 10.

30 George Glazebrook, interview, 12 January 1977, 95, DFAIT Special Registry.

31 Ibid.

32 During the Second World War and immediately after, Canada had neither the time nor the intellectual resources to develop ciphers that would meet its security standards.

33 See note 10 at 20.

34 See note 2, vol. 4, chap. 17, 1-2.

35 Ibid., 3.

36 See note 2, vol. 4, chap. 16, 1-2.

37 See note 10 at 21-22.

38 See note 2, vol. 4, chap. 14, 14; and see note 10 at 24.

39 See note 10 at 24.

40 Ibid., 21.

41 Ibid.

42 Ibid.

43 Ibid., 23-42.

44 Matthew M. Aid and Cees Wiebes, eds., *Secrets of Signals Intelligence during the Cold War and Beyond* (London: Frank Cass, 2001), 102.

45 Lt. Col. E.M. Drake, Memorandum, to Chairman, CJIC, "Canadian Post-War Intercept Facilities," 16 January 1946, Library and Archives Canada [LAC], RG24, vol. 8088, file 1274-10, pt. 1.

46 Ibid.

47 Lt. Col. E.M. Drake, Memorandum, to Chairman, CJIC, "Canadian Post-War Intercept Facilities," 2 May 1946, LAC, RG24, vol. 8088, file 1274-10, pt. 1.

48 Ibid.

49 Ibid.

50 Bradley F. Smith, *The Ultra-Magic Deals and the Most Secret Special Relationship, 1940-1946* (Shrewsbury, UK: Airlife Publishing, 1993), 218.

51 Matthew M. Aid, "All Glory Is Fleeting, The U.S. Communications Intelligence Effort: 1945-1950," paper presented at the Annual Conference of Society for Military History, Calgary, Alberta, 25-27 May 2001, 10. Made available by the author.

52 See note 50 at 217-18; Jeffrey T. Richelson, *The U.S. Intelligence Community,* 3rd ed. (Boulder, CO: Westview Press, 1995), 277; Christopher Andrew, "The Making of the Anglo-American SIGINT Alliance," in *In the Name of Intelligence,* eds. Hayden B. Peake and Samuel Halpern, 95-109 (Washington, DC: NIBC Press, 1994), 106; and see note 47.

53 Matthew M. Aid and Cees Wiebes explore the motivation for the alliance in the conclusion of their book. See note 44 at 314.

54 Stephen Dorril, *MI6: Inside the Covert World of Her Majesty's Secret Intelligence Service* (New York: Free Press, 2000), 52.

55 See note 51 at 2-3.

56 Ibid., 9.

57 Ibid., 54.

58 Ibid., 10.

59 Richelson, see note 52 at 277; and Dorril, see note 54 at 56.

60 See, for example, Jeffrey T. Richelson and Desmond Ball, *The Ties That Bind: Intelligence Cooperation Between the UKUSA Countries,* 2nd ed. (Boston: Unwin Hyman, 1990), 5; James Bamford, *The Puzzle Palace: Inside the National Security Agency, America's Most Secret Intelligence Organization* (New York: Penguin Books, 1983), 399; and Christopher Andrew, "The Growth of the Australian Intelligence Community and the Anglo-American Connection," *Intelligence and National Security* 4, 1 (1989): 213-56 at 224. Nicky Hager, *Secret Power: New Zealand's Role in the International Spy Network* (Nelson, NZ: Craig Potton, 1996), 61, specifically calls attention to the fact that the 1947 date, so often cited, is incorrect.

61 See note 44 at 314.

62 Information received from Matthew Aid, email dated 12 December 2003.

63 Christopher Andrew, *For the President's Eyes Only: Secret Intelligence and the American Presidency from Washington to Bush* (New York: HarperCollins, 1995), 163.

64 Hager, see note 60.

65 Richelson, see note 52 at 277.

66 Aid, see note 51 at 12.

67 See note 44 at 315.

68 See note 10 at 7.

69 See note 44 at 108.

70 Ibid., 315-16.

71 Bill Robinson, "The UKUSA Community," Granite Island Group, Technical Surveillance Counter Measures, 3 March 2003, http://www.tscm.com/cseukusa.html.

72 Jeffrey T. Richelson, *The U.S. Intelligence Community*, 4th ed. (Boulder, CO: Westview Press, 1999), 284.
73 Ibid.
74 See note 62.
75 Ibid. The signing of CANUSA in 1949 is also clearly recorded in Copies of the CSSI (Canadian SIGINT Security Instructions) of 2 November 1976, DND ATIP No. (A) 98/0109, Introduction, 2.
76 See note 71.
77 See note 24 at 297.
78 C.M. Drury, Minister of State for Science and Technology, admitted in 1975 before a House of Commons Standing Committee on Miscellaneous Estimates that Canada had communications intelligence agreements with the United Kingdom and the United States, although in his view the purpose was "to ensure effective collaboration between these three countries in security matters." See Richelson and Ball, see note 60 at 6. Another partial acknowledgment was made by Jean-Luc Pépin, Minister of State for External Relations, on 22 September 1983; the acknowledgement focused on security and the support of foreign and defence policies. See Philip Rosen, "The Communications Security Establishment: Canada's Most Secret Intelligence Agency" (Ottawa: Library of Parliament/Research Branch, Background Paper BP343E, 1993), 5.
79 Canada, Parliament Committees of the House of Commons, "Statement of 2 May 1995 by Deputy Clerk, Security and Intelligence, before the House National Defence Committee," http://www.parl.gc.ca/committees/defa/evidence/22_95-05-02/defa22_blk101.html. Other details of Canada's foreign intelligence program were equally slow to emerge. It was only in 2002 that the first acknowledgment of Canadian overt foreign HUMINT collection occurred. For details, see Kurt F. Jensen, "Canada's Foreign Intelligence Interview Program, 1953-90," paper presented at the annual meeting of the Canadian Association of Security and Intelligence Studies, Ottawa, Ontario, 26-28 September 2002. See also Jensen's article of the same title in *Intelligence and National Security* 19, 1 (2004): 95-104.
80 Richelson and Ball, see note 60 at 333-57.

Bibliography

Government and Manuscript Records

Department of National Defence, Canada [DND]
Directorate of History and Heritage files

Foreign Affairs Canada [DFAIT]
Select departmental files

Library and Archives Canada [LAC]
Department of External Affairs [DEA], RG25
Department of Labour, RG27
Department of Mines and Resources, RG28
Department of National Defence [DND], RG24
Manuscript Division, MG
  MG26 J2 and J4: W.L.M. King
  MG26 L: L.S. St. Laurent
  MG26 N: L.B. Pearson
  MG27: Wartime Cabinet Ministers
  MG30 D33: Oscar D. Skelton
  MG30 E101 (D9): Hume Wrong
  MG30 E133: Gen. A.G.L. McNaughton
  MG30 E140: Arnold D.P. Heeney
  MG30 E151: Laurent Beaudry
  MG30 E163: Norman A. Robertson
  MG31 E31: Marcel Cadieux
  MG31 E102: Hugh D. Keenleyside
  MG42: Great Britain, Dominions Office
Privy Council Office, RG2
Records of Royal Commissions, RG33

National Archives and Records Administration, United States [NARA]
RG457: National Security Agency [NSA] Records: Historic Cryptographic Collection: primarily boxes 766, 798, 800, 843, 1123, 1292, 1358, and 1395.

Public Record Office, United Kingdom [PRO]
Foreign Office records

Solicitor General's Department, Canada
Select departmental files

Other Sources

Aid, Matthew M. "All Glory Is Fleeting, The U.S. Communications Intelligence Effort: 1945-1950." Paper presented at the Annual Conference of Society for Military History, Calgary, Alberta, 25-27 May 2001. Made available by the author.

Aid, Matthew M., and Cees Wiebes, eds. *Secrets of Signals Intelligence during the Cold War and Beyond*. London: Frank Cass, 2001.

Aldrich, Richard J. "British Intelligence and the Anglo-American 'Special Relationship' during the Cold War." *Review of International Studies* 24, 3 (1998): 331-51.

–. *The Hidden Hand: Britain, America and Cold War Secret Intelligence*. Woodstock, NY: Overlook Press, 2002.

Allan, Catherine E. "A Minute Bletchley Park: Building a Canadian Naval Operational Intelligence Centre, 1939-1943." In *A Nation's Navy: In Quest of Canadian Naval Identity*, edited by Michael L. Hadley, Robert Huebert, and Fred W. Crickard, 157-72. Montreal: McGill-Queen's University Press, 1996.

Anderson, Scott. "The Evolution of the Canadian Intelligence Establishment, 1945-1950." *Intelligence and National Security* 9, 3 (1994): 448-71.

Andrew, Christopher. *For the President's Eyes Only: Secret Intelligence and the American Presidency from Washington to Bush*. New York: HarperCollins, 1995.

–. "The Growth of the Australian Intelligence Community and the Anglo-American Connection." *Intelligence and National Security* 4, 1 (1989): 213-56.

–. *Her Majesty's Secret Service*. New York: Viking Penguin, 1986.

–. "The Making of the Anglo-American SIGINT Alliance." In *In the Name of Intelligence*, edited by Hayden B. Peake and Samuel Halpern, 95-109. Washington, DC: NIBC Press, 1994.

–. "The Mobilization of British Intelligence for the Two World Wars." In *Mobilization for Total War: The Canadian, American and British Experience, 1914-1918, 1939-1945*, edited by N.F. Dreisziger, 87-101. Waterloo, ON: Wilfrid Laurier University Press, 1981.

Andrew, Christopher, and Oleg Gordievsky. *KGB: The Inside Story of Its Foreign Operations from Lenin to Gorbachev*. London: Hodder and Stoughton, 1990.

Aronsen, Lawrence R. "American National Security and the Defence of the Northern Frontier, 1945-1951." *Canadian Review of American Studies* 14, 3 (1983): 259-77.

Bamford, James. *The Puzzle Palace: Inside the National Security Agency, America's Most Secret Intelligence Organization*. New York: Penguin Books, 1983.

Barros, James. *No Sense of Evil. Espionage: The Case of Herbert Norman*. Toronto: Deneau, 1986.

Beesly, Patrick. *Very Special Intelligence: The Story of the Admiralty's Operational Intelligence Centre 1939-1945*. London: Greenhill Books, 2000.

Bercuson, David J. *Maple Leaf against the Axis*. Toronto: Stoddart, 1998.

Bloch, Jonathan, and Patrick Fitzgerald. *British Intelligence and Covert Action*. Kerry, Ireland: Brandon Book Publishers, 1984.

Bothwell, Robert, and J.L. Granatstein, eds. *The Gouzenko Transcripts*. Ottawa: Deneau, 1982.

Boutilier, James A., ed. *RCN in Retrospect, 1910-1968*. Vancouver: UBC Press, 1982.

Bowen, Roger. *Innocence Is Not Enough: The Life and Death of Herbert Norman*. Vancouver: Douglas and McIntyre, 1986.

Brand, E.S. "Not All the Work Was Done at Sea." In *Salty Dips Project*, vol. 3, edited by Mack Lynch. Ottawa: NOAC, 1988.

Bryden, John. *Best Kept Secret: Canadian Secret Intelligence in the Second World War*. Toronto: Lester Publishing, 1993.

–. *Deadly Allies: Canada's Secret War, 1937-1947*. Toronto: McClelland and Stewart, 1989.

Calvocoressi, Peter. *Top Secret Ultra*. London: Sphere Books, 1981.

Canada. Communications Security Establishment (CSE). "Canadian SIGINT Security Instructions." Ottawa: CSE, 1976 (Access to Information Program [ATIP] released version).

–. Communications Security Establishment. *History of the CBNRC*. Ottawa: CSE, 1987 (ATIP released version).

–. Communications Security Establishment. *25 Years of Signals Intelligence and Communications Security*. Ottawa: CSE, 1971 (ATIP released version).

–. Department of External Affairs (DEA). *Documents on Canadian External Relations*. Vol. 6, *1936-1939*. Ottawa: Information Canada, 1972.

–. Department of External Affairs. *Documents on Canadian External Relations*. Vol. 7, *1939-1941, Part 1*. Ottawa: Information Canada, 1974.

–. Department of External Affairs. *Documents on Canadian External Relations*. Vol. 8, *1939-1941, Part 2*. Ottawa: Supply and Services Canada, 1976.

–. Department of External Affairs. *Documents on Canadian External Relations*. Vol. 9, *1942-1943*. Hull: Supply and Services Canada, 1980.

–. Department of External Affairs. *Documents on Canadian External Relations*. Vol. 10, *1944-1945, Part 1*. Ottawa: Supply and Services Canada, 1987.

–. Department of External Affairs. *Documents on Canadian External Relations*. Vol. 12, *1946*. Ottawa: Supply and Services Canada, 1977.

–. Department of External Affairs and International Trade. *Documents on Canadian External Relations*. Vol. 11, *1944-1945, Part 2*. Ottawa: Supply and Services Canada, 1990.

–. Department of External Affairs and International Trade. *Documents on Canadian External Relations*. Vol. 13, *1947*. Ottawa: Supply and Services Canada, 1993.

–. Department of Foreign Affairs and International Trade (DFAIT). *Documents on Canadian External Relations*. Vol. 14, *1948*. Ottawa: Supply and Services Canada, 1994.

–. Department of Foreign Affairs and International Trade. *Documents on Canadian External Relations*. Vol. 15, *1949*. Ottawa: Supply and Services Canada, 1995.

–. Department of Foreign Affairs and International Trade. *Documents on Canadian External Relations*. Vol. 16, *1950*. Ottawa: Supply and Services Canada, 1996.

–. Department of National Defence, Directorate of Heritage and History. *Notes on the History of Operational Intelligence Centre*. Ottawa, n.d. (ATIP released version).

–. Parliament. Committees of the House of Commons, "Statement of 2 May, 1995 by Deputy Clerk, Security and Intelligence, before the House National Defence Committee," http://www.parl.gc.ca/committees/defa/evidence/22_95-05-02/defa22_blk101.html.

–. *Report of the Royal Commission to Investigate ... Confidential Information to Agents of a Foreign Power*. Ottawa: King's Printer, 1946.

–. Statistics Canada. *Canada's Balance of International Payments: Historical Statistics 1926 to 1992*. Ottawa: Statistics Canada, 1993.

Cleroux, Richard. *Official Secrets: The Story behind the Canadian Security Intelligence Service*. Toronto: McGraw-Hill Ryerson, 1990.

Cradock, Percy. *Know Your Enemy: How the Joint Intelligence Committee Saw the World*. London: John Murray, 2002.

Craig, Bruce. "A Matter of Espionage: Alger Hiss, Harry Dexter White, and Igor Gouzenko – The Canadian Connection Reassessed." *Intelligence and National Security* 15, 2 (2000): 211-24.

Creighton, Donald. *The Forked Road: Canada 1939-1957*. Toronto: McClelland and Stewart, 1976.

Darling, Arthur B. *The Central Intelligence Agency: An Instrument of Government to 1950*. University Park: Pennsylvania State University Press, 1990.

Davies, Philip H.J. "From Special Operations to Special Political Action: The 'Rump SOE' and SIS Post-War Covert Action Capability 1945-1977." *Intelligence and National Security* 15, 3 (2003): 55-76.

–. "Organizational Politics and the Development of Britain's Intelligence Producer/Consumer Interface." *Intelligence and National Security* 10, 4 (1995): 113-32.

Donaghy, Greg, ed. *Canada and the Early Cold War 1943-1957*. Ottawa: DFAIT, 1998.

Dorril, Stephen. *MI6: Inside the Covert World of Her Majesty's Secret Intelligence Service*. New York: Free Press, 2000.

Douglas, W.A.B., ed. *The RCN in Transition 1910-1985*. Vancouver: UBC Press, 1988.

Douglas, W.A.B., and Jürgen Rohwer. "'The Most Thankless Task' Revisited: Convoys, Escorts, and Radio Intelligence in the Western Atlantic, 1941-43." In *RCN in Retrospect, 1910-1968*, edited by James A. Boutilier, 187-234. Vancouver: UBC Press, 1982.

Eayrs, James. *The Art of the Possible: Government and Foreign Policy in Canada*. Toronto: University of Toronto Press, 1961.

–. *In Defence of Canada*. Vol. 2, *Appeasement and Rearmament*. Toronto: University of Toronto Press, 1965.

–. *In Defence of Canada*. Vol. 4, *Growing Up Allied*. Toronto: University of Toronto Press, 1980.

Elliot, Maj. S.R. *Scarlet to Green: A History of Intelligence in the Canadian Army, 1903-1963*. Toronto: Canadian Intelligence and Security Association, 1981.

Evening Citizen (Oshawa), "Protest Cuts to Power Sent to Army," 14 October 1948.

Foot, M.R.D. *SOE: An Outline History of the Special Operations Executive 1940-46*. London: BBC, 1984.

Fraser, Blair. *The Search for Identity: Canada, Postwar to Present*. Toronto: Doubleday, 1967.

Gannon, James. *Stealing Secrets, Telling Lies: How Spies and Codebreakers Helped Shape the Twentieth Century*. Washington DC: Brassey's, 2001.

Granatstein, J.L. *Canada's War: The Politics of the Mackenzie King Government, 1939-1945*. Toronto: University of Toronto Press, 1990.

–. *A Man of Influence: Norman A. Robertson and Canadian Statecraft, 1929-68*. Toronto: Deneau, 1981.

–. *The Ottawa Men: The Civil Service Mandarins, 1935-1957*. Toronto: Oxford University Press, 1982.

–, ed. *Towards a New World*. Toronto: Copp Clark Pitman, 1992.

Granatstein, J.L., and David Stafford. *Spy Wars: Espionage and Canada from Gouzenko to Glasnost*. Toronto: McClelland and Stewart, 1992.

Gray, S.A. *Getting to the Roots of a 291er*. Ottawa: DND, 1993 (ATIP released version).

Grose, Peter, *Gentleman Spy: The Life of Allen Dulles*. New York: Houghton Mifflin, 1994.

Hadley, Michael L. *U-Boats against Canada: German Submarines in Canadian Waters*. Kingston: McGill-Queen's University Press, 1985.

Hager, Nicky. *Secret Power: New Zealand's Role in the International Spy Network*. Nelson, NZ: Craig Potton, 1996.

Hannant, Larry. *The Infernal Machine: Investigating the Loyalty of Canada's Citizens*. Toronto: University of Toronto Press, 1995.

Herman, Michael. *Intelligence Power in Peace and War*. Cambridge: Royal Institute of International Affairs, 1996.

Hilliker, John. *Canada's Department of External Affairs*. Vol. 1, *The Early Years, 1909-1946*. Montreal: McGill-Queen's University Press, 1990.

Hilliker, John, and Donald Barry. *Canada's Department of External Affairs*. Vol. 2, *Coming of Age, 1946-68*. Montreal: McGill-Queen's University Press, 1995.

Hillmer, Norman, ed. *Partners Nevertheless*. Toronto: Copp Clark Pitman, 1989.

Hillmer, Norman, Robert Bothwell, Roger Sarty, and Claude Beauregard, eds. *A Country of Limitations: Canada and the World in 1939*. Ottawa: Canadian Committee for the History of the Second World War, 1996.

Hillmer, Norman, and J.L. Granatstein. *Empire to Umpire: Canada and the World to the 1990s*. Toronto: Copp Clark Longman, 1994.

Hinsley, F.H. *British Intelligence in the Second World War*. Abrid. ed. New York: Cambridge University Press, 1993.

–. *British Intelligence in the Second World War*. Vol. 1. London: HMSO, 1979.

–. *British Intelligence in the Second World War*. Vol. 2. New York: Cambridge University Press, 1981.

–. *British Intelligence in the Second World War*. Vol. 3, pt. 1. London: HMSO, 1984.

–. *British Intelligence in the Second World War*. Vol. 3, pt. 2. London: HMSO, 1988.

Hinsley, F.H., and C.A.G. Simkins. *British Intelligence in the Second World War*. Vol. 4. London: HMSO, 1990.

Hodges, Andrew. *Alan Turing: The Enigma*. New York: Simon and Schuster, 1983.

Howard, Michael. *British Intelligence in the Second World War*. Vol. 5. London: HMSO, 1990.

Jensen, Kurt F. "Canada's Foreign Intelligence Interview Program, 1953-90." *Intelligence and National Security* 19, 1 (2004): 95-104.

–. Review of *British Security Coordination: The Secret History of British Intelligence in the Americas, 1940-45* by Nigel West. *Intelligence and National Security* 15, 3 (2000): 163-65.

–. Review of *The True "Intrepid": Sir William Stephenson and the Unknown Agents*, by Bill Macdonald. *Bout de papier* 16, 1 (1999): 44-45.

Kahn, David. "Nuggets from the Archives: Yardley Tries Again." *Cryptologia* 2, 2 (1978): 139-43.

–. *The Reader of Gentlemen's Mail: Herbert O. Yardley and the Birth of American Codebreaking.* New Haven, CT: Yale University Press, 2004.

–. *Seizing the Enigma: The Race to Break the German U-Boat Codes, 1939-1943.* New York: Barnes and Noble, 1998.

Kealey, Greg S., and Reginald Whitaker, eds. *R.C.M.P. Security Bulletins: The War Series, 1939-1941.* St. John's, NL: Committee on Canadian Labour History, 1989.

Kelly, John Joseph. "Intelligence and Counterintelligence in German Prisoner of War Camps in Canada during World War II." *Dalhousie Review* 58, 2 (1978): 285-94.

Knight, Amy. *How the Cold War Began: The Gouzenko Affair and the Hunt for Soviet Spies.* Toronto: McClelland and Stewart, 2005.

Little, C.H. "Early Days in Naval Intelligence, 1939-41." In *Salty Dips Project.* Vol. 2, edited by Mack Lynch, 111-18. Ottawa: NOAC, 1985.

–. "Now It Can All Be Told." In *Salty Dips Project.* Vol. 3, edited by Mack Lynch, 213-37. Ottawa: NOAC, 1988.

Littleton, James. *Target Nation: Canada and the Western Intelligence Network.* Toronto: Lester and Orpen Dennys, 1986.

Lux Ex Umbra. http://luxexumbra.blogspot.com/.

Lyon, Peyton V. *The Loyalties of E. Herbert Norman.* Ottawa: DEA, 1990.

Macdonald, Bill. *The True "Intrepid": Sir William Stephenson and the Unknown Agents.* Surrey, BC: Timberholme Books, 1998.

Margolian, Howard. *Unauthorized Entry: The Truth About Nazi War Criminals in Canada, 1946-1956.* Toronto: University of Toronto Press, 2000.

McKnight, David. *Australia's Spies and Their Secrets.* St. Leonards, Australia: Allen and Unwin, 1994.

Montreal Gazette. "Canada's Joint Intelligence Bureau Depends on U.S., U.K. for Intelligence Data," 25 April 1966, 7.

Mount, Graeme S. *Canada's Enemies: Spies and Spying in the Peaceable Kingdom.* Toronto: Dundurn Press, 1993.

Murray, Gil. *The Invisible War: The Untold Story of Number One Canadian Special Wireless Group, Royal Canadian Signal Corps, 1944-46.* Toronto: Dundurn Group, 2001.

Naftali, Timothy J. "Intrepid's Last Deception: Documenting the Career of Sir William Stephenson." In *Espionage: Past, Present, Future?* edited by Wesley K. Wark, 72-99. Essex, UK: Frank Cass, 1994.

Nolan, Brian. *King's War: Mackenzie King and the Politics of War, 1939-1945.* Toronto: Random House, 1988.

Overy, Richard. *Interrogations: The Nazi Elite in Allied Hands, 1945.* New York: Viking, 2001.

Page, Don. "Tommy Stone and Psychological Warfare in World War Two: Transforming a POW Liability into an Asset." *Journal of Canadian Studies* 16, 3-4 (1981): 110-20.

Pearson, Lester B. *Mike: The Memoirs of the Right Honourable Lester B. Pearson.* 3 vols. Toronto: University of Toronto Press, 1972-75.

Pickersgill, J.W. *The Mackenzie King Record.* Vol. 1, *1939-1944.* Toronto: University of Toronto Press, 1960.

Pope, Maurice A. *Soldiers and Politicians: The Memoirs of Lt.-Gen. Maurice A. Pope.* Toronto: University of Toronto Press, 1962.

Ranelagh, John, *The Agency: The Rise and Decline of the CIA.* London: Sceptre, 1988.

Richelson, Jeffrey T. *A Century of Spies: Intelligence in the Twentieth Century.* New York: Oxford University Press, 1995.

–. *Foreign Intelligence Organizations.* Cambridge, MA: Ballinger Publishing, 1988.

–. *The U.S. Intelligence Community.* 3rd ed. Boulder, CO: Westview Press, 1995; 4th ed. 1999.

Richelson, Jeffrey T., and Desmond Ball. *The Ties That Bind: Intelligence Cooperation Between the UKUSA Countries.* 2nd ed. Boston: Unwin Hyman, 1990.

Robinson, G. de B., ed. *A History of the Examination Unit 1941-45.* Ottawa, 1945 (ATIP released version).

Rosen, Philip. *The Communications Security Establishment: Canada's Most Secret Intelligence Agency.* Ottawa: Library of Parliament/Research Branch, Background Paper BP-343E, 1993.

Sawatsky, John. *For Services Rendered.* Markham, ON: Penguin Books, 1982.

–. *Gouzenko: The Untold Story.* Toronto: Macmillan of Canada, 1984.

–. *Men in the Shadows: The RCMP Security Service.* Toronto: Doubleday, 1980.

Sebag-Montefiore, Hugh. *Enigma: The Battle for the Code.* London: Weidenfeld and Nicolson, 2000.

Simpson, Christopher. *Blowback.* New York: Weidenfeld and Nicolson, 1988.

Skaarup, Maj. Harold. *Canadian Military Intelligence: Short History.* Winnipeg: CFTMPC, 2000.

–. *Out of Darkness – Light: A History of Canadian Military Intelligence.* 3 vols. New York: iUniverse, 2005.

Smith, Bradley F. *The Ultra-Magic Deals and the Most Secret Special Relationship, 1940-1946.* Shrewsbury, UK: Airlife Publishing, 1993.

Smith, Denis. *Diplomacy of Fear: Canada and the Cold War 1941-1948.* Toronto: University of Toronto Press, 1988.

Smith, Michael. *The Emperor's Codes: Bletchley Park and the Breaking of Japan's Secret Ciphers.* London: Bantam Press, 2000.

Stacey, C.P. *Arms, Men and Governments: The War Policies of Canada 1939-1945.* Ottawa: Queen's Printer, 1970.

–. *Canada and the Age of Conflict: A History of Canadian External Policies.* Vol. 2, *1921-1948.* Toronto: University of Toronto Press, 1981.

–. *The Canadian Army 1939-1945: An Official Historical Summary.* Ottawa: King's Printer, 1948.

–. *Six Years of War: The Army in Canada, Britain and the Pacific.* Ottawa: Queen's Printer, 1955.

Stafford, David. *Camp X: Canada's School for Secret Agents 1941-45.* Toronto: Lester and Orpen Dennys, 1986.

Stafford, David, and Rhodri Jeffreys-Jones, eds. *American-British-Canadian Intelligence Relations 1939-2000.* London: Frank Cass, 2000.

Standard (Ottawa). "They Lock Up Their Wastepaper Baskets," 28 February 1950, 1 and 17.

Starnes, John. *Closely Guarded: A Life in Canadian Security and Intelligence.* Toronto: University of Toronto Press, 1998.

Steury, Donald P., ed. *Intentions and Capabilities: Estimates on Soviet Strategic Forces, 1950-1983.* Washington. DC: Central Intelligence Agency (CIA), Center for the Study of Intelligence, 1996.

Stinnett, Robert B. *Day of Deceit: The Truth about FDR and Pearl Harbor.* New York: Free Press, 2000.

St. John, Peter. "Canada's Accession to the Allied Intelligence Community 1940-45." *Conflict Quarterly* 4, 4 (1984): 5-21.

Syrett, David. "The Infrastructure of Communications Intelligence: The Allied D/F Network and the Battle of the Atlantic." *Intelligence and National Security* 17, 3 (2002): 163-72.

Taylor, Graham D., and Peter A. Baskerville. *A Concise History of Business in Canada.* Toronto: Oxford University Press, 1994.

Thompson, John Herd, and Stephen J. Randall. *Canada and the United States: Ambivalent Allies.* Montreal: McGill-Queen's University Press, 1994.

Toohey, Brian, and William Pinwill. *Oyster: The Story of the Australian Secret Intelligence Service.* Port Melbourne, Australia: Mandarin, 1990.

Troy, Thomas F. *Donovan and the CIA.* Washington, DC: CIA, Center for the Study of Intelligence, 1981.

–. *Wild Bill and Intrepid.* New Haven, CT: Yale University Press, 1996.

United States. Department of State. *Foreign Relations of the United States 1945-1950: Emergence of the Intelligence Establishment.* Washington, DC: Government Printing Office, 1996.

Wark, Wesley K. "Creating a Cold War Intelligence Community: The Canadian Dilemma." In *Intelligence in the Cold War,* edited by Lars Christian Jenssen and Olav Riste, 103-14. Oslo: Norwegian Institute for Defence Studies, 2001.

–. "Cryptographic Innocence: The Origins of Signals Intelligence in Canada in the Second World War." *Journal of Contemporary History* 22, 4 (1987): 639-66.

–. "The Evolution of Military Intelligence in Canada." *Armed Forces and Society* 16, 1 (1989): 77-98.

–. "Security Intelligence in Canada, 1864-1945: The History of a 'National Insecurity State.'" In *Go Spy the Land: Military Intelligence in History,* edited by Keith Neilson and B.J.C. McKercher, 153-78. Westport, CT: Praeger, 1992.

Warner, Michael, ed. *The CIA Under Harry Truman.* Washington, DC: CIA, Center for the Study of Intelligence, 1994.

West, Nigel. Introduction. *British Security Coordination: The Secret History of British Intelligence in the Americas, 1940-45.* New York: Fromm International, 1999.

–. *The SIGINT Secrets.* New York: Quill, 1988.

Whitaker, Reginald. "Origins of the Canadian Government's Internal Security System, 1946-1952." *Canadian Historical Review* 65, 2 (1984): 154-83.

Whitaker, Reginald, and Gary Marcuse. *Cold War Canada: The Making of a National Insecurity State, 1945-1957.* Toronto: University of Toronto Press, 1994.

Yardley, Herbert O. *The American Black Chamber.* Indianapolis, IN: Bobbs-Merrill, 1931.

–. *The Chinese Black Chamber.* Boston: Houghton Mifflin, 1983.

Index